NUCLEAR WAR
The Moral Dimension

SOCIAL
PHILOSOPHY
& POLICY CENTER

NUCLEAR WAR
The Moral Dimension

James W. Child

Transaction Books
New Brunswick (USA) and London (UK)

Published by the Social Philosophy and Policy Center
and by Transaction, Inc. 1986

Library of Congress Cataloging-in-Publication Data

Child, James W. 1941-
  Nuclear war.

  (Studies in social philosophy & policy; no. 6)
  Bibliography: p.
  1. Nuclear warfare--Moral and ethical aspects.
I. Title.   II. Series.
U263.C46   1986   172.42   85-63440
ISBN 0-912051-09-4
ISBN 0-912051-10-8 (pbk.)

For my children, Laura and Jim, in the hope they may inherit a safer world than ours, and one that is at least as free.

i

ACKNOWLEDGEMENT

I owe my gratitude and thanks to a former colleague, Dr. Fred Young, who patiently listened to many of my views while they were in their earliest and murkiest form, and to Professor Robert Pfaltzgraff from whom I learned an immense amount in several enlightening discussions and who showed me that tough-minded pragmatists do, indeed, have consciences.

I am grateful to John Ahrens and his staff at the Social Philosophy and Policy Center for all their editorial help.

But my most profuse thanks must go to two people. Ellen Frankel Paul, my former student, long-time friend, and editor, who believed in this project and lent it her persistent encouragement and keen critical intellect. Without her, it would not have been done. Lynn Roeder Child, my wife, provided me the emotional support to delve into an always difficult and sometimes painful subject matter. With intelligence and sensitivity, she saw the project through with me. Without her, it could not have been completed.

TABLE OF CONTENTS

I. Introduction

Our country possesses one of the two great nuclear forces presently deployed upon the globe. Our government tells us, and most of us believe, that we need this force to protect ourselves. Indeed, some of us believe, the author included, that our present nuclear forces are inadequate and that we need to divert more of our scarce tax dollars to modernizing them. On the other hand, those who criticize our present nuclear defense policy tell us that the mere possession of nuclear weapons is either immoral or insane or both. If this is so, then we must be rid of them, if we are to be both sane and moral. But doesn't ridding ourselves of nuclear weapons open us up to nuclear blackmail at the hands of nuclear powers who do not elect to do the same? Must we maintain our nuclear arsenals at the cost of immorality and insanity or give them up at the cost of nuclear blackmail?

Other critics of our nuclear defense policy don't go quite so far. It may be morally acceptable to possess nuclear weapons, they tell us, but it can never be morally justifiable to use them, for any use would, with a high probability, precipitate an unlimited nuclear war and that is the most awful of possible outcomes. And if we are subject to nuclear attack and the worst has happened (an unlimited nuclear war has started), then all we can do is kill millions of innocent civilians in our adversary's country, while doing nothing to "defend" ourselves.

Even some of the most conservative and hawkish defense analysts seem recently to have become enamored of the view that the use or even the possession of offensive nuclear weapons is immoral. These include both President Reagan and Secretary of Defense Weinberger. For them, the new solution to our terrible dilemma is to be the Strategic Defense Initiative. Indeed, in the very long run it may well offer a partial substitute for offensive nuclear weapons and the consequent threat to millions. At least, it deserves very serious study. But it is not a panacea. We will be wholly dependent upon our offensive strategic nuclear forces for at least another fifteen years and partially dependent upon them for the foreseeable future.

Given this fact, it is incumbent upon us to resolve the moral questions raised by our possession and possible use of these offensive weapons. Is our possession of this strategic force immoral? Is its threatened use immoral? Is our policy and strategy *necessarily* immoral, so long as it is based upon these weapons? If the answer to these questions is "yes," then we are in a most profound dilemma. For if we cannot ever under any circumstances use these terrible weapons in genuine self-defense, what are they for? Why not be rid of them, for all they do is pose the threat of Armageddon without making us one scintilla safer or more secure. Thus, the critics who say we must never be willing to use nuclear weapons seem to be at one with those who say we ought not even to possess them. Both seem quite clearly to be saying that we cannot ever use our nuclear weapons to defend ourselves; such "defense" is irrational and, even if we were to make rational sense of such a notion, it would still be massively immoral, tantamount to mass murder.

If both logic and morality require that we never use nor, it would seem, even sincerely threaten to use, our nuclear weapons, are we not impotent to respond to attack or threat of attack by a power immoral or insane enough to use its nuclear weapons? Are we not fair game for nuclear blackmail? Dare we allow ourselves to be so threatened? Wouldn't we put in danger our most cherished freedoms, our very way of life? We might call this the "dilemma of nuclear weapons." Possess them and be irrational and immoral, or do not and be subject to nuclear blackmail. Then again what is "nuclear blackmail"? Is it really so inevitable or so terrible as those partisans of a strong defense tell us it is?

Finally, we must have some nuclear defense policy, even if it is unilateral disarmament. What, when everything is said and done, ought we to do? Is our present nuclear defense policy immoral? Must we fundamentally change it? Among our choices, is there any course of action which is both practical and moral? One thing is certain: doing nothing is doing something by default, so hard decisions must be made.

The central thesis of this book is that strategic nuclear weapons do have a potential *use,* one which is both rational and moral. Based upon this legitimate use, a perfectly coherent policy and strategy of *defensive nuclear war waging* can be built. Thus, our terrible "offensive" weapons can play justifiable defensive roles. What is more surprising is that this policy and strategy is not so very different from the one we are actually pursuing; it needs only to be viewed from the proper perspective.

A key part of that perspective is moral in nature. Far too many partisans of a strong defense abjure talk of morality and speak as "hard headed pragmatists," as if there were something weak or effete about appeal to moral considerations. This is nonsense and has led the public to the false but sadly understandable conclusion that only those critics who find our nuclear defense policy to be immoral care about morality or have it on their side. These critics have at least one thing right. Moral issues are not only important, they are absolutely central.

But we must do more than justify past policy, for great choices remain to us in the arena of defense policy. Without confronting moral issues, we literally do not know what to do. Ought we to modernize our nuclear forces? Ought we to unilaterally disarm, completely or partially? Ought we to engage in arms control talks with the Soviets? If so, what ought to be negotiable? What ought not to be?

Even if our policy to this point can be morally justified, this does not guarantee that it will be jusitifiable in the future. We must understand why we do what we do and how what we do might be permissible within a common-sense moral philosophy. Once we have a *theory* of what purposes our nuclear weapons serve and how those purposes are morally justified, we can formulate a specific nuclear defense policy.

In order to complete our work, we shall have to go to the root of the matter and question many of the first principles that underlie the debate. What sorts of conditions justify resort to force in the international arena? Could any of those conditions ever justify resort to nuclear weapons? What would the effects of a nuclear war be? Just how bad would it be? Would it be so bad that it could never be justified under any imaginable circumstances? Do we have a right to defend ourselves using nuclear weapons? Does the notion of self-defense even make sense in a nuclear context? What is nuclear blackmail? Finally, what would the world really be like if the United States unilaterally divested itself of nuclear weapons? How would this work in real world circumstances? Why would it be so bad?

Only when we have answered these questions can we formulate a moral theory which explains and justifies our present policy of nuclear defense, or one very close to it. Only then can we rationally set a course for the future.

II. Permissible Resort to War

A. *The Just War Tradition: A Brief History*

Although the glorification of war and violence is as old as Homer and the Bible, we are by no means the first generation to challenge the morality of war and other violent human conflict. There is a long history of moral analysis of war and conflict in Western thought. One strand of it, well-known, honorable, and important to be sure, is pacifism: the complete rejection of violent force in human affairs. But there is another tradition, one also based on an *appeal to morality:* the just war tradition.

The just war tradition is younger than pacifism.[1] In this is an important lesson, for just war theory is a philosophically sophisticated and morally sensitive viewpoint. It rejects the glorification of war as completely as does pacifism. Just war theory recognizes that war produces great human misery and, as a result, erects a strong presumption against it. Given this presumption, the theory asks two very deep questions: "Are there ever any *reasons* which morally justify waging war?" and "Are there any *means* whereby it can be waged morally?" It differs from pacifism precisely because it answers both questions affirmatively.

Just war theory finds its philosophical roots in the early Roman Catholic thought of St. Ambrose and, especially, St. Augustine.[2] Unlike such earlier church fathers as Clement, Origen, or Tertullian, these two men could not accept a radical and absolute pacifism. By their time, the Roman Empire had been Christianized and, at least in their eyes, it stood for civilization and an ordered life against barbarian forces and heathen values. Thus, the exercise of force to preserve those values was permissible. Yet Augustine excoriated martial values and the glorification of war, and there were clear limits to what could be justified in waging war. Nonetheless, in the end good men must be willing to wage war because "....it would be worse that the injurious should rule over the more righteous."[3]

Augustine's distinction between the reasons for fighting a war and the way a war was fought was later to become the crucial distinction between *jus ad bellum* (justice of war) and *jus in bello* (justice in war). It was important that justice in both be obtained. To the latter end there must be no gratuitous violence or bloodshed. Since Augustine also believed that a proper Christian attitude, "right intention," should be maintained in war, vengeance, hatred, and what we might today call the "dehumanization" of the enemy were forbidden.

St. Thomas Aquinas was the next important philosopher to discuss just war theory and the prerequisites for *jus ad bellum,* i.e. the justice of war. He concluded:

1. War must be waged by legitimate authority.

2. It must be waged in a just cause.

3. It must be waged with the proper Christian attitude or intention.[4]

Aquinas went on to ask who the proper combatants were, whether ambushes were an acceptable means of waging war, and whether it was acceptable to fight on holy days.[5] Here Aquinas was deep into issues of *jus in bello,* justice in war.

One other notable figure who formulated his own theory of just war was Thomas More, whose Utopians detested war but found it sometimes unavoidable.[6]

However, just war theory also had roots in the harsh world of medieval politics as well as in theology and philosophy. Many of its tenets were worked out by popes and bishops in the canon law as they tried to limit and civilize war. Thus, there emerged the Truce of God which prohibited war on Sundays and Christian holidays, and the Peace of God which gave immunity from military violence at first to the clergy and later to many other peaceful pursuits. The Second Lateran Council banned certain weapons from warfare among Christians, including the crossbow and seige machines, albeit without much success.[7]

From Aquinas, the theological and philosophical branch of just war theory passed to two Spanish theologians, Vitoria and Suarez. In their hands the tradition took an interesting and important turn. While they still drew deeply from the philosophical and theological traditions of Augustine and Aquinas, they also drew from the practical canon law tradition mentioned above. What emerged was the beginning of an international law of war, as well as the explicit formulation of just war theory.[8]

Francisco De Vitoria (1492/1493-1546) was the first to deal explicitly and by reference to actual cases with the two central questions of just war theory: what makes a war a just war (*jus ad bellum*), and what is justice in war waging (*jus in bello*)? He distinguished between offensive and defensive wars, although he found the former to be sometimes justifiable. And he asked penetrating, specific questions about the Spanish conquests in the new world and the wars waged upon the American Indians. Indeed, he reached some surprisingly candid and critical conclusions about this enterprise. Vitoria also inquired more thoroughly than Aquinas into what the actual rules of war ought to be. Francisco Suarez (1548-1617) followed in the footsteps of Vitoria. His signal achievement was to formulate the conception of a society or community of sovereign states submitting themselves to a law that controls their behavior.

Succeeding Vitoria and Suarez was the great seventeenth century Dutch theorist of international law, Hugo Grotius (1583-1645). It has been said simplistically that Grotius invented international law. This ignores the canon law tradition which preceded him and the two Spanish theologians. Nonetheless, Grotius was of monumental import in Western thought for two reasons. First, he was a Protestant, but he thought in lay rather than in religious terms. More importantly, he perceived, even anticipated, the emergence of the nation state and created codes for its behavior. His first work dealt with the laws of prize and booty and was extended to freedom of the seas. His master work, *The Law of War and Peace,*[9] however, spanned the entire gamut of issues faced by nations at war or contemplating war. He went into far more detail than Vitoria on the legal ramifications of military campaigns, that is, on the topic of justice in war. He discussed the treatment of prisoners, the status of hostages, rules for the siege of cities and for the treatment of noncombatants, requirements of good faith in truces and under rights of safe conduct, notions of neutrality, treaties, and freedom of the seas.

Grotius made a distinction in the sources of international law: that between natural law and custom or treaty. Grotius believed that both are legitimate sources of international law, although, the former is more basic than the latter. Treaties and customs are generally called *positive law.* They are entered into voluntarily by nation states. Positive law is based upon the pure discretion of completely sovereign legal entities and, thus, forms the basis for the ultimately conventional nature of any standards of international behavior.

Natural law, on the other hand, is derived by reason from one or another set of first principles.[10] As such, it tends to limit sovereign discretion by a ''higher law.'' Natural law places contraints upon sovereign nations in the sense that they can only reach agreements or act in ways which conform to the parameters set by this ''higher'' moral law.

Natural law theory is of vast importance in the history of Western political and moral philosophy, going far beyond issues of international relations. Natural law theory has its roots in both Greek philosophy and Christian theology. It is at the base of American political philosophy, i.e., the view that men have "inalienable rights" based upon "self-evident truths."[11] The foundation of natural law and natural rights doctrines may be in God's rational will, as Aquinas argued, or in the ultimate rationality of man and the universe, as Jefferson argued, or in a variety of other related notions.

For our purposes, the source of its foundations makes no difference. I will not undertake to defend the notion of natural law as such. Needless to say, such a defense is philosophically very difficult. However, my analysis is based upon natural law theory, and I take natural law to be a set of moral first principles. The important point for natural law theory is that certain moral first principles are not reducible to convention nor, therefore, to positive law. They are fixed and objective, and they give us a standard by which to judge governments and their actions.[12] (Indeed, they give us a standard by which we can judge positive law itself.) The importance of natural law to just war theory cannot be overestimated because without it, the notion of just war waging is reduced to a question of abiding by formally enacted rules (primarily treaties), whatever they happen to contain. In international relations, particularly, this is a fragile and variable foundation at best. Without natural law as a limitation, there is precious little which controls or judges the behavior of sovereign nations, save their own unbridled pursuit of "national interest."

The notion of natural law as used by Grotius is captured nicely in the following passage:

> Natural law is the dictate of right reason, showing the moral necessity or moral baseness of any act according to its agreement or disagreement with rational nature, and indicating that such an act is therefore either commanded or forbidden by the author of nature, God.[13]

Emeric de Vattel (1714-1767), an important Swiss international lawyer who followed Grotius, formulated the natural law foundations of international law this way:

> We call that the *Necessary law of Nations* which consists in the application of the law of nature to *Nations*. It is *Necessary* because nations are *absolutely* bound to observe it. This law contains the precepts prescribed by the *law of nature* to *States,* on whom that law is not less obligatory than on individuals, since states are composed of men, their

resolutions are taken by men, and the law of nature is binding on all men, under whatever relation they act....Several writers term it the *Natural law of Nations.*

Since therefore the necessary law of nations consists in the application of the law of nature to states,—which law is immutable, as being founded on the nature of things, and particularly on the nature of man,—it follows, that the *Necessary* law of nations is *immutable* (emphasis in original).[14]

The successors to Grotius and Vattel began to take sides between the natural law and the positive law doctrines. The latter are called "positivists." The positivists soon rose in influence, since their views accorded well with the growing claims of nation states to unlimited sovereignty and complete legal and political autonomy. International law, the positivists taught, was what nations said it was, nothing else.

The results were that the just war theory went into abeyance. People no longer asked if the waging of a given war was justified (*jus ad bellum*). No one questioned war aims, for to do so would be to question the sole authority and full discretion of a sovereign nation to make those sorts of decisions. What this conception of international law did allow, however, was a piecemeal approach to some of the more technical rules of war that constituted justice in war (*jus in bello*). For it was clearly within the authority of the sovereign state to enter treaties and voluntarily apply rules, each to itself.

Thus, the Geneva and Hague Conventions made significant progress, or appeared to, in this area of technical detail.[15] The original Geneva Convention was signed in 1864. Another followed in 1906, two more in 1929 and 1949. They spoke extensively to the treatment of prisoners of war, as well as to the treatment of noncombatants, the immunity of wounded combatants and medical personnel, and the facilities and activities of the International Red Cross. The Hague Conventions of 1898 and 1907 covered some of the same ground but aimed primarily at defining neutrals and belligerents and setting out the respective rights and duties of each.

It was the horrible human carnage and bestial conditions in the trenches on the Western Front in World War I that changed forever the way modern man thought about nations and their sovereignty. It is hard for us, children of World War II and the nuclear era, to empathize with the profound disenchantment that shook a generation.[16] It was the experience of World War I which led Western powers to give up on the piecemeal attempts to make war more civilized and humane. Long before the atomic bomb, it was clear that technology would always outstrip such vain efforts. Instead, in the post World War I era, there were valiant efforts to outlaw war in the Covenant of the League of Nations (1920), and the Kellogg-Briand Peace Pact (1928). They failed, of course, as did the attempt to outlaw war in the 1945 United Nations Charter.[17]

However, it is interesting that even these efforts to outlaw war were based on legal positivism. No one questioned that nations have *a right* to wage war for any reason whatever and that only the voluntary assumption of treaty obligations and prohibitions could limit this right.

Over the last several decades, however, there has been a renaissance of traditional just war theory and the use of its categories in analysis. Most of all, we have seen a return to the natural law upon which it was based. Nuremberg was the first reason for this. For here we were confronted by monstrous crimes which had been committed, yet no positive laws were broken. Only a natural law analysis could make sense of it. Since then, the advent of nuclear weapons and the growth of insurgency and counterinsurgency warfare have driven us back to first principles, that is, principles based upon some notion of natural law.

Perhaps nations do not have a discretionary *right* to wage war. Perhaps there are only very narrow sorts of things which justify resort to war. Perhaps there is a strong presumption against waging war and very good reasons indeed must be adduced to overcome it. Perhaps in the absence of those justifying reasons, waging war is a crime. Likewise, perhaps it is possible that preexisting moral strictures put certain weapons and certain ways of waging war beyond the legal and moral pale.

Whatever the reason, there surely has been a renewed interest in just war theory over the last two and one-half decades. Its early manifestation was in the work of Protestant theologians Reinhold Niebuhr[18] and Paul Ramsey,[19] and the Jesuit theologian, John Courtney Murray.[20] Important books by Michael Walzer,[21] William V. O'Brien,[22] and James Turner Johnson[23] are very much in this tradition. These thinkers ask not only, or even primarily, what *are* the rules governing nations at war but, rather, what *ought* they to be, given basic moral assumptions about the dignity and worth of human beings and the morally objectionable character of human suffering and death. The most recent product of this renewed tradition is the pastoral letter of the American Catholic Bishops Conference on nuclear weapons and war.[24]

Today, this rediscovered conceptual framework seems indispensable for the discussion of war and national security policy. It is this tradition and this conceptual framework which I shall assume and use throughout this book in the moral analysis of nuclear war.

B. *Just War Theory: A Primer*

What is "justified war" or "war waging"? It strikes one as sounding odd, or much worse, to ask if war is just. War is a monstrosity about which very little good can be said. It has been the bane of man's existence and threatens to be his ultimate undoing. How can we ask if it is just? Of course, we can't, and it is on this misnomer that much ignorant rejection of just war theory is based. Wars are not justified, only acts or policies of waging war are. Thus, though it sounds morally objectionable even to ask if World War II was a just war, it makes perfectly good moral sense to ask if the allied side was behaving in a morally justifiable way in waging it. Was the allied cause just? Yes, most of the world believes that it was, and even those who disagree would admit that it is a morally legitimate question, open to dispute by reasonable people.

It is noteworthy that under a natural law theory, only one side's cause can be just. For if both sides were justified, it would imply a contradiction in our basic moral principles, or a relativity in them. That is, Hitler had his moral principles and Churchill his, and who can say which were right? We want to answer, "We can, that is who!" However, under the positivist (conventional) theory discussed above, both sides may be morally right, so long as neither side breaks specific treaties or other formally enacted international rules. There is only positive law and all else is relative or indeterminate. To arrive at our answer, that someone is right and someone is wrong, we adopt the consequences of natural law theory. Both sides cannot wage a war with *jus ad bellum*.

"Just" or "Permissible" War

Another confusion over language draws even more fire from critics of just war theory than the one considered above. In modern parlance we tend to speak of just institutions or just policies or procedures as ones that are fair and without irrational or arbitrary prejudice. 'Just' commends or praises those institutions, policies, or procedures. We talk about justice, whether economic or legal and procedural, as that situation in which people get what they deserve, whether reward or penalty. How, then, can war waging be "just"? It sounds strange to our ears, as it should. William V. O'Brien translates the archaic terminology of just war theory into modern terms as well as anyone. "The *jus ad bellum* lays down conditions that must be met in order to have permissible recourse to armed coercion."[25] Likewise, we can say that *jus in bello* sets out conditions for the way armed coercion may permissibly be used. So it is what we may do, what is permissible, not what is laudatory or good, that delineates a set of rules for determining "just war theory." It is a theory that sets out the rules for the permissible resort to international coercion and violence, surely a less controversial sounding definition of "just war theory."

The Prerequisites of Permissible War Waging (Jus ad bellum)[26]

The requirements for the permissible recourse to war have traditionally been these:

1. The war must be waged by a politically legitimate authority.

This requirement is more obviously problematic in the area of civil war and revolution than in wars between sovereign states. Nonetheless, as we shall see, the Soviet Union adopts a theory of war with capitalist states which throws the political legitimacy of those states into question. Likewise, in assessing the liability to attack of noncombatant civilians under dictatorships, I shall question the moral legitimacy of their governments.

2. All reasonable efforts to avoid war must have been made.

This is a notion close to the legal doctrine of the exhaustion of remedies. "Did you try everything else first?" is the question. It fits perfectly with the presumption against war waging discussed above. If you can ever permissibly wage war, it is only after you have tried everything else that is reasonable.

The moral duty this condition imposes has enormous consequences for our present situation. A failure to discharge it constitutes a kind of moral neligence. Members of the "peace movement" would argue that we are morally bound to make every effort to negotiate disarmament with the Soviets and try to formulate nonviolent means of conflict resolution. Within some limits, this may well be true. However, there is another duty imposed by this rule, the duty of military preparedness. I shall argue that military power is a deterrent to war and that we have a moral obligation to possess it in a sufficient amount to deter.

A good example of such immoral negligence is found in the French Third Republic's inability to raise and exert the military power necessary to stop Hitler. It is fairly clear that France and France alone could have done it.[27] Think about the moral import of that. There were several such opportunities, from the time Germany reoccupied the Rhineland in 1936 through the Munich affair, right up to the pathetic collapse of the French in the face of the Blitzkrieg during May and June of 1940.

A state must take present measures to avoid future war. It may be peaceful means like negotiation, or it may be possession of military strength for deterrence or, more probably, both. The important philosophic point is that by failing to take indicated preventive measures now, a state can put itself into a moral *cul de sac,* where any action it takes to either fight or surrender is morally wrong. This is of vast importance and we shall see it occur several times in the course of this investigation.

    3. The purposes or ends for which the war is to be fought must be morally justifiable.

This is an obvious but crucially important requirement. There is a strong presumption against war. It is impermissible, unless what you are trying to accomplish is morally important enough to overcome that presumption. We shall look further into sufficient and insufficient reasons for waging war shortly.

    4. There must be a reasonable proportion between the good of the purposes aimed at by waging the war and the harm (cost in human terms) that will result.

In other words, even if 3 is satisfied and the war aims are morally acceptable, they must justify the human cost (in death, pain, and privation) that will be involved. We shall meet this rule of proportionality again in considering the requirements for *jus in bello,* i.e., the means used in war. But here we must weigh benefit and harm in deciding *whether to wage war at all.*

Obviously, nuclear war poses a nearly insurmountable problem of proportionality. Would anything be worth fighting a nuclear war? Is there any war aim so valuable that it would justify such carnage? These are the central questions of this study and of just war theory in our time. I shall devote considerable effort to answering them.

    5. The purposes or ends sought must be practicable and achievable as well as morally permissible.

The satisfaction of 3 and 4 above guarantees only that the war will be waged for the right ends. But that is not enough. Those ends must not be so unlikely of achievement that, in all probability, the cost in human suffering will be borne and the end in human good will not be attained. The end must not only be permissible and worth the cost if it can be brought about; it must also be reasonably probable that it can be brought about. This rule is sometimes put in the form, "victory must be possible."

However, especially in nuclear war, the notion of victory confuses more than it clarifies. Again, in nuclear war we must ask, what end could possibly be achieved? Wouldn't the means, *viz.*, nuclear weapons, frustrate any rational end? A very tough question!

    6. The war must be waged by just (permissible) means.

This is, of course, *jus in bello*. It merely says that to have *jus ad bellum* you must also have *jus in bello,* if not absolutely and perfectly, then at least in large part.

C. *Permissible War Aims*

The third requirement of *jus ad bellum* held that the reasons or purposes for which the war is fought must be permissible. Why might a nation choose to fight a war? There have been many such reasons throughout history, some adequate and some pathetically inadequate. Sometimes the "reasons" given have been only outrageous rationalizations for yet other, unspoken reasons. A few which we would likely find morally objectionable are (the historical claims are of necessity simplistic):

1. To open up or keep open markets for trade and to dominate those markets once they are open: the Punic Wars, the Opium War.

2. To establish the claims of one royal family to the crown of some other nation: the Hundred Years War, the War of the Spanish Succession.

3. To uphold a nation's "honor": World War I for most combatants, e.g., Serbia, Russia, Germany, France.

4. To extend national and racial suzerainty over an alien and "inferior" people: Nazi war aims in Eastern Europe.

5. To prevent a neighboring people from establishing the government of their choice because it is not sufficiently friendly: the Soviet War in Afghanistan, the Soviet invasions of Hungary and Czechoslovakia.

Another list of reasons for war which we might find more agreeable would include:

1. To establish self-government on republican principles: the American war aim in the Revolutionary war.

2. To preserve the Union and extirpate slavery: Lincoln's proclaimed war aims in the American Civil War.

3. To save Western Civilization: Churchill's proclaimed war aim in his fight against Nazi Germany.

Yet another list we would likely find morally equivocal and fraught with problems is:

1. To "stop Communism": the American involvement in Vietnam.

2. To protect the sovereignty of a neighbor and thus, ultimately, oneself: Britain's reasons in World War I (the neighbor was Belgium).

3. To protect freedom of the seas from interference: the U.S. reason for the War of 1812 and World War I.

What a confusing variety of reasons, motives, and justifications. Is there any reasoned and orderly way to sort them out? Yes, but we must begin by narrowing our purview. We are ultimately interested in analyzing nuclear war between the United States and the Soviet Union. Thus, we can constrain our examination to the behavior of nations and safely ignore the fascinating but complex issues of permissible rebellion and civil war, as well as the historical issues of dynastic or religious conflict.

As for the other examples, it is fairly easy to observe the distinction first made by Francisco de Vitoria: that between defensive and offensive war. Surely, the Opium War was offensive on the British part, as was the invasion of Eastern Europe by the Nazis. Justice Robert Jackson, a Supreme Court justice and the American chief justice at Nuremberg, held that resistance to aggression against one's own nation or allies constitutes the *only* legitimate aim in war.[28] Indeed, Jackson's position has gained wide acceptance. Telford Taylor, himself a prosecutor at Nuremberg, characterizes the twentieth-century development of international law as the substituting of "defensive war" for "just war" and "aggressive war" for "unjust war."[29]

But the scope of "resistance to aggression" or "self-defense" as the only legitimate war aim may be both too broad and too narrow. It is too narrow in that it may fail to include war aims which we would intuitively believe were permissible. The most obvious is the prevention of crimes against humanity. Imagine that Hitler had not invaded Poland in 1939 but, instead, publicly announced a program to exterminate all Jews, Slavs, Gypsies, and other "mongrel races" from Greater Germany (i.e., Germany, Austria, and the Sudetenland). It seems a morally outrageous conclusion that the allies could not lawfully and morally have intervened. Or imagine that today a new ultraracist regime in South Africa announces a similar "final solution" to the problem of twenty-three million black South Africans. Would the United States be an aggressor under international law and morality if we intervened militarily to put a stop to it? Clearly, the notion of resistance to aggression is too narrow a base for all permissible recourse to international violence.

Is it also too broad? Yes, it seems that it is. There are at least four contexts in which acts or policies undertaken by a country in its own defense are or might be impermissible.

I. Cases in which the power that is aggressed upon is in the process of committing crimes against humanity.

II. Cases in which the defense is not of "self" and the aggression is indirect and against one or another "national interest" rather than against territory or population.

III. Preemption of perceived but objectively unreal threats.

IV. Cases in which the power that is aggressed upon desires, after the aggression is stopped, to *punish* the aggressor.

From I, it seems that Nazi Germany or South Africa in the hypothetical cases cited above would not be justified in waging a war against their aggressors. This is an interesting case because it seems to require of a government that it meet at least some minimal level of human decency if it is to be able to use justifiable violence in its own defense. Note, this is close to the condition that war be waged by a morally legitimate government.

This criterion, however, is open to serious abuse, for it is easy to say of your adversary that it is a morally illegitimate government or "system" and, as such, may be (should be) aggressed upon willy-nilly. We shall see that the Marxist-Leninist theory of war makes this sort of argument and is subject to the corresponding abuse.

With regard to II, it is generally accepted in international law that defensive alliances are permitted and that, acting under such an alliance, one power can treat an invasion of its alliance partner as an invasion of itself. But suppose a nation A feels that its security is threatened by the invasion of neighbor B by nation C, and suppose that A does not have an alliance with B. By invading B, C put A's security at greater risk than it was before. Is nation A justified in attacking nation C?

One way to analyze this question is to ask if A has a "national interest" in B's security and if A has a right to protect that national interest. What is a national interest? Which national interests are morally worthy of protection by resort to armed violence? On the one hand, A's protection of its own territorial integrity seems a clear, almost trivially obvious, national interest. Protecting the lives of its own citizens in their homeland is even more so.

But what of A's interest in B's territorial integrity or B's system of government, e.g., the British in Belgium in 1914, the Soviets in Poland or Afghanistan, the U.S. in Nicaragua? What of freedom to trade or freedom of the seas? What of economic necessity, e.g., the Western Alliance's interest in the Persian Gulf? What of more tendentious claims, e.g., "Manifest Destiny," "Lebensraum" or the liberation of the world's proletariat? Obviously we are on a slippery slope toward a view which justifies warmaking whenever it suits a nation to make war, surely a view which trivializes any moral or legal limits. Indeed, Justice Jackson's categorical assertion can be seen as directed against such a license for warmaking. Whatever its problems, Jackson's strict limitation to warmaking in response to aggression has the virtue of refusing to step on the slippery slope of "national interest."

Let us return to A's attack upon C for invading A's neighbor B. Another way of interpreting A's behavior is to view it as preemptively preventing C from invading A (as in III above). In general, can a nation act *before the fact* to prevent an attack upon itself? There is generally a ban on preventive war and a presumption against first use of armed force, although relevant issues involve the clarity of the indications of an attack, the immediacy of the threatened attack, and the existence of alternatives to preemption.[30] For our purposes, one key element stands out. What is the cost of waiting to be attacked? In nuclear war, the answer may be that it is vast indeed. This is true in part because nuclear weapons have a frightful capacity to do violence, but also because nuclear war could happen with so little warning, as little as a few minutes.

Historically, punitive wars (IV) were deemed justified. Both Thomas More and Grotius, for example, believed this. But today we must certainly question this sort of war aim. Truly punitive wars can in no way be considered an act of self-defense because, by hypothesis, the aggression has been arrested. Furthermore, it could well lead from an effort to punish the government to an effort to punish "the people," with all the frightening human consequences that might entail. In general, international law rejects reprisals and punitive war.[31] Again, the notion of punitive wars is relevant to our concern, for many have claimed that once a nuclear first strike is launched, the only possible purpose of a second strike would be "retaliation" (presumably, solely for punishment or vengeance).

Indeed, the whole question of self-defense in the context of nuclear war is fraught with deep confusions and problems, and much of our enterprise is just one of clarification and resolution. To simplify our present task, however, we can assume that the only kind of war which may permissibly be fought is a war against an aggressor, a war in self-defense, or a war in defense of alliance partners. We have seen that this position is problematic, and some of the problems will return to bother us later. Furthermore, we have as yet not analyzed self-defense in the necessary depth. Still, we have made a beginning. We have at least some idea of *why* we might permissibly wage war. But what are the limits upon *how* we may do it?

D. *Permissible Means of Waging War*

Waging war is a goal-directed activity which must be carried out by a set of practices and procedures. The use of immoral or impermissible practices is a separable question from the legitimacy of the policy or its aims. A two-by-two matrix with some examples will clarify this.

		Jus in bello (means)	
		Present	Absent
	Present	A	B
Jus ad bellum (aims)			
	Absent	C	D

A. An example might be the invasion of Normandy. The allies were justified in waging war against Nazi Germany and an amphibious operation of this sort is certainly within the ambit of a legitimate means of waging it.

B. An example might be the allied raid on Dresden. I would claim that the aim and policy, i.e., the destruction of the Nazi government, was legitimate, but attacking an undefended, open city that was without significant military targets and full of refugees must be deemed a failure of *jus in bello*. On what specific grounds we shall see later.

C. A good example was Irwin Rommel's treatment of Hitler's infamous Commando Order. Frustrated by the British Eighth Army's refusal to give up North Africa, Hitler ordered that all British soldiers caught behind German lines be shot as spies (commandos). In a desert war with the great speed of armored columns and a fluid front, this was tantamount to an order to execute all prisoners, a clear violation of the Geneva Convention and a moral outrage. Rommel is said to have burned the order in front of his men, while uttering a few choice epithets. If he really did this, it was a clear case of the practice of just war waging while waging it in the wrong cause.

D. The instances of D are, unfortunately, far too numerous to list, but Nazi Germany's brutal treatment of Russian prisoners or the Japanese "rape of Nanking" would surely suffice.

Proportionality

The law of war is an extensive body of moral principles and specific procedures expressed in custom, tradition, and explicit international agreements, including the Hague and Geneva conventions. Much of it is technical and detailed, having to do with treatment of prisoners, the wearing of uniforms, the immunity of medical personnel and wounded, and the activity of the International Red Cross. We will be concerned with only the most basic tenets of *jus in bello*. The *Rule of Proportionality* says:

> No means of waging war should be utilized which does not produce
> more good or benefit than it costs in human terms.

We met this rule in considering *jus ad bellum* when deciding whether or not to wage war. Now we meet it in deciding how to fight a war. A commander must choose weapons, targets, objectives, strategies, and tactics. In each case, this rule tells us he must ask, "Which of my choices will create the most benefit over harm?"

Now, it is immediately obvious that this rule is replete with problems. Harm to whom? The enemy army? But isn't it the role of a commander to inflict the *maximum harm* possible on the enemy army?

The rule fits better when applied to noncombatants or to one's own forces. A commander will usually follow it with respect to his own troops, as much to conserve his power and attain victory as for moral reasons, although any soldier will tell you that there are commanders who sincerely care for the health and well-being of their troops, and there are commanders who do not. And most soldiers perceive that difference in moral terms.

With regard to noncombatants, either the enemy's, a neutral's, or an ally's, the rule takes on clear moral force. The rule tells us not to do something that will cause more collateral death and suffering than the value of the objectives to be achieved. This rule was almost certainly violated in the allied bombing attack upon Dresden and probably in the atomic bombings of Hiroshima and Nagasaki.

In general, nuclear weapons seem on the surface always to violate the Rule of Proportionality. We saw previously that the decision to wage nuclear war, as a question of *jus ad bellum,* appeared always to do so. Here, we might imagine a field commander facing a decision to use one nuclear weapon. "Is it worth it?" he asks; "If I use it I might attain my objective. But at what cost to noncombatants?" More importantly he might ask, "What risk of escalation to an unlimited nuclear war does my action pose?" For risk of cost is a cost.

The Rule of Proportionality, whether it arises in *jus ad bellum* or *jus in bello,* provides almost insuperable problems for the use of nuclear weapons. Almost but not quite. We shall see why soon enough.

Two related principles are really special cases of the Rule of Proportionality. The *Principle of Humanity* says:

> The infliction of death or suffering not necessary to attain a military objective is forbidden.[32]

This merely forbids gratuitous violence and would seem to be the minimum required of civilized men in war. The *Rule of Least Harm* says:

> Among various means of accomplishing your objective or mission, choose that which causes the least death and suffering.

One principle that modifies the Rule of Proportionality is the *Principle of Necessity,* which can be formulated as:

> Those measures are justified which are necessary to accomplish a legitimate (according to *jus ad bellum*) objective.

Authors differ greatly on whether the Principle of Necessity has any place at all in moral war waging. Some argue that to ignore it is to render any restraint on war nugatory, for in the real world commanders will operate in accord with it in any case.[33] Others argue that by accepting the Principle of Necessity, we make the moral restraint of war vacuous, because we make permissible anything so long as it helps accomplish the mission.[34]

Among those who have in the past argued for the moral legitimacy of nuclear deterrence, almost all have used some form of the principle of necessity.[35] But this is just too easy. To say we may deter with nuclear weapons because we must, advances the issue not at all. I shall eschew the Principle of Necessity. I am interested in determining if resort to nuclear war waging could ever be justified under any set of circumstances and to reach conclusions about our nuclear defense policy based upon that answer. Thus, it behooves me to make the use of nuclear weapons pass an acid test of morality, not to beg the question. So for my puposes, I shall reject the Principle of Necessity and hold that merely because a certain measure is necessary to accomplish a legitimate end in warfare, it is not thereby justified.

Noncombatant Immunity

The Rule of Proportionality is one of two key rules for *jus ad bellum*. The other central principle is the *Principle of Noncombatant Immunity,* which holds that:

> Noncombatants are not the legitimate subject of intentional attack.

This principle, sometimes also known as the *Principle of Discrimination,* is absolutely central to any discussion of aerial bombardment, strategic devastation, and certainly of nuclear weapons.

This principle, as much as the Rule of Proportionality, raises numerous difficult problems. Is the immunity absolute? What about munitions workers, civilian employees of the armed forces, and other borderline cases? What about enemy politicians guilty of launching an aggressive war? I shall not belabor these issues now, for a great deal of our enterprise is wrapped up in this issue as it applies to nuclear weapons and policy.

There are two important ways in which the Principle of Noncombatant Immunity might be hedged or limited. The first is the use of the Principle of Necessity, which we met above. It is appropriate, this argument would hold, to violate intentionally the immunity of noncombatants, if a legitimate military objective is being pursued. I shall reject this applica-tion of the Principle of Necessity, as I did the earlier one. Military necessity is *not* adequate justification for the intentional violation of the immunity of noncombatants.

A far more important, and conceptually more difficult, candidate for the limitation of the immunity of noncombatants comes from the old principle in theology and moral philosophy of *double effect. A Dic-tionary of Philosophy* defines it this way:

> A principle characteristic of, but not confined to, Roman Catholic moral theology. Where some course of action is likely to have two quite different effects, one licit or mandatory and the other illicit, it may be permissible to take that course intending the one but not the other; for

example, to give a terminally ill patient a dose of morphine to relieve pain knowing that it might perhaps also prove fatal.[36]

As it applies to the immunity of noncombatants in warfare, the Principle of Double Effect would hold that:

> It is permissible to launch attacks (or undertake other measures) which might have as an unintended (double) effect the injury or death of civilians, as long as the intended purpose of the attack is morally legitimate.

The Principle of Double Effect differs from the Principle of Necessity in that the latter justifies the *intentional* killing of noncombatants as a military necessity. The Principle of Double Effect, on the other hand, justifies only collateral, unintended killing in pursuit of some *other*, legitimate goal.

For example, imagine that you are a commander preparing a defense of your national capitol against an enemy army which has already invaded your country. There is a key bridge in the enemy nation's territory which is being used to supply the invading army. However, it is also used by civilians. You know that if you bomb the bridge you will probably kill some civilians. You do not want to kill them, and in that sense you do not intend to do so. The doctrine of double effect would hold that if you do bomb the bridge, your killing the civilians will not be wrong, because the purpose of your act—stopping the enemy army—was permissible. The probability of collateral deaths does not prohibit it. As we shall see, double effect holds a crucial place in the analysis of nuclear weapons.

E. *Moral Nihilism and Pacifism*

It may strike the reader that all of this theorizing about just wars, permissible war waging, and morality applied to war is so much poppycock. War is not the kind of thing that can be moral, and talk about its possible morality is either confused and perverse or, worse, morally perverted.

This is a natural reaction. Warfare, as we shall see in some detail, is and always has been a bloody and terrible business. We ought to be revolted by it. The question though is, what do we do with this feeling of revulsion? One answer is that it might give rise to a particular moral approach to war, which in turn might be articulated as one of two moral theories.

One might hold that all war is so destructive of human life and human values that, regardless of reason or justification, it is irredeemably evil and, therefore, morally prohibited. This is *pacifism*, a view which cannot be understood without contrasting it to a right we often claim for ourselves, a right to use violence in self-defense.

Another, even more basic way of rejecting just war theory is to claim that warfare is simply beyond the purview of morality, that it is a clash of power pure and simple, in which moral distinctions have no relevance. This is the view described by Richard Wasserstrom as "moral nihilism in regard to war," a view he defines as holding "it is not possible to assess war in moral terms."[37] It is to this latter alternative to just war theory, a superficially attractive but deeply problematic alternative, that we now turn.

Moral Nihilism in Regard to War

It is not uncommon for "hardheaded" practical types to tell us that war has nothing to do with morality, nor morality with war. Former Secretary of State Dean Acheson said:

> Those involved in the Cuban crisis of October, 1962, will remember the irrelevance of the supposed moral considerations brought out in discussion....Moral talk did not bear on the problem."[38]

A true hardhead was W.T. Sherman, the Union general, who said:

> War is simply power unrestrained by compact or constitution....You cannot qualify war in harsher terms than I will. War is cruelty and you cannot refine it.[39]

Well, what of those claims? Are they correct? Can one say *anything* about the morality of war? Well, yes, one surely can, and even the two hardheads quoted above would have to agree. Is war bad? Most of us would agree that it is. Just war theorists would say that it is sometimes a necessary evil, but an evil nonetheless. Why is it an evil at all? It is productive of a very great deal of human pain and death, of privation and other human suffering, and those things are bad. Indeed, we know that Sherman quite explicitly believed this.[40] But to say that a certain kind of activity is morally bad or evil is to make a moral judgment. Try as we might, eliminating moral judgment from talk about war is nearly impossible.

Note that because he denies that moral concepts apply to war the nihilists cannot say that war is morally bad. We saw that just war theory begins with a presumption against war, i.e., that war is an evil to be avoided if at all possible. But such a presumption is a moral claim and the moral nihilists in regard to war cannot make moral claims. War, it would seem for the nihilist, can be waged willy-nilly, without justification.

Another consequence of a thoroughgoing moral nihilism in regard to war is that even the most basic moral distinction about wars will not hold. Aggressive wars are no different from defensive ones. War waged by Hitler was no different from war waged by Churchill.

Indeed, it seems that Acheson and Sherman, as quoted above, believed what they were doing was morally right: Sherman in waging war, Acheson in risking it. Neither would argue that they were doing what they were doing for the fun of it, or to enrich themselves, or for the aesthetic pleasure of it. They wouldn't even have said that they were doing it because they were ordered to. They were doing something which *had to* be done (as they saw it, at least), and that "had to" was a moral imperative, followed in the service of a morally greater end. Intuitively, we know we make moral judgments about why wars are fought. Indeed, if we can ever meaningfully pass moral judgment on anything, we can pass it on the reasons wars are fought. If anything is ever immoral, then Hitler's war waging was immoral. If it was not, nothing is.

If the reasons wars are waged can be judged morally, does the activity of war waging have moral limits? Can we make moral claims about it? Just war theory, as we have seen, claims that *jus in bello,* justice *in* war, establishes limits on permissible war waging. Are those limits meaningful or is war so "unrestrained by compact or constitution" that literally anything goes? Surely not. Even W.T. Sherman made moral judgments about the way wars are waged. Sherman believed he was *right* in destroying crops, livestock, and buildings, and inflicting the consequent privation upon belligerent peoples. Others disagreed. A moral disagreement? Certainly! Moreover, Sherman expressly rejected even "crueler" practices such as the execution or torture of prisoners of war and noncombatants. Why? They must often have appeared expedient options to one who waged such total war. It is hard to see what else but moral compunction restrained him.

Many people who would reject moral nihilism as applied to most wars would strongly assert it when it comes to nuclear war. This is a favorite view of both extreme hawks and extreme doves. The former say "When you decide to wage nuclear war you have already transcended morality, and there can be no limits upon what you do." The latter say "There can never be any moral justification for the use of nuclear weapons; one is not even conceivable or imaginable. They are too terrible to have anything to do with morality."[41] I shall demonstrate that both are quite wrong, but the burden of proof is on me.

Let us assume, however, that moral claims can be made about wars in general, about why they are fought and how they are fought. Let us proceed to the closely cognate position that all war waging is not beyond moral evaluation, but instead is irredeemably wrong, *viz.,* pacifism.

Pacifism and Self-Defense in the Domestic and International Context

Pacifism has been defined broadly as a rejection of all violence, or all lethal violence, as irredeemably evil and never justified.[42] A crucial point must be made here: pacifism is not merely the view that violence is bad, or that we ought not to engage in it without justification, or that we ought to discourage its use. The vast majority of us would subscribe to those claims. We do not thereby subscribe to pacifism, although some rather confused individuals apparently think that they do. We must remember that just war theory shares, indeed, must share on pain of incoherence, the view that both individuals and societies have a *prima facie* duty not to engage in violence; otherwise, why must it especially be justified?

Pacifism differs from this uncontroversial claim precisely because of its categorical and unlimited rejection of violence under *any* circumstances. The consequences are obvious. If one cannot employ violence for any purpose, then one cannot employ it in self-defense, no matter how outrageously unjust is the attack. Similarly, one cannot employ violence in defense of others when they are attacked. This is true even when you are especially responsible for their welfare, as a parent is for a child's, for example, or when they are helpless to defend themselves, and all this regardless of how wrong the attacker is.

Little wonder, then, that pacifism conceived as the wholesale rejection of all violence, domestic as well as international, personal as well as national, has received rough treatment at the hands of philosophers and theologians. Pacifism has been held variously to be:

> Irresponsibly naive about human nature.[43]
>
> Logically contradictory.[44]
>
> Immoral in its consequences.[45]

I shall not launch general philosophic arguments against pacifism here. However, since the notion of just war turns crucially on notions of defensive war and self-defense, we must examine the converse of pacifism, i.e., that as individuals and nations we have rights to defend ourselves and to defend others when they are unjustifiably attacked.

Self-defense and the defense of alliance partners has become so central to the justification of war that some of the most outrageous examples of aggressive war making in our time have begun with claims of resistance to aggression. Consider:

1. Japan's invasion of China in 1937 commenced with an "attack" by Chinese troops across the Marco Polo Bridge.

2. Hitler actually staged a mock attack on German radio stations along the Polish border in September 1939. This little drama was complete with S.S. troops firing blanks while dressed in Polish uniforms, and dead bodies (of concentration camp inmates), also dressed in Polish uniforms.

3. North Korea's attack across the 38th parallel in 1950 was a response to a fictitious South Korean attack.

4. The Soviet Union entered Afghanistan to counter so massive an infiltration of American and Pakistani "agents" as to amount to an invasion.

It has been rare indeed when an aggressor in this century has admitted to other than "defensive" motives.

As we move closer and closer to the principle that only resistance to aggression justifies waging war, the analogy of self-defense in domestic law takes on a central role. In the Anglo-American legal tradition, at least, we take the doctrine of self-defense and the defense of innocent third parties as an obvious part of the law of assault, battery, and homicide (in both tort and crime).[46] Yet to build the solid ground that this notion requires for our purposes, it is necessary to look beyond the law to a moral justification for this use of violence.

Perhaps the most traditional argument for a right of self-defense (and the one most consonant with the moral stance taken in this book) is that based upon natural rights. Everyone has a natural right to life, that is, a right to personal security from injury or harm or coercive threat of harm at the hands of another. I can act under that right to protect myself from attack or threat with whatever force is necessary. Similarly, others have a right to life, and if they are the innocent victims of attack, and especially if they are unable to defend themselves, I have a right (or perhaps, more strongly, a duty) to defend their lives and safety.

Charles Fried has drawn upon the moral theory of Immanuel Kant to elaborate, and I believe strengthen, this natural-rights based argument.[47] When you intentionally harm another, you are using that person as a means to some end of your own. You might want his wallet, or it might be that his injury will be of particular advantage to you (he can't compete with you for a prize, perhaps), or you may simply enjoy beating people up. Regardless of the specific motive, you obviously do not care at all for that person's well-being. You are using him only as a means to your own ends. But such treatment fails of the respect that human beings are due simply because they *are* human beings. Another way of saying the same thing is to say that the aggressor asserts his moral priority over the victim. This denies the victim's right to moral equality and thus his worth as a person. When the victim resists the aggressor, however, he is not committing the same wrong as the aggressor, i.e., asserting *his* priority over the aggressor. On the contrary, he is asserting the *equality* of his moral worth. He is saying that he is not worth *less* than his attacker.

The moral right of self-defense is not a right to use unlimited force. How much force may we use? The natural-rights argument, or Fried's variant of it, justifies only the application of enough force to arrest or frustrate an attack, to right the moral imbalance, if you will. There is certainly *no right to apply gratuitous amounts of force.* There is also, from the argument for self-defense alone, *no right to punish* after the attack is arrested. One can stop the attack, and that is all. Thus, the conclusion of either the natural-rights argument, or Fried's variant of it, fits perfectly with the Anglo-American legal tradition. The law of self-defense is no more than an elaboration of this simple point: one may legitimately resist an attack, using the minimum force reasonably necessary to frustrate or arrest the attack.[48]

Now, let us extrapolate that right to life we all possess to the level of nations. We organize ourselves into political entities, some of which are called nations. We do this to attain a number of ends but the most obvious ones, and most political philosophers would say the most important, are to protect our lives, our safety, our freedom, and our property from arbitrary and unjustified violence or coercive threats of violence. In such political organizations, we give up a lot. We must abide by many rules (laws), and we must pay (via taxes) for the services we receive.

There is, then, a *quid pro quo* between what we obtain and what we give up; i.e., we enter a *contract* with each other, or the political organization, to give up something in order to get something. This conception of political organization is usually called *social contract theory.*[49] Combined with the notion of natural law, which justifies our original rights (against all, including the political organization itself) to life, liberty, and property, it is the theory which forms the foundation of Western political philosophy.

There are two ways that our lives, our liberty, or our property can be invaded. First, we can have our liberties removed or threatened with removal from within our society by fellow citizens. We have police forces to protect us from that. Second, we can have our liberties threatened by people from outside our society, often (although certainly not always) organized as nations. Thus we have armed forces.

Now comes a crucial move. The right of a nation to defend itself and to launch any military operation to that end is justified *only because it is protecting its people in their homeland*. The state can defend its territory with violent force *only because* that territory is also the property of its citizens and is indispensable in defending their lives and liberty. National territorial integirty is derivative, protection of citizens in their homes fundamental.[50] For the present, we shall merely assume that in recognizing a right to self-defense, international law recognizes, as logically contained therein, a right of a nation to defend its citizens within its boundaries.

Thus, if a nation's people are attacked by artillery firing over a border, for example, the nation, even though its territory is not in imminent threat of conquest, clearly has the right to stop the attack with counterfire. For it has the right to protect its citizens' lives from the artillery fire. It would seem that similar defensive strikes by conventional missiles or bombers against missile or bomber bases launching attacks would be justified on the same grounds. Certainly, the use of nuclear weapons complicates the question deeply because of such issues as the immunity of noncombatants and proportionality, but the defensive counterfire seems justified.

Let us take an example. Country A has for a long time been making threats to attack country B. There is no moral justification even claimed for these threats. One day the attack comes. Bombers and missiles (for simplicity, assume that they are armed with conventional warheads) attack B, killing many of its citizens. The national command authority of B knows where the attacks are coming from and knows that, unless it counterattacks, more attacks will be launched. Furthermore, B has the capability to attack those bases and arrest subsequent attacks. Let us further assume that the bomber and missile bases are remote and that *no* noncombatants will be killed (a highly convenient assumption to be sure). Could anyone besides a strict pacifist contest the right of B to launch such counterattacks? It would be hard! Why? Precisely because B would be defending its citizens' right to life, their right not to be gratuitously murdered as a means to A's morally objectionable ends. I will call the right of a nation to fire over a border in direct defense of its people the *Principle of Justified Defensive Counterfire,* and I will discuss its importance below.

It would seem, then, that so long as a nation or other political organization is pursuing those legitimate ends for which it is organized, it has a right to exist. That right is derivative and is based upon its citizens' rights to protect their lives, liberty, and property, and on their right to organize themselves to secure these rights. Vattel makes precisely this argument in *The Law of Nations* when he says:

> In the act of association, by virtue of which a multitude of men form together as state or nation, each individual has entered into engagements with all,...To facilitate for him the means of supplying his necessities and to protect and defend him..., it thus follows that every nation is obliged to perform the duty of self preservation.[51]

A right of existence as such has never been explicitly articulated in covenants or treaties. Perhaps, as von Glahn says in *Law Among Nations,* "no such right can exist, for obviously existence represents an essential characteristic of a state rather than a right."[52] Certainly a number of areas of international law seem to presuppose a right to existence or, with von Glahn, a right to *continued* existence. Recognition of a nation (or government) is an acknowledgement of its existence, if not its right to exist.[53] Rights to self-determination and equality with other nations before international law are guaranteed to all members of the United Nations Charter (in Article 1), as is a right to territorial integrity (in Article 2(4)). These rights seem clearly to presuppose a right to existence. Furthermore, various treaties for collective defense, such as the NATO treaty, the Rio Treaty, and the Warsaw Pact, seem to confer guarantees of existence upon signatories. From these rights the right to self-defense seems to follow logically and, indeed, international law recognizes this, most explicitly in Article 51 of the U.N. Charter.

The foregoing theory of the legitimacy of states and their actions in international affairs is terribly constraining. States are legitimate only when they serve the legitimate interests of their people. Furthermore, their use of violent force or the threat of violent force is legitimate only when they are protecting the rights of their citizens to life, liberty, and property. One can go a step further and allow for the right of the state to enter alliances which protect itself and its citizens and subsequently to honor those alliance commitments with the use of force in defense of alliance partners.[54]

However, one move we explicitly *do not* want to make is to reify the state as something other than the aggregate interests and rights of its citizens. There is no "national interest" beyond the rights of citizens. National honor and various theories of the messianic role or the historical purpose of nations must be rejected. Obviously, not all philosophers would agree with this severe limitation on the actions of states. Hegel and Treitschke, for example, believed that states (or, more accurately, nations) had their own historical destiny which had virtually nothing to do with the citizens' lives or interests. This destiny permits, or even mandates, recourse to international violence without reference to citizens' rights. Marx and Lenin, as we shall see, believed that certain classes and, derivatively, states which represent those classes, have similar historical roles to play. These historical roles justify recourse to international violence without specific justification based upon reference to the defense of individual human beings and their rights. Indeed, these morally prior roles also justify the supression of individual rights within the nation. My theory rejects all of this.

At the practical, historical level we have already seen that in just war theory, many wars fought for trade or trading rights, for colonies, for influence or spheres of influence, would be ruled out as aggressive and not defensive. Notably, this would probably include several wars in which the United States has fought: the Mexican War, the Spanish-American War, perhaps the War of 1812, or the Vietnam War.

There are fascinating questions about the permissibility of fighting wars to prevent crimes against humanity, the permissibility of fighting wars to protect so called "vital" national interests (such as freedom of the seas), or the permissibility of wars to enforce international law. However, our inquiry concerns nuclear weapons and nuclear defense policy. So we shall neglect these issues and set up a very stringent standard for permissible resort to international violence or threat of violence.

F. *The Standard of Permissible War Waging*

Permissible resort to armed force exists when and only when a nation wages defensive war. 'Defensive war' requires that:

1. The nation waging war is protecting the life or liberty of its citizens in their homeland;

or

2. The nation waging war is defending its own right to exist so as to be able to continue protecting the rights to life and liberty of its citizens in their homeland;

or

3. The nation waging war is defending an alliance partner's existence and

a. the existence of that alliance partner is necessary to the protection of the rights to life and liberty of the citizens of the nation in question;

and

b. the treaty creating the alliance and obligating the nation to defend its alliance partner was arrived at by a politically legitimate process in both nations.

G. *The Dilemma of Nuclear Defense Revisited*

Unless one is a strict pacifist, the above standard must delineate permissible war waging. One might want a broader (or weaker) standard, that is, one which makes it easier to justify war waging. One could not want a narrower (or stronger) standard. For a more restrictive standard would make the permissible use of force so difficult, no matter what the circumstances, that it would be tantamount to pacifism. If there is any such thing as permissible war, the *Standard of Permissible War Waging* spells it out. The Standard is based upon powerful rights of individual human beings to protect their lives and to be free from arbitrary, and unjustified, coercive interference with their lives. If we have such rights, we may morally wage war in defense of them.

Ask yourself: do *you* have rights to life and liberty? I feel certain that I do. I also feel certain that the vast majority of the American people feel that they do as well. Of course, I have made no arguments in favor of either natural rights or the social contract theory of a state designed to protect these rights. And arguing that a majority of the American people believe themselves to have certain rights does not establish that they do in fact have such rights. But it does describe the huge burden of proof that anyone carries who might wish to argue that we cannot wage morally permissible war in our own protection, either because moral judgment is not applicable to war (moral nihilism in regard to war) or because it is always irredeemably wrong (pacifism). Proponents of both of these views, thus, would have to dispute the natural rights-social contract tradition.

But what of nuclear weapons and nuclear war? Could it ever be permissible that we wage nuclear war? The overwhelming answer provided by conventional wisdom is no.

The conventional wisdom is usually framed either as nuclear pacifism or moral nihilism in regard to nuclear war. The argument is either that any use of nuclear weapons, regardless of the situation or purpose, is morally wrong, or that one cannot even put the use of nuclear weapons into a moral context. Now, as we have seen, this bit of conventional wisdom poses some horrendous problems. Any nuclear aggressor, i.e., a nation willing to use nuclear weapons to coerce and, in the last resort, to attack another nation, cannot be resisted by nuclear force or threats of it. This is for four interrelated reasons:

1. Nuclear weapons are so devastating and so dangerous in the risk of escalation that their use imposes that, as a matter of fact, they do not constitute a defensive weapon. They might be used to punish. They could never be used to defend.

2. Nuclear weapons, even if they could, as a matter of fact, be used in defense, are totally unable to discriminate between combatants and noncombatants. Thus, many (millions, probably) of innocent noncombatants would be killed.

3. The devastation caused by the use of even one nuclear weapon plus the risk of escalation and the near total devastation of an unlimited nuclear war would, of necessity, violate the Rule of Proportionality, at both the level of *jus ad bellum* and *jus in bello*. Put simply, nothing would be worth the cost or risk of cost in using even one nuclear weapon.

4. A separate moral requirement of *jus ad bellum* is that the ends sought must be practicably achievable (requirement 5 on p. 13). A nuclear war would never achieve the protection of life and liberty of the citizens of the defending nation, since most would be killed anyway. There is no other end permissible in war. So you could not achieve what you were fighting for.

This is one horn of the dilemma of nuclear weapons: we cannot morally use nuclear weapons. The other horn is a factual claim I shall investigate below. For now, we will suppose it only. What if, as many military thinkers believe, there is no meaningful nonnuclear defense against nuclear weapons? If that is true, the consequence is ugly indeed: effective defense against a nuclear aggressor is immoral; moral defense is ineffective. We cannot morally and effectively defend our lives and our liberty.

Thus the dilemma: either we must not resist a nuclear aggressor and, thus, must surrender our rights to protect our lives and liberty, or we must resist immorally. I shall grasp the second horn of the dilemma. I shall argue that, given some crucial strictures upon *how* we do it, defensive nuclear war waging is both factually possible and morally permissible.

To show this, however, we must understand a good deal more about nuclear weapons and nuclear war.

III. The Effects of Nuclear War

Robert McNamara and Hans Bethe have recently written:

> Throughout history war has been the final arbiter of disputes and a finite disaster. Unbounded calamities — the apocalypse, Armageddon — were left for mythology.[1]

Are nuclear war and its consequences morally measurable? Or is it truly an *infinite* evil, "unbounded" as McNamara and Bethe say? The answer has profound consequences for moral analysis. To assess the moral cost of nuclear war we must begin by conceiving of it. Can we? For a long time we told ourselves that we could not. And if it would impose truly infinite human costs, it is little wonder. We called it "the unthinkable" and works of fiction skirted its boundaries. Nevil Shute, in *On the Beach*,[2] wrote about consequences occurring well after a nuclear war, exclusively from radiation effects and only in the Southern Hemisphere. Even that was frightening enough. Terry Southern took us right to the edge in the film, *Dr. Strangelove,* then left us to try to conceive it for ourselves. Not so any longer! Numerous works of nonfiction have been written about the effects of nuclear war, from the Office of Technology Assessment's sober *The Effects of Nuclear War*[3] to Jonathan Schell's rather frantic *The Fate of the Earth*.[4] Several attempts have been made to assess the medical consequences, including *Last Aid*[5] and *The Final Epidemic*.[6] At long last, popular fiction and drama have begun to grapple directly with nuclear war, rather than to dance around its edge. Examples include General Sir John Hackett's *The Third World War*,[7] the novel *Warday*,[8] and the films *The Day After, Testament,* and *Threads*. Though the definitive fictional account of an unlimited nuclear war has yet to be published, we can begin, through these fictional accounts, to see the outlines of what it might be like.

The truth is that nuclear war is quite conceivable, although doing so takes hard work and is profoundly disturbing.

A. *The Notion of Moral Commensurability*

Can the effects of nuclear war be related to our history in a meaningful way? Can they be compared to past catastrophes? If the answer to the two previous qustions is yes, then moral analysis and evaluation can at least begin. Furthermore, we can employ the categories and concepts of previous moral thought about human conflict and, in particular, just war theory. If, however, nuclear war is fundamentally different, geniunely new under the sun, then new categories and a new conceptual framework might well be required.

Which is it? The antinuclear movement has answered without much inquiry that nuclear war is *sui generis,* and that is a handy answer. But is it the right one? As we shall see, that is a complex question. What kinds of nuclear wars are we referring to and what are their consequences? How much human death, suffering, and privation does, or might, a given kind of nuclear war produce? Is it commensurable with the human experience of other wars or the Black Plague, for example? Can it be measured on *the same scale* of human cost?

A word about the notion of moral measurement. We work here with a concept familiar to economists, game theorists, and business planners. It is known as "utility." Utility is just some good or value. It may be pleasure, happiness, self-expression and self-development, or one of several other things, depending upon the moral theory of value one holds. The important thing is that it is abstract and, by definition, quantifiable and, therefore, measurable.[9]

Since we are working with bad things here, like wars and the bombing of cities, we will speak more of negative utility. It is interesting that philosophers and moralists more often agree about negative utility than about positive. It seems obvious to most of us that human pain, suffering, privation, and death are bad (have negative utility). I will refer to this negative utility as "human cost." Some would say that there are bad things other than those which can be measured in terms of human cost, such as blaspheming God or making animal species which have no utility to man extinct. Others, like me, would say that violating the rights of people, or failing to carry out duties owed to them, is also bad, never mind that no human cost may result. But whether it is the *only* bad thing or not, nearly universal agreement exists that human cost is very bad, indeed.

Note also that while we often cannot measure instances of human cost directly, we certainly can (and often do) rank them in order of severity. A ruptured appendix is worse than a hangnail. A child being hungry is worse than a child being deprived of television, and the hunger of ten children is worse than that of one. One thousand human deaths are worse than ten, and (to go to a far more difficult moral claim) we intuitively feel that the death of an innocent person is worse than the death of a person who somehow "deserves it": a terrorist who is killed in his own effort to kill many other innocent people, for example.

As we approach the consequences of nuclear war and attempt to get a conceptual grip upon a catastrophe of such large human proportions, we must knock down one very large bogyman raised by the antinuclear defense movement. The philosopher Michael Dummett says:

> Those who devise nuclear strategies and talk of megadeaths are already insane.[10]

In describing the numerical proportions of a U.S. attack on the Soviet Union, Helen Caldicott tells us, "These numbers are obscene,"[11] and by implication she calls "obscene" anyone who analyzes nuclear war by using such numbers. The actress, Coleen Dewhurst, at a meeting of the Cambridge Union, has said that defense planners who think about nuclear war are "pure evil."

It is not evil, nor obscene, nor insane to think and talk about the consequences of nuclear war. To be told that it is can only be understood as name-calling and bullying. The reader should note that those who use such abusive *ad hominem* arguments almost always go on to discuss nuclear war and its effects. They do not deem themselves to be insane, obscene, or evil, only those who might use such numbers to disagree with them.

To talk about quantities of human cost—death, pain, and suffering —and to reason about them, does not necessitate a callous or indifferent attitude toward that suffering and death. Nor does it indicate approval of the actions which cause it, whatever they may be. We may talk of tens of thousands of deaths in conventional bombing raids in World War II or millions of deaths in a nuclear war. The horror felt at the deaths, often painful, of many of our fellow humans ought never to leave us. For myself, at least, it never does. We must not become inured to the horror by using numbers, but neither should we let it paralyze our thinking process. We are not less humane or human for pushing beyond the horror we feel to use what tools of reason we have, to think and to analyze. We must, after all, decide what we shall *do,* for great decisions about nuclear war and peace remain to be made. Time and events dictate that these decisions will be made. But it is our choice whether they are made thoughtfully and carefully or by default. Unexamined horror and reactive revulsion alone will make for very poor decisions, and perhaps dangerous ones.

Now for the commensurability of wars. Wars are great producers of all sorts of human cost and, thus, of massive amounts of disutility. We can compare those disutilities and measure them (at least rank them in order of their severity, if not on an exact metric scale). Wars (or any other events productive of human cost) are commensurable *if they can be measured on the same scale.* That is all that is at issue here! 'Commensurable' does *not* mean "no worse than." I shall argue that the consequences of any practically possible nuclear war are indeed commensurable with past human catastrophes. This claim, if satisfactorily established, has important moral consequences. Indeed, it leads to answers to seemingly unanswerable moral questions. For there is little wonder that "unbounded calamities" are mythic in nature. They are very difficult to think about any other way. But a bounded, finite catastrophe, however vast, however unequaled in our history, is commensurable and thus comparable.

The near term effects (within the first ninety days) of various possible nuclear wars are, within very broad but meaningful limits, known; thus, we can arrive at approximations of commensurability. The long term effects, on the other hand, are almost completely unknown. Indeed, the theory of the nuclear winter appears to hold that in important sorts of ways, nuclear war might be truly incommensurable. And I shall examine the theory and these apparent claims. But let us look first at the consequences that would occur in the first ninety days following a nuclear war.

B. *The Commensurability of Nuclear War in Historical Perspective*

In thinking about wars in history, one is inclined to think of the neat, orderly battlefields of Frederick the Great or the Duke of Marlborough, where each army formed neat lines, and each soldier was in a colorful uniform which clearly identified him as a combatant. In these kinds of battles, noncombatants were nowhere to be seen—or threatened. But we must remember that battles are like this only in Hollywood epics. Grapeshot was a vicious weapon which often struck off heads or limbs, or disemboweled its victims. An asymmetric, tumbling musket ball behaved much like a modern dum-dum bullet, which was outlawed at Geneva as inhumane. Wars kill brutally and painfully! They always have.

Still, wars, like those of Frederick or Marlborough, made up of a series of battles between professional armies, often mercenaries and always predominantly (before the French Revolution) volunteers, on isolated fields, are not even a good paradigm. Wars have always been worse than that, far worse.

Whole peoples have made war their primary cultural activity, or source of livelihood, or both. The Yanomamo of the Orinoco Valley in Venezuela live to fight.[12] War and plunder (more often than not visited upon noncombatants) were central to the tribal existence of the Mongols, the Norse raiders, and numerous American Indian tribes.

Of more relevance to our purposes, total war—defined as the obliteration of whole societies and the enslavement or slaughter of whole peoples—did not arrive with the nuclear weapon or even with the strategic bomber. It is literally as old as recorded history. Sargon of Akkad, for example, conducted strategic devastation throughout Mesopotamia around 2250 B.C.

If one activity captures the essence of war in history it is not the battlefield, but the siege and sack of cities and the devastation of the countryside: total war carried out upon civilians. The Second Punic War (218-201 B.C.) matched two of the greatest generals of the ancient world, Hannibal and Scipio Africanus. The battles they fought are still studied in military schools. Less often remembered is the horrible devastation that resulted in Southern Italy, the locus of most of the campaigns, devastation that resulted from the marching armies, rather than the historic battles. Some claim that 50 perecent of the population was killed or died of hunger or disease in the seventeen years of the war.[13]

Genghis Khan (1162?-1227), one of the greatest conquerers of all time, quite consciously used terror to prompt surrender. In one particularly brutal campaign, he attempted to slaughter the entire population of the Khorezin Empire of Persia.[14] He did not quite succeed, although millions must have died and scores of cities and towns were completely destroyed in the process.

Desmond Seward, in his excellent book, *The Hundred Years' War: The English in France 1337-1453,* gives us a frightening account of strategic devastation on a smaller scale, but one which is completely characteristic of military campaigns throughout history.

> On 13 July 1346 the English armada landed at La Hogue, on the north of the Cherbourg peninsula....The following day the King launched a *chevauchee* through the Cotentin, deliberately devastating the rich countryside, his men burning mills and barns, orchards, haystacks and cornricks, smashing wine vats, tearing down and setting fire to the thatched cabins of the villagers, whose throats they cut together with those of their livestock. One may presume that the usual

atrocities were perpetrated on the peasants—the men were tortured to reveal hidden valuables, the women suffering multiple rape and sexual mutilation, those who were pregnant being disembowelled. Terror was an indispensable accompaniment to every *chevauchee* and Edward obviously intended to wreak the maximum *'dampnum'*—the medieval term for that total war which struck at an enemy King through his subjects....

On 26 July Edward's army reached Caen, larger than any town in England apart from London, and soon stormed their way through the bridge gate. When the garrison surrendered, the English started to plunder, rape and kill, 'for the soldiers were without mercy'. The desperate inhabitants then began to throw stones, wooden beams and iron bars from the rooftops down into the narrow streets, killing more than 500 Englishmen. Edward ordered the entire population to be put to the sword and the town burnt, 'and there were done in the town many evil deeds, murders and robberies'—although Godefroi d'Harcourt persuaded the King to rescind his order. The sack lasted three days and 3,000 townsmen died.[15]

And so goes the grim tale throughout Edward's entire campaign in France.

Closer to our own time, it is estimated that in the Thirty Years' War (1618-1648) as much as 40 percent of the population of Germany was wiped out either directly by siege or by strategic devastation with its consequent disease and hunger. Reports of starvation and cannibalism were not uncommon.

What was almost certainly the greatest human cost ever expended in human conflict before the dawn of the twentieth century is almost unknown in the West. China in the middle of the last century was wracked by a series of revolutions and outbursts of civil violence on a scale never seen anywhere before. They lasted from 1850 until 1878. The cost in lives can never be known within even a worthwhile approximation, but it was vast. The worst outbreak, called the Taiping Revolution, lasted from 1850 to 1864. It has been estimated that forty million people died, perhaps 10 percent of the entire population of China. Much of this monumental human cost resulted from the conscious policies of both the rebels and the Imperial Manchu armies as they killed civilians and induced starvation by strategic devastation.[16]

To get a measure of the ethnocentrism we practice in these matters, consider the fact that this titanic human cataclysm does not even merit its own article in most English language encyclopedias. As we shall see, this ethnocentrism is a key feature of our assessment of nuclear war.

In general, wars throughout history were characterized by armies marching from siege to siege and laying waste to the countryside along the way. Moreover, one is constantly struck while reading in primary historical sources just how casually such brutality was accepted. Hugo Grotius, whom we have met before, did as much as anyone to civilize and humanize war. Nonetheless, in his *The Law of War and Peace,* he blithely comments that after a city falls to siege the commander *ought* to turn it over to his troops for three days of plunder (always unavoidably attended by rapes and killings).[17] It is after all, he assures us, a conventional law of war, honored throughout history. He was quite correct, of course. And besides, he continues, it is their due! Just three days though, no more.

Quite simply, most wars in history have been total wars waged without quarter against combatants and noncombatants alike, with the level of destruction *limited only by the means* available. Sometimes this viciousness and brutality was part of the conscious use of terror; sometimes it was completely without rational purpose. Whether purposive or not, it occurred over and over throughout history. Of course, fact does not translate to value; the frequent occurrence of such frightful events does not render them justifiable: most certainly not. It only sets the stage for consideration of what we face today. It tells us that our problems might not be without precedent in history. The siege and sack of cities and the devastation of rural areas made the whole population of a city and the surrounding countryside hostage to their leaders' policies and their enemies' mercy. Constant risk of total war—the stakes being death or enslavement—seems to have been an element of the human condition.

Quite simply, the period between the Thirty Years' War and the advent of the strategic bomber in World War II represents a short hiatus, while the era of strategic bombing and nuclear weapons is a return to the norm. If the military historian Michael Howard is correct, even this relatively humane respite from an otherwise horrifying tale of brutality was not due to the moral values of the West but, instead, to the meager national treasuries that funded wars during that time.[18]

But surely, we want to say that, however regrettable this sad tale is, nuclear war is worse than these examples of human cruelty and stupidity. An unlimited nuclear war between the super powers would, quite simply, be the worst catastrophe in human history, substantially worse than anything that has preceded it. But there are comparable, commensurable experiences of global or at least hemispheric magnitude that snuffed out vast numbers of lives and dislocated and altered the subsequent life histories of even more people, and that profoundly shocked whole cultures and destroyed, at least temporarily, organized polities and societies.

The Black Death[19]

The most catastrophic human experience, at least until the twentieth century, was not man-made. In 1338 and 1339 there arose in Central Asia a new strain of bubonic plague that became, in the next twenty years, the greatest epidemic in history. The plague devastated India and China, though we have not even a vague idea of the extent of human cost there. We know a bit more about its effects in Europe. As many as twenty-five million people, and perhaps more, died in the years 1345 to 1351. That is a staggering number in any case, but it takes on even greater significance when we consider the size of the total population. Estimates generally agree that one in three Europeans died of the plague in that time. One can imagine the havoc that such a death rate would cause to organized society and to the continuity and regularity of human existence.

Yet it was even worse than this, for like war, and especially nuclear war, the effects of the plague were geographically variable. Some areas remained more or less untouched, while in others more than two-thirds of the people died.[20] At least two-thirds of the citizens of Florence died, as did the same proportion of the populations of most of Northern Italy and Southern France. Portions of England and Northern Europe experienced that same mortality rate. Yet some cities, like Milan or Liege, were spared almost completely.[21] Similarly, in rural areas some villages were totally wiped out and ceased to exist while others were passed by with a few deaths or, in a few cases, none.

But the thirteenth century offers even more pointed parallels with what might be the aftermath of a nuclear war. Europe was cursed during that time with a significant cooling of the climate and a series of extremely harsh winters, sometimes called the "little ice age." The cold weather caused a series of famines. Moreover, the plague returned at frequent intervals throughout the remainder of the century. All in all, the population of Europe might have fallen by as much as 40 percent from 1300 to 1400 due to the "die off."[22]

Indeed, one might argue that the thirteenth century offers an excellent historical model of the effects of a nuclear war after the initial blasts upon detonation, with the plague standing in for radioactive fallout and the little ice age for the nuclear winter. But we will see this parallel more clearly only after an examination of the twentieth century's two commensurable phenomena. Certainly, we must also remember that there is no parallel in the thirteenth century to the immediate blast effects of an unlimited nuclear war in which most cities would be struck. Still, we do not seek equivalence, only commensurability.

The First World War[23]

At first blush, the First World War might be seen as the last of the old style wars, not comparable to World War II and certainly not to a nuclear war. After all, there was no significant strategic bombing. Civilians were largely immune from attack. There was none of the ideological fury that existed on the Russian front in the Second World War and which accounted for so much brutalization of civilians and prisoners. There was no equivalent of the Nazi genocide. Yet the First World War must rank with the Black Death and World War II as one of the great global (or, at least, hemispheric) spasms of human death and suffering.

World War I increased the carnage wreaked upon soldiers on the battlefield to an unparalleled level, not to be equaled even on the western front in World War II. This was due primarily to the development in the decades prior to 1914 of rapid firing artillery, the breach loading, repeating rifle and especially the machine gun.[24] These developments gave a huge advantage to the defense.

The generals of World War I, with one or two brilliant exceptions, were in the thrall of an idiotic, doctrinal obsession with the offensive (at the worst possible moment in the history of weapons technology), or were simply stupid. In either case, their solution to the revolution in fire power was to hurl even more human flesh at its tools. Nearly half a million men, French and German, died in the eleven months it took to fight the battle of Verdun. The Battle of the Somme, which resolved nothing and barely moved the front at all, cost the French, the Germans, and the British nearly one million casualties.[25]

All in all, some nine million men died in World War I, with more or less triple that number wounded or missing. Although this war was far less costly of civilian lives than World War II would be, it is estimated that another five million civilians died as a direct result of the war, primarily from starvation and disease. As if this horrible human cost were not sufficient, an influenza epidemic broke out in 1918 that, over the next two years, took another twenty million lives. It is difficult to connect this pandemic disease directly to the war. However, war has always brought disease in its wake, due to increased human movement and dislocation, interrupted or completely destroyed public health and sanitation measures, and lowered resistance brought on by malnutrition and war wounds. It is best to remember that nuclear war might well produce its own set of epidemics.[26]

We are constantly told that a nuclear war would be the end of the United States and the end of organized society. This may be so, but it is not as if the destruction of social structures is new in the works of war. World War I saw the complete disintergration of the Hapsburg state of Austria-Hungary and the empire of the Ottoman Turks, and the destruction of the German and Russian monarchies. Russia fell into complete anarchy and revolution, followed by a bloody civil war and a brutally repressive regime, the human cost of which must be reckoned in the millions of lives. Germany faced anarchy and revolution for several months until the Wiemar leaders obtained at least a semblance of control. The map of Europe and, more profoundly, the way European man organized himself politically were changed forever.

World War II

If history prior to 1939 does not make nuclear war conceivable, then human experience in World War II should. World War II was a total war, almost a war of annihilation. It is primarily the strategic bombing carried out against civilian targets that occupies the focus of Western moral analysis of World War II, but that is pure ethnocentrism. I shall have much more to say of the Allied conventional strategic bombing campaign. The real war, though, the really hair-raising horror, was fought out on the Eastern front.[27] Millions of men died in engagements that dwarfed anything in the West. Prisoners on both sides were summarily shot or systematically starved to death. Civilians were swept up in massive searches for partisans and killed indiscriminately (by both sides). Hostages were taken and killed regularly. Whole peoples were eradicated by both sides, the Jews of Poland and Russia being only the most well-known. Stalin committed virtual genocide on the Volga Germans and Crimean Tatars for suspected disloyalty, transporting the survivors to Siberia. He summarily executed vast numbers of soldiers and officers for retreating or because they had been prisoners.[28] In Leningrad, more people died under siege—approximately one and one-half million—than in all the strategic bombing raids carried out over both Germany and Japan.[29] Many of the survivors were reduced to cannibalism.[30] In the end, Germany was destroyed as a civilization, European Russia and the Ukraine very nearly so. The recovery of both Germany and the Soviet Union is testimony to the recuperative powers of modern society and to the help they both received from the United States.

The "Rape of Nanking" by the Japanese Army in 1937 was one of the most brutal atrocities in history, with perhaps 250,000 Chinese civilians killed in a few days.[31] In the Pacific, once the United States joined the war, a nearly universal *de facto* policy of no prisoners existed on both sides. As we shall see, several of the conventional fire raids on Tokyo were as devastating as the atomic bombs.

World War II was a war of annihilation pure and simple. Yet brutal as it was, could we say it should not have been fought? Would we have been morally more praiseworthy had we stood back and allowed Hitler his vicious predations? Certainly not! Whatever else it was, the European effort in World War II was permissible war waging, exemplary of *jus ad bellum,* of just war aims. Not all the means were morally justifiable, e.g., the Dresden raid or the summary execution of many prisoners by the Soviets, but the aims of self-defense and the defense of whole peoples who were helpless to defend themselves can only be questioned by a confirmed pacifist.

One could argue a bit more over the Pacific War. The final strategic bombing, including the two atomic bombs, might well not have been morally justifiable. (One can arrive at that judgment, however, only after taking into account the attitude of the adversary toward surrender and the human cost of alternatives.[32]) But the war itself seems just, a war to stop a conqueror in his conquests. Japan attacked first and with surprise throughout the Pacific, and practiced total war against a nearly helpless enemy, China. Furthermore, Japan imposed an imperial yoke far more brutal than any the British or French ever had on all of its conquered territories.

If we are prepared to say that we waged war permissibly in World War II, think carefully on this: fifty million souls perished in that war. That is the population of France, or of two Californias, or of seventeen Chicagos. More people died as a direct result of that war than from any cause in a similar time span in history. Body count is not only a gruesome way to keep score morally; it also lacks complete accuracy. One must ask *how* those who died did so and what happened to those who lived. One must weigh other deprivations and the moral value of goals achieved. As we have seen above, more is involved even than the mere calculation of the human cost and human benefit of the consequences. There are rights and duties to be considered. Certainly some, a few at least, in an important sense "deserved" their fate: the Nuremberg criminals and perhaps the brutal prison camp guards whom General Patton was reported to have had summarily executed.

Some large portion of this dreadful human cost would have been incurred almost regardless of whether or not we Americans (or the British) had entered the war. We did not choose to wage war in the first instance. The German and Japanese leaders were dedicated at least to territorial conquest, and perhaps to waging war for its own sake. A large number of those lives would have been lost in any case, given only that some people in Poland or China or Russia would have chosen to resist aggression and conquest. We chose to increase the human cost in order to stop that aggression and end those aggressive regimes. By what amount we increased it we can never know, but we did not originate it. There is a deep lesson here. Faced with an obdurate and determined adversary, one can only react; one's choices are constrained. No decent person or nation makes choices to incur terrible human costs in a moral vacuum.

Still, fifty million dead is a staggering number. Place it against casualty estimates for a nuclear war. A pure counterforce strike (where each side targets only the offensive nuclear weapons of the other) might cause less than twenty million deaths.[33] It makes the blood run cold to speak of millions of human deaths, and it is best to remember that you yourself might well be among any such statistics. Yet, numbers are by definition commensurable, and twenty million is less than fifty million.

The real issue, of course, is that counterforce strikes, a kind of highly limited nuclear war, may well not be containable. What kind of casualties might an unlimited nuclear war impose? Some say extinction of human life on the planet, others permanent reversion to the Stone Age. And we will have to consider these possibilities. But let us rather arbitrarily (but not unreasonably) assume for the moment that an unlimited nuclear exchange between the super powers would kill, within three months of the attack, 60 percent of the population of the United States, 40 percent of the population of the Soviet Union (a more rural society) and 20 percent of the population of Europe, where the nuclear war might be more tactical and less costly of human or, at least, civilian life. That kind of truly devastating strategic nuclear war would cost around 400 million dead. This is far more than fifty million, but on the same scale: it is commensurable, conceivable, and perhaps most important, within our abilities to calculate morally, to make sense of, to denominate right or wrong. At least it is imaginable (and only that) that some events might justify our involvement in such activities, for some chose to pay a smaller but comparable price to stop Hitler and the Japanese military, and thought that it was right to do so.

C. Of Ethnic and Contemporary Bias

We must be brutally honest. There is in our attitude toward the comparison of nuclear war with World War II, and with all the cataclysms which went before it, more than a little ethnocentrism. Nuclear war means the infliction of millions of deaths upon *us*—Americans—upon *our cities* and *our people*. We are the last great insular power, and nuclear devastation is completely without parallel in our own short history. But surely a moral point of view must ignore this. If the war aims of the allies in World War II justified engaging in a war which produced fifty million deaths, including twenty million Soviet citizens, ten million Germans, and 400,000 Americans, then it would surely have been as justifiable if the distribution had run the other way. Yet for the Soviet Union and Germany, World War II was an experience commensurable with many possible sorts of nuclear wars.

It is an ignorant or insensitive person whose palms never sweat at the sound of an especially piercing siren in the middle of the night or who never feels a twinge of panic at the announcement of a low-level "precautionary" nuclear alert. Our lives and those of the ones we love *are* at risk. There is no doubt of it. But is that so different from other peoples in times past? Imagine that you are a member of a tenth century Irish fishing family who could not sleep on moonlit nights knowing that Norse raiders, who kill all the men and carry all the women into slavery, choose such times to strike. Or imagine that you are a fifth century Slavic farmer watching the dust rise on the horizon, wondering if it is caused by a herd of sheep or murderous Hunnic cavalry on the move.

In general, as twentieth-century North Americans attempting to get a conceptual grip on the consequences of nuclear war, we are faced with a twofold limitation. Like all people at all times, we tend to see the entirety of the human story from a contemporary perspective, a kind of "contemporcentricity" if you like. If we are safe and secure, then all men have always been safe and secure. If something new by way of weapons technology distrubs that safety and security, then it is new under the sun, removing that God-given right to safety and comfort that man always had and presumably deserves.

Thus, we forget or studiously ignore, or at least do not attempt to genuinely understand and empathize with, the fear and horror that Southern Italians faced during the Second Punic War or that Germans faced during the Thirty Years' War. But they and most of our fellow men throughout history never had that safety and security we attribute to them. They were always at risk and constantly fearful, as much so as we have recently become again.

Beyond this sort of "contemporcentricity," we Anglo-Americans are profoundly ethnocentric. Man's experience, we tend almost unconsciously to believe, is the experience of the Anglo Saxon, the experience of the United Kingdom, Canada, and the United States. Neither England nor America have been conquered in modern history (let us arbitrarily say since 1500); nor have they even been invaded in force. To be sure, the British landed troops a few places on our shores in 1812, and the Scots made several minor incursions into England over the years, but neither England nor America has suffered anything remotely like the invasions that France, Germany, Italy, Russia, and China have experienced in modern times (most more than once). England has had some rational reason to fear invasion three times: from Spain in 1588; from Napoleon intermittently from 1800 to 1812; and from Hitler in 1940 and 1941. But in each case, the great British fleet made the threat relatively remote. Large-scale invasion of the United States by a world power has been laughable since Yorktown. We have never even had to take it seriously. Think of the significance of that in historical perspective.

England and the United States both fought bloody civil wars but neither produced the massive human cost in death, devastation, and economic and social dislocation of the Thirty Years' War, or the Taiping Revolution, or the Russian or Spanish Civil Wars. Sherman's or Sheridan's campaigns in the South to the contrary, neither country has ever experienced strategic devastation on a large scale, as practiced by both Hitler and Stalin on the Russian front in World War II, or by Japan on China.

Britain was subject to serious and damaging air attacks in World War II, but they were puny when compared to what happened later to Germany and Japan. Before the age of the intercontinental bomber (the 1950s), the United States was beyond the technological reach of any possible attacker.

The conclusion seems inescapable: the Anglo-American world view is one which offers nothing comparable to nuclear war. But then, it offers nothing comparable to the Russian front in World War II, or Japan's war with China, or the Thirty Years' War, or so many other cataclysms. We have lived in a gentle, calm little pool of safety and security, while all around us historically and geographically our fellow humans have faced the omnipresent danger of violent death, or the wrenching dislocation of their ordinary lives, or both. It is we who are different. It is we who departed for a few centuries from the norm and have returned to it—to what can only be described as part of the human dilemma.

It is profoundly sad that this is so, and it demeans our civilization that we could not keep the security we had. We should work very hard to bring it back and to share it with our fellow humans. But we cannot let our privileged status of these last five centuries paralyze our minds when seeking to comprehend nuclear war. Reinhold Niebuhr, the great Protestant theologian, has put it as clearly and as starkly as anyone:

To understand life and history according to the meaning given it by Christ is to be able to survey the chaos of any present or the peril of any future, without sinking into despair. It is to have a vantage point from which one may realize that momentary securities are perennially destroyed both by the vicissitudes of history and by the fact of death which stands over all history.[34]

Nuclear war is commensurable with, though worse than, the worst experiences of human kind, if not those of ourselves as a people. But to grasp this fully, we must probe deeper into the nature of nuclear weapons and their effects.

D. *Nuclear War as Conceivable and Survivable*

The destructive capacity contained in the nuclear arsenals of the two superpowers is immense. It exceeds the energy contained in any natural phenomenon with which we have a high probability of having to contend. The Mount St. Helens volcano, for example, expended approximately the energy contained in a one hundred kiloton bomb (100,000 tons of TNT), or five Hiroshima bombs. Astronomical events, however, could easily dwarf our poor efforts to destroy ourselves. The energy contained in even a 10% increase in the sun's radiant energy or the impact of a moon-sized asteroid upon the Earth, for example, makes our nuclear arsenal appear as a mere firecracker. These events do not appear likely, although they are not beyond imagining. They also would very likely extinguish life or, at least, higher life forms on this planet. But imagine, instead, a fraction of a percent increase in the sun's energy or a collision with a large comet. There are in such speculations comparisons, if we look long enough.

However, our efforts to understand what the nuclear arsenals mean have historically centered upon comparisons with conventional arms; it is not for nothing that "megaton" and "kiloton" have become part of our language. Kosta Tsipis, an MIT nuclear weapons expert, attempts to explain how much explosive force is in a one megaton bomb by comparing it to a train full of TNT. To carry enough TNT to equal a megaton, the train would have to be three hundred miles long.[35] Traveling at fifty miles per hour it would take six hours to pass you. In a manner much like Tsipis, some experts tell us that in the U.S. nuclear arsenal alone we have the equivalent of ten tons of TNT for every person in the world.[36] Overkill! Yes, that is surely overkill—if it means anything at all. It is worth noting that at one point during World War I, there were an estimated nine billion rifle bullets in existence, or six for every man, woman, and child then living on the planet.[37] This was overkill and about as meaningful. There weren't enough rifles, nor enough soldiers to use them. The bullets were not in the right place to kill all the people on earth, and that is not what they were for in any case.

Sometimes one is struck with the feeling that these efforts to help us "comprehend" the magnitude of nuclear weapons and nuclear war are really ways of celebrating its very inconceivability, of paralyzing the mind.

Another similar statistic is that the combined arsenals of the superpowers contain approximately 6,000 times the explosive power of all the bombs dropped in World War II.[38] Within very rough measures of accuracy this is true. But explosive power is not the best measure for capacity to kill or injure people. In any explosion, conventional or nuclear, a great deal of the energy is wasted. The target lies roughly on a plane and the energy of the explosion goes up and down as well as out along the plane where the people are. It is destructive force along two dimensions (forward and backward, right and left) that we are interested in. The destructive force extending along the third dimension (up and down) is of less relevance. Thus, it is two out of the three dimensions that we are interested in, and, therefore, the important (human killing and injuring) portion of the total explosive power varies as taken to the two-thirds power. Indeed, that notion, i.e., $y^{2/3}$, is the definition of the 'equivalent megaton', the most important measure of the deadly effects of nuclear explosions.

If we take the 6,000-times-the-explosive-power by the two-thirds power, we find it equals 330. So, the combined superpower arsenals contain 330 times the explosive power of the bombs dropped in World War II. This is still a vast increase over World War II, but certainly more conceivable. In general, those who write to inform people about nuclear war talk in terms of the more accurate 'equivalent megatons'; those who write to frighten speak of 'simple megatons'.

Weapons must be deliverable to be usable, and nuclear warheads stored in bunkers kill no one. All of our strategic launchers taken together could deliver approximately 3,800 equivalent megatons (EMT) upon the Soviet Union.[39] Compare this to the destructive equivalent of 400 Hiroshima-sized bombs delivered upon Germany in World War II by allied conventional bombing.[40] Four hundred Hiroshima bombs equal approximately 3.9 EMT. Thus, we have a capacity to wreak upon the Soviet Union approximately *974 times* the destruction we visited upon Germany in World War II.

Now we must take into account that the Soviet Union is a much bigger country than is Germany—approximately 63 times as big. Thus, in terms of EMTs per square kilometer, our present strategic arsenal is about *15.5 times* more devastating than what we delivered upon Germany. The population of Germany in 1939 was approximately 69 million, and roughly five hundred thousand Germans died in Allied air raids. If we multiply five hundred thousand times 15.5 and compare it to the total population, we find that if a nuclear war had been visited on Germany in 1939, 7.75 million souls would have perished—only 11 percent of the population.

Do you believe this? Perhaps you shouldn't. These last calculations are not particularly meaningful. Much of the land mass of the Soviet Union is strategically insignificant and the amount of strategically significant target area is not nearly 63 times greater in the Soviet Union than it was in Germany. And the relation between EMTs per unit of area and the number of deaths is probably not linear. Nonetheless, the fifteen times factor and the 11 percent figure are of at least as much value in making comparisons as is the 6,000 times figure with which we started. The real lesson is that these sorts of numbers are not especially helpful. Remember the old saw: "Figures don't lie, but liars figure."

We do know that two factors will substantially mitigate damage in a nuclear war. Improved missile accuracy and the advent of MIRVing (mounting many independently-targeted warheads on one missile) have rendered nuclear weapons themselves subject to attack, so called *counterforce* attack. This is a dangerous, destabilizing development, for it tends to give a much greater advantage to the side which strikes first. But counterforce capability does have another side. It destroys weapons which would otherwise kill people. It is impossible to estimate how many such weapons would be destroyed in a nuclear war (or, more ominously, *whose*) but they would be the *primary target* in any attack, so many of them would be lost. It has been estimated that an attack carried out with complete surprise upon the strategic nuclear forces of the United States could knock out virtually all of our bomber force, up to 90 percent of our land-based ICBM force, and 50 percent of our ballistic missile submarine force (those in base, not those on station). This would reduce the number of deliverable warheads we could launch by two-thirds and the number of EMTs from 3800 to 1260. This reduces the EMT per square kilometer to only slightly more than five times greater than what was delivered on Germany. Be careful! As we have seen, these numbers can be tricky. Also, a complete surprise attack is merely a thought experiment, almost impossible to carry out. So the damage-mitigating effects of a counterforce first strike would, in reality, be more in the range of 10 to 50 percent. Nonetheless, these numbers require reflection. They serve to reduce one's capacity to destroy the adversary's country and populace to terms both more conceivable and more commensurable with World War II.

Let us remember what commensurability does and *does not* mean. No one in his right mind would claim that an unlimited nuclear war would be no more destructive than World War II. That is simply false. The argument I am making is only that it is conceivable in the same terms and measurable on the same scale, though many, many times worse. It bears repeating also that commensurable horror is not *ipso facto* justified horror. It only brings the subject within a recognizable moral ambit.

E. *Jonathan Schell's Nuclear War*

Could we ever conceivably recover from a nuclear war? Could the United States even survive it as an organized society? Would *anybody* in America survive? Conclusive answers to these questions are beyond the scope of this essay; indeed, they are beyond the limits of present human knowledge. I will argue, however, that commensurability and survivability are, at the very least, highly plausible outcomes, and I will frame the first set of moral issues within these plausible assumptions.

How to test this plausibility? The best way I know is to examine a description of a nuclear war put forth by someone who holds a diametrically opposite position. Jonathan Schell, in *The Fate of the Earth*,[41] has argued that the United States could not possibly survive a nuclear war. Indeed, all human beings living in the United States would be killed within the first three months. Nuclear war would bring "the annihilation of the United States and its people" (p. 58) and the United States "would be a republic of insects and grass" (p. 65). Schell goes further with respect to the long-term effects and argues that there is a substantial chance that the human race would be extinguished from the planet. But I shall reserve an examination of these alleged long-term effects until we consider the nuclear winter.

I shall try to show how Schell's arguments are deeply flawed and fail completely to carry us to his conclusions. Certainly, as a matter of logic, by showing that Schell's arguments about the near-term effects fail, I will not thereby have shown that nuclear war is survivable. However, the substance of the examination will indicate just how exaggerated Schell's assumptions are. The measure of that exaggeration will increase the plausibility of the contrary view: that such a war, however horrible, would be survived by many Americans and would be morally commensurable with some past human experiences.

A comment about Schell's style of argument is in order, precisely because he shares it with so many in the antinuclear movement.[42] They practice a kind of fallacious argument based upon emotion which might be called *argumentum ad metum,* appeal to fear. Now make no mistake, nuclear war is fearful in the extreme. No sane person who understands it could or would want to deny that. This mode of argument, however, does not merely describe; it also attempts to paralyze the critical faculties with fear and horror, precisely to *stop* the thought process. It is as if to say "you see how horrible you feel, how fearful...then you see I must be right." In the process of committing this fallacy Schell and others irresponsibly exaggerate the already fearful horror of nuclear war.

There is another related fallacy committed both in Schell's book and by others making a similar point. It is a curious kind of *ad hominem* fallacy and it goes like this:

> No matter how bad I say the effects of nuclear war would be, and no matter how poorly I substantiate the claims I make, if you question my evidence or my conclusions, you are in favor of nuclear war and are therefore a wicked person.

Suffice it to say that no person who is both moral and sane is in favor of nuclear war or thinks it is a worthwhile activity. Our concern is with how to think clearly about nuclear war in moral terms and, thus, how to make both rational and moral decisions about it, *not* to decide if it is a good thing or a bad thing.

In addition to the commission of these two fallacies, Schell's entire analytic framework is symptomatic of a certain blindness, I believe a moral blindness, particularly to the fate of survivors of a nuclear war. Thus, a consideration of his views will advance the larger moral analysis while lending credibility to my factual assumptions.

Schell begins his examination of nuclear war with a description of the atomic bombing of Hiroshima (pp. 36-45). He is not the first to attempt to illustrate the horror of nuclear war by describing the horror of the attack upon Hiroshima.[43] And horrible it was! No one would argue that point. What is lost, I fear, in these renditions is the feature of commensurability. We are treated to far fewer accounts of the horror imposed by conventional weapons upon civilians in World War II. However, if one compares the accounts of the great Tokyo firebomb raids or the combined Allied raid on Dresden or the RAF raids on Hamburg, one finds precious little difference in the ghastly human experience produced by each. John Toland's description of the largest Tokyo raid in particular is startling in its similarity to descriptions of the attack on Hiroshima.[44]

Indeed, accounts by witnesses of each are virtually indistinguishable. Casualties in the Toyko raid Toland describes were somewhat more numerous than those at Hiroshima, and one can be sure that each victim died as horribly. In one of the thousand bomber raids the RAF visited on Hamburg, the asphalt in the streets caught fire and ran along the gutters as it burned. Hell is hell, however we bring it about.

Schell's next step is the hypothetical description of a one megaton blast over New York City (pp. 45-54). This account begins with general accuracy, but it betrays a tendency to bend specific details to his favor so that the accumulated small inaccuracies build up to plainly false conclusions. To put it bluntly, it is not a particularly honest form of argument. But let us consider some examples.

At one point Schell tells us that:

> As far away as ten miles from ground zero, pieces of glass and other sharp objects would be hurled about by a blast wave at lethal velocities [p. 47].

This is simply false. The blast wave of a one megaton blast, ten miles from ground zero, would be traveling at approximately 50 miles per hour.[45] Almost all of us have been in wind storms with winds of that velocity. You have only to ask yourself if you felt pursued by glass and sharp objects hurled at lethal velocities. Such winds are not even classified as "storms" on the Beaufort scale, but are "strong gales." Storms have winds of from 64 to 73 MPH and hurricanes from 74 and above.

Schell further informs us that:

> Anyone caught in the open within nine miles of ground zero would receive third degree burns and would probably be killed [p. 48].

This, too, is false. Third degree burns would occur only inside an 8 mile radius. At 9½ miles most people (82 percent) would receive first degree burns and 18 percent would receive second degree burns.[46] That means they almost certainly would not "be killed" by their burns. Lest the reader believe that the 1 mile addition to the radius is insignificant, it actually overstates the *area* where people would be subject to third degree burns by 26 percent. That means a large number of people (26 percent if the population were evenly distributed) that Schell says would have third degree burns and die simply would not.

There is another inaccuracy in Schell's claim. Not "everybody caught in the open" would be burned at all. The flash of light and heat from a nuclear blast is just that, pure radiant energy. It does not have time to heat surfaces through conduction or air through convection. This curious fact would lead to "profile burns," where only the half of the face or the portion of the body pointed toward the blast would be burned.[47] This means that only those people who were in a direct line of sight to the blast would be burned. Thus, standing behind a building or a hillock or even a tree, anything that casts a "shadow" with respect to the line of sight from the blast, would constitute protection. In addition, the kind of clothing worn, the weather conditions, and many other things can reduce the risk of burn. All in all, most authorities estimate that anywhere from 99 percent to 75 percent of people in the blast area would be protected from flash burns (the higher number on a winter night and the lower on a clear summer day).[48]

Schell reports that in the aftermath of a nuclear bomb blast:

> individual fires would coalesce into a mass fire, which, depending largely on the winds, would become either a conflagration or a firestorm [p. 49].

There is no generally accepted definition of a firestorm, although the physics of one is clear.[49] As a result, there is disagreement over whether the fire at Hiroshima reached the proportions of a firestorm. Schell asserts that it did. The definitive text, *The Effects of Nuclear Weapons,* sits on the fence.[50] This may seem to be a trivial terminological difference, but it is not. Firestorms are far more deadly to a city than lesser fires, since they move more rapidly, burn far more thoroughly, and force hot combustion fumes far higher into the stratosphere.[51] (And the last is a crucial point when we come to discuss the nuclear winter hypothesis.)

What is clear is that, if there was a firestorm at Hiroshima, it was of much lesser intensity than earlier ones caused by conventional incendiary raids over Hamburg, Dresden, and Tokyo. Specifically, the intensity of the winds blowing into the center of the fire give a firestorm its unique cyclonic character. At Hiroshima, those winds reached a maximum velocity of thirty to forty miles per hour.[52] At the Hamburg raid on July 27, 1943, winds reached 150 miles per hour,[53] and at the Dresden raid they were described as being of tornado force, presumably well in excess of 200 miles per hour.[54]

Far more important, there is strong evidence, totally neglected by Schell, that the building materials and type of construction in typical American and Soviet cities *cannot* produce a firestorm.[55] One necessary condition for a firestorm is the presence of eight pounds of combustibles per square foot. Hamburg had 30 lbs/ft². This compares to 2.1 lbs/ft² in a typical American suburb and to 5.1 lbs/ft² in an American urban row house neighborhood. Although Schell claims he used both books cited (pp. 4-5), he neglects to mention this and proceeds to assume a mass fire or firestorm simply *will* break out in all cases (p. 49).

After the rendition of the horrors of an air burst which would maximize the damage done by blast and heat but produce little radioactive fallout, Schell quickly shifts to a ground burst to describe the effects of fallout (p. 50). He tells us of all the additional devastating effects of radioactivity that a ground burst would create but virtually neglects to mention the ways in which a ground burst ameliorates blast effects. All he says is:

> but the range hit by a minimum of five pounds per square inch of overpressure would be less [p. 50].

To put it mildly! As we saw, he systematically exaggerated the blast and heat effects of an air burst. Now he neglects to tell us that a ground burst would reduce the radius of damage from 5 psi of overpressure from 4.4 miles to 2.7 miles and the area so damaged from 61 square miles to 23, that is, by 2.7 times or 62 percent.[56] All of the damage and death connected with blast effect, directly or indirectly, including the spread of fires, he thus overstates by that much.

While the blast effects of a ground burst are considerably less than those of an air burst, the radioactivity spread as a result is much greater. (This is due to the irradiated dust and particulate matter which is injected into the atmosphere by the explosion.) In his effort to demonstrate this undeniable fact, however, Schell gets a bit carried away. He tells us that within the twenty-four hours following a nuclear explosion, if the wind were blowing at 15 MPH:

> fallout of lethal intensity would descend in a plume about one hundred and fifty miles long and as much as fifty miles wide [p. 51].

A bit further on, he reiterates this:

> Doses of around five hundred rems, which would be delivered as far as a hundred and fifty miles downwind...would kill half of all exposed able-bodied young adults [p. 52].

A rem is a unit that measures the intensity of radiation as it affects living tissue. Most authorities agree that somewhere between 350 and 500 rems, by definition, is a "lethal" dosage, precisely because, as Schell rightly points out, that dosage will kill 50 percent of those exposed.

Where Schell is completely wrong is in the claim that one hundred and fifty miles downwind, the dosage within twenty-four hours will reach anything close to a lethal level. Within twenty-four hours, the dosage from a one megaton surface burst will in fact only reach 30 rems, which is well below even the minimal amount that will make one sick.[57] Indeed, the radiation 150 miles downwind will only reach 100 rems after a week, and it will *never* reach 500 rems, or even come close. (A 100 rems dosage will also not produce any sickness or visible symptoms in most normal people.) Using Tsipis's figures, the distance lethality extends downwind is between fifty and fifty-five miles.[58] Schell has exaggerated the distance of lethality by a factor of *three times*. Indeed, this is the beginning of a series of what will lead to the most glaring exaggeration in Schell's account of nuclear war: his account of the effects of radioactivity.

At this point (p. 52), Schell informs us that all of his discussion of the effects of a one megaton bomb on New York City are moot because "...a weapon that is more likely to be used against New York is a twenty megaton bomb." How Schell concludes this is a bit of a mystery, as we shall see. Why he concludes it is no mystery at all. It is extremely scary to talk in terms of twenty megaton bombs. He tells us that "the Soviet Union is estimated to have at least a hundred and thirteen twenty megaton bombs in its nuclear arsenal..." (p. 52). He does not tell us how he knows this. In a way he is probably right because, during the era of the manned bombers and gravity bombs (roughly 1950-1965), both superpowers had lots of these huge bombs. The U.S. arsenal contained hundreds of 20 and 25 megaton bombs.

But Schell can have no possible idea of how many of these horrible old weapons the Soviets deem to be part of their active arsenal. However, the *Military Balance: 1980-1981*, to which Schell refers (p. 55) does attribute 113 Bear heavy bombers to the Soviet Long Range Air Force.[59] (The *Military Balance* is, as Schell says, as authoritative as anything published in the West on Soviet armaments.)

It must be from the presence of these bombers in the Soviet inventory that Schell infers the existence in their arsenal of 113 twenty megaton bombs. From this first dubious inference, Schell leaps to the conclusion:

Since the explosive power of the twenty-megaton bombs greatly exceeds the amount necessary to destroy most military targets, it is *reasonable to suppose* that they are meant for use against large cities [p. 52, emphasis added].

So now we have an inference upon an inference to support the horror of a twenty megaton bomb upon New York.

What is truly "reasonable to suppose" is that these bombs, if they are in the Soviet arsenal at all, are not "intended for" anything. If there, they are residuals from the heyday of the manned bomber and the gravity bomb. What Schell neglects to tell the reader is that the Bear bomber is propeller driven and first entered service in 1955. Indeed, the *Encyclopedia of World Air Power* reports that the Bear became obsolete in the late 1950s and has been largely reassigned to maritime patrol duty.[60]

It is also instructive that Secretary of Defense Weinberger reports that he believes that the day of the American B-52 heavy bomber, an aircraft far superior to the Bear, is over, at least as a manned penetrating bomber.[61] Its future is as a cruise missile platform only. The day of the subsonic bomber and the gravity bomb is over; it is as simple as that. We should be so lucky that the Bear and its gravity bombs were the only threat posed to our cities. (One last thought: Schell might have asked himself what our fifteen jet interceptor squadrons would be doing as the ancient Bear bomber ground its way slowly toward its target.)

Schell rightly reports that some Soviet ICBMs can carry 20 megaton warheads. (Actually, the SS-18 Mod 1 and Mod 3 can carry in excess of 20 megatons.[62]) However, few of their heavy missiles are believed to be tipped with such giant warheads,[63] and most authorities believe that those which are seem intended for earth penetration of hard targets such as the North American Aerospace Defense Command in the middle of Cheyenne Mountain in Colorado.

As I observed earlier, the cumulative effect of Schell's individually small inaccuracies becomes profoundly misleading when he summarizes the effects of a single bomb. When they are extrapolated to assess the results of a nuclear war (pp. 54-61) they get completely out of hand. He quotes Dr. Henry Kendall, of M.I.T. (p. 55), as saying that "without serious distortion" we could assume a Soviet attack of 10,000 warheads, each of one megaton. This immediately overstates the Soviet strategic arsenal by at least 15 percent, even if we assume that they would expend all their warheads in the initial attack.[64] But let us begin with Schell's (and presumably Kendall's) scenario and see what is wrong with it.

Does Schell exaggerate the effects of a 10,000 warhead attack? Yes. Much of the exaggeration comes from his already overstated analysis of a single nuclear detonation. In calculating the area devastated by the blast effects of the bomb, he chooses a circular area defined by 5 pounds per square inch and 40 calories of heat per square centimeter (pp. 56-57). That converts to a circle with a radius of 4.5 miles.[65] That area times 10,000 warheads does equal, as Schell says (p. 56), approximately one-sixth of the land area of the United States, or approximately 600,000 square miles. However, bomb blast areas are circular rather than square and thus must overlap and "overdestroy" some areas while not destroying adjacent areas outside of the circles, so to speak. This effect alone would cut down the area devastated by a minimum of 20 percent, and possibly much more. Having overstated the area of destruction, Schell proceeds to overstate what would occur in it. The flash effect would indeed inflict serious third degree burns on anyone *not sheltered*. But we earlier saw that shelter constitutes any "shadow" and that anywhere from 75 to 99 percent of the populace would be sheltered.

Schell also tells us that:

> the six hundred thousand square miles already scorched by the forty or more calories of heat per centimeter squared would now be hit by blast waves of a minimum of five pounds per square inch and virtually all habitation, places of work and other man made things would be vaporized, blasted or otherwise pulverized out of existence [p. 54].

This is an extreme exaggeration of a grim reality. Five psi overpressure would completely collapse light frame construction but most heavy construction would endure, though damaged, as would basements, vehicles, and numerous other "man made things."[66] At Hiroshima, two-thirds of the buildings were destroyed within the 5 psi circle and casualties approached 50 percent dead and 30 percent wounded.[67] This is frighteningly grim, but it is not being pulverized out of existence. Moreover, many of those killed and wounded at Hiroshima, even within the 5 psi circle, died as a result of the fires, rather than from direct effects of the blast. Five pounds per square inch of overpressure is below the threshold that creates even burst eardrums. Massive traumatic injury is imposed by 20 to 50 psi.[68] Thus, overpressure alone within Schell's 5 psi circle (4.5 miles) would kill almost no one directly. But collapsing buildings and flying glass would. It is undeniable that blast and heat damage would cause staggering casualties within this area, as it did at Hiroshima. Furthermore, we must remember that the area in which Schell postulates the impacts (the one-sixth of the land area of the U.S.) is by far the area in which the largest part of the population lives. Thus, his assumption that survival would be impossible within immediate blast areas, using the Hiroshima results, consigns perhaps 27 million uninjured Americans who live in those areas and 40.5 million who are injured but still alive to the ranks of the annihilated.

Indeed, he tells us that however you present these initial effects of an attack, the conclusion is the same—"the annihilation of the United States and its people" (p. 58). But this is profoundly wrong. When casualty figures are so high a strange mind numbing effect sets in. We are inclined to say: if so many die, then it is as if everyone dies. But it is not.

If 50 percent of the population within the blast area will survive, as the Hiroshima results would indicate, we must think of them. They count morally. It is *not* as if they will be dead. Remember also that, even on Schell's assumptions, some additional number of Americans do not live in the areas of blast (the most populated one-sixth of the land area) and thus would, in large measure, escape blast effects completely unscathed. We owe these survivors some thought and planning.

Let us try to reconstruct Schell's scenario without his exaggerations. Some 27 percent of Americans live in rural areas, outside of any metropolitan area. Surely they would suffer much lower casualty rates than those who live in urban areas. There would, however, be casualties among these Americans because of their proximity to some of our more remote military bases. We shall somewhat arbitrarily, but plausibly, assume that of the 27 percent of Americans living in rural areas, 55 percent (15 percent of the total U.S. population) would be unhurt and another 20 percent (5 percent of the total U.S. population) would be wounded but alive. All in all, under Schell's own hypothetical attack scenario, reconstructed without exaggeration and using the Hiroshima results, there would be a good chance that fifty million Americans would survive the blast effects unhurt and another fifty million would survive with injuries. That is one hundred million living human beings whom Schell treats as though they would be dead.

After describing the effects of a 10,000 megaton attack calculated to maximize blast effects, he abruptly shifts to a fallout maximizing attack made up solely of ground bursts (pp. 58-59). He tells us:

> However, calculations on the basis of figures for a one-megaton ground burst which are given in the Office of Technology Assessment's report show that ten thousand megatons would yield one-week doses around the country *averaging more than ten thousand rems* [p. 59 emphasis added].

This is a most mysterious claim. The OTA's study gives no "figures" on which such "calculations" could be based. Schell gives us no page reference, nor does he state any further what his assumptions are or where they come from. Suffice it to say that his figure of 10,000 rems is wildly inconsistent with anything else ever produced upon the subject. Using the maps included in the OTA study of a one megaton surface burst on Detroit, and extrapolating to a 10,000 warhead attack made up solely of surface bursts, one gets a one week dosage of 3,000 rems for approximately 60 percent of the area of the United States.[69] So even given the OTA results, Schell has overstated the fallout by *3.3 times*. However, the OTA study predicts considerably more severe fallout levels than almost any other authority. I calculated on the basis of Glasstone and Dolan's text that in a similar fallout maximizing attack, the whole of the United States would be subjected to a minimum of 1,300 rems, with areas closer to the blast site receiving more.[70] So, Schell has overstated the radiation effects of this kind of an attack by as much as *7.7 times*. It is worth noting that Tsipis predicts even less severe results than those which I calculated from Glasstone and Dolan.[71]

Not only does Schell exaggerate many times over the effects of a fallout maximizing attack, he completely ignores the effects of shielding or shelter. Although it would save the lives of vast numbers of Americans, he simply does not bring it up. A dosage of 1300 rems would be fatal to virtually all human beings who were completely exposed (that is, *outside all the time during the full exposure period*). But, unlike Schell's 10,000 rem exposure, there are many things one could do to mitigate it. So called "territorial masking"—being to the leeward of a hill, for example—would cut exposure by 30 to 60 percent.[72] By simply staying inside an ordinary residence, one would reduce the exposure to 40 percent of the outside dosage.[73] This could bring the level of exposure below the 50 percent fatality level (450 rems). Taking shelter in a residential basement would reduce the exposure to 5 to 10 percent of the outside level, which takes it under the threshold for any form of manifest radiation sickness. Surprisingly, the dose rate for a typical apartment house is 10 percent of outside exposure on the ground floor (a reduction of 90 percent) and as little as 1 percent in upper floors (a reduction of 99 percent). All of this mitigation occurs without any sort of preplanned fallout shelter, merely staying inside or staying in a basement. In short, even in so theoretical a radiation maximizing attack as Schell postulates, a very large proportion of the population could and would survive.

Keep in mind that even if the Soviets had the means of carrying out this fallout maximizing attack, it would never happen. For the Soviets to launch a radiation maximizing attack they would have to give up much of the blast destruction of air bursts and detonate all devices merely for fallout effect. Blast effect and fallout effect are mutually inconsistent and competing effects (technically, "conjugate parameters"). One is maximized only by minimizing the other. Schell's constant switching back and forth between the scenarios he is considering confuses the reader as between his blast maximizing attack and his fallout maximizing attack. We must remember that Schell is talking about two different, mutually inconsistent nuclear wars, one which maximizes blast effect and one which maximizes fallout. Through his own confusion and the reader's, it is easy to get the impression that he *combines their worst effects* and calls them *one* attack.

In addition to overstating the effects of attacks that are mere thought experiments in any case, Schell overstates the size of a realistically possible Soviet attack in a number of ways. He does this by neglecting several vital considerations. Schell interprets unlimited thermonuclear war as each power unleashing its entire arsenal instantaneously at the other (p. 55). This defies any account of nuclear strategy, even for a so-called "unlimited" war. An unlimited nuclear war has a clear and practical definition in the literature. It means a war in which targets or types of weapons used are not limited by mutual and reciprocal restraint. As one component of its meaning, then, it would include strategic targets, i.e., targets in the homelands of the primary combatant powers. It does not mean a thought experiment in which the worst of all logically possible wars would be fought, where the entire aresenal of each side is instantaneously released upon the other. Even a practically unlimited nuclear war would reach a range of natural limits defined by a series of discounting factors.

1. Counted in Schell's attack are the twenty megaton gravity bombs carried by the Bear bombers referred to earlier. It is very doubtful that they would ever be used in *any* attack upon the U.S. Yet this dubious "force" constitutes 2,000 of his 10,000 megatons, or 20 percent of the explosive power of the attack. Then, by verbal legerdemain, he converts the 10,000 megatons to 10,000 one megaton warheads. Thus, 113 old propellar driven bombers become 2,000 missile warheads. This is roughly equivalent to all the warheads carried by all the Soviet ballistic missile submarines, a significant, if highly dubious, addition to the Soviet strategic forces.

2. Almost no conceivable attack could be staged that would constitute a complete surprise. There are deep decision-theoretic and systemic planning reasons why this is so. Suffice it to say that time would be available for some utilization of American counterforce weapons against some Soviet strategic weapons prior to their launch. Such a response would mitigate damage by destroying some significant percentage of the Soviet missile force—perhaps 10 to 30 percent.

3. Virtually any nuclear strategy that either side might adopt would require a large reserve of strategic weapons to be used in subsequent stages of the battle. Under no conceivable circumstances would either side launch everything it had all at once. Yet this is exactly what Schell supposes. The notion of a strategic reserve is unequivocally part of Soviet strategy.[74] As we shall see below, the existence of those reserves will create important moral imperatives upon the

attacked country to defend itself. At present, we shall only observe that Schell's hypothesized 10 percent reserve of Soviet weapons (p. 54) would be woefully inadequate for Soviet purposes.

In reality, Schell provides for no reserve at all because, as we have seen, he has assumed the Soviets have 15 percent more warheads than they do. He plays the same game with megatonnage (p. 54). Beginning with a total maximum possible megatonnage in the Soviet arsenal (which he neither attributes to a reliable source nor justifies), he concludes that the Soviets have 11,500 megatons to deliver, again without any justification. Then he equivocates between megatons of explosive energy and the far more important 'equivalent megatons', telling us finally that he assumes that they will use 10,000 megatons for their attack and reserve 1,000. The 500 megatons apparently get lost. In fact, the best sources put the total Soviet strategic arsenal at somewhere between 6505 Emts[75] and 4535 Emts.[76] This means that Schell has overstated the destructive power of the Soviet arsenal by somewhere between 77 and 154 percent.

4. Schell must assume that all submarine-launched ballistic missiles in the Soviet armory would be launched and strike their targets. Yet, the Soviets keep only about 7 to 10 percent of their subs on station[77] and they are constantly monitored by U.S. antisubmarine forces.

The Soviets would risk preemption by the U.S. if they began to put many more subs on station. Furthermore, even if they did and we did not preempt, we would monitor them through various "choke points," track them, and, in the first minutes of an attack, would unquestionably destroy many. American antisubmarine capability is one of the least advertised but most potent arms of our military establishment. It is almost inconceivable that the Soviets could utilize much more than 50 percent of their submarine-launched ballistic missiles, and perhaps no more than 10 percent. That component of their strategic forces represents 16 percent of their total number of warheads. (It should be reported that the newer long-ranged Soviet submarine-launched ballistic missiles can be fired from home waters. However, as of now, only a few Soviet submarines are able to carry these larger missiles.)

5. Schell makes no provision for Soviet strategic launchers that are not operational due to maintenance, a number that often runs higher than 30 percent in any complicated weapons system. Furthermore, he makes the grossly simplistic assumption that so incredibly complicated an attack could take place with weapons never tested in combat conditions, over trajectories never fired before, with zero loss from mechanical malfunction, targeting error, or command or communication breakdown. But any person familiar with complicated systems knows that some such failures *must* occur and that they will

probably be substantial in number. This factor is, indeed, one of the significant mitigating factors of the damage created by a possible nuclear war, and it is one which is ignored or dramatically understated by almost all commentators regardless of ideological bent. Put simply, many of the damned things won't work! Chant and Hogg, in *Nuclear War in the 1980's,* try to assess the probability of everything from the silo doors failing to open to the failure of warheads to detonate upon impact. They conclude that a shockingly high 65 percent of ICBMs will malfunction.[78] In a penetrating analysis of Soviet (and, by implication, U.S.) missile reliability, Andrew Cockburn concludes that the rate of malfunction may even be higher.[79]

Indeed, a related argument is frequently made by those who deny the existence of a U.S. "window of vulnerability" to a Soviet first strike.[80] They argue that, given all the technical and operational uncertainties, the Soviets would never launch a counterforce first strike against our land-based ICBMs because of the great chance that such failures as discussed above would occur. In addition, there are unsolvable timing problems with such an attack. Thus, the theoretical vulnerability of our ICBMs to counterforce attack is not real. (Those who make such arguments are critics of the Reagan Administrations efforts to close that window of vulnerability by strategic force modernization and are generally of dovish inclination.)

It is interesting that Schell ignores even the arguments of his own allies and implicitly sets the malfunction factor for Soviet forces at 0 percent. A related issue to keep in mind is that the more surprise the attacker attempts to achieve, the less visible preparation he dares permit himself, and the higher will be the malfunction factor. Thus surprise, which allows for the destruction of one's adversary's nuclear weapons before they can be used, and reliability, which cuts down on the malfunction of weapons, are inconsistent and competing parameters. *Increasing surprise decreases reliability.* One way or the other, nuclear destruction is mitigated because fewer weapons are available for use, either through counterforce destruction or lack of preparedness.

6. Schell also assumes that the Soviets would not reserve or use any of their strategic nuclear inventory for China or Western Europe. It is true that their theater nuclear weapons would largely take care of those nuclear battles but certain targets would require strategic weapons: China's southern rim, for example.

Thus, when the practical world of real nuclear war is considered, it is clear that Schell has exaggerated the effect of a nuclear attack in warheads and megatons striking the United States by at least 60 percent and perhaps as much as 85 percent. Indeed, he has engaged in a thought experiment about as relevant as the overkill calculations that we considered earlier. Perhaps such a thought experiment is valid, though I do not know for what. It certainly is scary!

Schell's conclusion is not surprising: "the annihilation of the United States and its people" (p. 58). "Annihilation" literally means reduction to nothing, and Schell's consequent assertion bears this out: we have no reason to consider life after nuclear war. There will be none. We certainly have no need to consider defense against further Soviet attack. We will all have been annihilated. We have no reason to consider long-term effects (although he does) because we will all be dead in the near term. Thus, his conception of the moral issues involved in a second strike become deceptively simple. An American president cannot face a moral question of a second strike because he is "the leader of no one." He commands no forces. There is nothing. The United States is a republic of insects and grass (p. 65).

But life is not so simple; we will not all be annihilated. Some Americans will be alive and that has moral consequences. The conclusion that we have reached, contrary to Schell, is shared by almost all scientifically responsible studies. The Office of Technology Assessment has compiled studies from the Department of Defense, the Arms Control and Disarmament Agency, and the Defense Civil Preparedness Agency.[81] The results range from 23 percent fatalities in the U.S. population to 88 percent, depending upon an array of assumptions including evacuation, fallout protection, and ratio of ground bursts to air bursts.[82] This means that in the worst case 195 million Americans would die in the near term. That is a staggering number, but still nearly 30 million would live. Herbert Abrams and William von Kaenel, writing in the *New England Journal of Medicine,* believe that in a practically unlimited Soviet attack, 133 million Americans would die within two months.[83] Kosta Tsipis projects 100 million near-term deaths.[84] The Federation of American Scientists estimates 150 to 190 million deaths, or 30 to 70 percent of the U.S. population.[85] The International Physicians for the Prevention of Nuclear War estimate that in the United States *and* the Soviet Union, 200 million would be killed immediately and another 60 million seriously injured or seriously sickened.[86] Assuming that all those injured would die within three months, that is almost exactly 50 percent of the combined population of both countries. A vastly important conclusion follows from all these studies: somewhere between 23 million and 150 million Americans would survive an unlimited nuclear war.

To be sure, the projected numbers of dead are mind-numbing. They measure the loss of human *lives* and contemplating them tends to shut down the thought process. But that is a reaction that, while understandable, is not justifiable. For it leads to grave mistakes in moral reasoning. Those who are most emotional in their reaction to nuclear war tend to forget (or deny, as in Schell's case) that there will be survivors. There will be many millions of them, perhaps more than there will be of the dead. Obviously, our first moral obligation is to avoid nuclear war. However, if war comes, we are under a strict obligation to those who survive to maximize their numbers and, if possible, make tolerable the quality of their postwar lives. They do not, by virtue of what has happened to their society, become moral ciphers. That there will be large numbers of survivors of the blast and fallout effects is clear. But will any survive the long-term climatic effects? It is to this question that I now turn.

F. *The Nuclear Winter*

On Halloween, 1983 Carl Sagan led a group of scientists in a press conference in Washington, D.C. The purpose was to announce the results of a study, at that time not yet published in a learned journal, which claimed to show that a nuclear war of any serious magnitude would immediately throw the Earth into a catastrophic climatic change turning daylight to darkness, causing temperatures to plummet to perhaps − 25 °C and stay there for as long as three years. All of this would occur over the Northern Hemisphere and very possibly over the remainder of the planet as well.

The press, as might be expected, had a field day. Sagan, Ehrlich, *et al.* did the rounds of the news and talk shows, appearing on ABC's *Nightline* and the *Phil Donahue Show*. All of this appeared to be carefully coordinated and professionally managed. No wonder! The public relations firm of Porter and Novelli had been retained and a budget of $100,000 earmarked for promotion, and all of this *before* any scientific study has been released.[87]

However, in time a pair of papers in *Science* and later a paper in *Scientific American* did report the results of a study. (The authors' names— R.P. Turco, O.B. Toon, T.P. Ackerman, J.B. Pollack, and Carl Sagan —make up the acronym TTAPS by which the papers, particularly the study in *Science,* are known in the literature. I will adopt this convention.[88]) Whatever our reaction might be to the carefully staged hoopla, the results, although highly tentative and somewhat speculative, deserve to be taken most seriously. But analysis will nonetheless dampen considerably what appears at first blush to demand a fundamental change in our thinking about nuclear war. In this section we shall see, first, that the nuclear winter actually predicted by the study is substantially "milder" than that which was bandied about by the press prior to the release of the study. Second, both scientific opinion and subsequent analysis since the original study was released have pushed even further in the direction of making the nuclear winter milder. Third, a great many questions have been raised which shed doubt upon any climatic effect of a nuclear war at all or suggest that it might even give rise to atmospheric heating. Finally, we shall see later in the book that the policy implications that are said to flow from the facts simply do not.

I should enter one caveat at this point. I am not a climatologist, nor even a physical scientist, although I am familiar enough with physical science. What follows is not a professional critique. It is an inquiry by a layman into questions which professionals will eventually have to address. That a layman can raise so many rather obvious questions should, however, throw considerable doubt upon the study.

Results of the Study: TTAPS Baseline Case

The cause of the nuclear winter is believed to be the large amount of particulate matter in the form of dust and smoke that nuclear detonations would hurl into the atmosphere. These materials, it is hypothesized, would reduce the sunlight reaching the Earth's surface, thereby causing a rapid cooling and a darkening of the daytime sky.

If one reviews the actual data and analyzes the studies, it is impossible not to get the impression that the effects of the nuclear winter have been seriously overstated, not only by the press, but by the investigators themselves in their popular pronouncements. There is no doubt that, if they are correct, the climatic effects will be dramatic. But dramatic effects are not necessarily catastrophic.

The results of their baseline case, a 5000 megaton (hereafter MT) war is instructive. They hypothesize a 4000 MT counterforce attack (by the two sides combined) coinciding with a 1000 MT countervalue attack.[89] This is a grim but realistic scenario of what an unlimited nuclear war between the superpowers might be like. This kind of nuclear war (hereafter, baseline case) would cause the sky to be darkened to the equivalent of a heavily overcast day or darker for approximately fifteen days following a nuclear war.[90] However, thereafter the sky would lighten rapidly toward normal, reaching near-normal within 100 days. The temperature would drop to a low of $-9\,°F$ ($-23\,°C$) within twenty days and remain there for another twenty days. Then the temperature would climb rapidly, reaching $32\,°F$ ($0\,°C$) in approximately 90 days and approximately $40\,°F$ within 120 days after the attack. Thereafter, the temperature would recover more slowly, reaching ambient average temperature ($56\,°F$) between 360 and 400 days after the war.

There are, of course, a wide variety of simplifying assumptions used in this analysis, but several are especially noteworthy. The temperature drop (although not the lowest temperature reached) would be greater in the summer, not so great in the winter. The variation from daytime temperatures to nighttime that we are used to would not occur, of course, because of the overcast conditions. So the low temperatures reported would indeed be lows, whereas ambient temperature in normal times is an average of daily lows and highs. This has the effect of overstating the temperature drops.

Let us imagine a nuclear war taking place in late spring. This is the worst time to get the most "winter" of very cold (below 10°) and very dark days that would last perhaps sixty days. This would be followed by an "autumn" of chilly temperatures and lightening skys that would last perhaps another ninety days. Soon a normal winter would commence. But by the following spring, one year after the nuclear war, most of the worst effects, *even by the authors' account,* would have passed.

Indeed, the authors discuss two strongly ameliorating effects which they did not take into account in their calculations. First, the model they use is a one-dimensional model. That is, it analyzes what occurs in a column of atmosphere.[91] As we shall see, this may seriously vitiate their entire study. Even Sagan admits it may cause their calculations of the effects to be overstated by up to 30 percent.[92] This means that in their baseline case the lowest temperature reached in continental interiors might be 11 °F, with the entire curve moderated accordingly.

Moreover, the authors believe that the oceans would drop in temperature only very little.[93] Thus, reduced effects in coastal areas might cause the general effects to be ameliorated by another 50 percent. Unlike the first ameliorating effect, this one is certain. The combined effects of the two overstatements means that for coastal areas the low point might reach only 33 °F, in which case we would be talking about a "nuclear autumn" which, for a war fought in late autumn or early winter, might almost be unnoticeable.

In any case, a nuclear winter which causes a few weeks at or below 0 °F, a few more at or a few degrees below 32 °F, and a few more which could best be described as a chilly autumn seems a far cry from the "new ice age" announced by the press and proclaimed by the antinuclear movement. It is hard to imagine that the ecosystem of the planet would be destroyed, or that human life on earth or even in the Northern Hemisphere would be extinguished.

However, such a nuclear winter would certainly be a greater short-term departure from normal weather patterns than any event heretofore experienced in recorded history. But would its effects be catastrophic? Yes, they would, but ironically they would not be catastrophic (or more properly, incrementally catastrophic) upon the countries attacked.

The authors rightly point out that the worst effects of such a nuclear winter would be on agriculture in the Northern Hemisphere. What would occur is fairly straightforward and simple. If a nuclear war occurred at any time other than late autumn, the Northern Hemisphere would miss *one entire crop year.* That effect in the already devastated combatant countries—the United States, the Soviet Union, and Europe— would very probably not be incrementally catastrophic. Imagine the consequences of a nuclear war as already described. The population would have been reduced to a relatively small precentage of the prewar population, say somewhat arbitrarily 20 to 50 percent. The economic infrastructure would be in ruins, making the transportation necessary for highly technological farming impossible at least in the first year after a war. In addition, the manufacturing capacity for fertilizers and pesticides would in all probability have been destroyed or severely damaged. It is very difficult to image how a substantial crop could be planted, reaped, and distributed with or without a nuclear winter.

To be sure, hunger would be a serious problem in the combatant countries, but that would be true even without a nuclear winter. All surviving communities or individuals would have to live at least one year on accumulated stores of food and that implies that hunger would be quite a desperate problem in some places. However, the pattern of death and damage would lessen the problem somewhat, and perhaps considerably; for rural areas, where most of the survivors would be, are also the areas where the largest amount of food is stored, in the form of food and feed grain stores.

The cold would impose very strenuous conditions upon the survivors, particularly upon those who were injured or who had received high doses of radiation, thus weakening their immune systems and making them especially susceptible to respiratory infections. But for the healthy, it would not be any worse than a typical winter, and it would be a bit shorter. Keep in mind, though, that most survivors would have to go through this artificial "winter" without central heating or electricity.

There is one salutary effect of the cold, however. Its presence would substantially reduce the risk of epidemics caused by unburied human and animal corpses. Indeed, it could provide a necessary respite in which smaller communities could make provision for such problems.

The truly devastating effects of the nuclear winter produced by the TTAPS baseline case would be in the Northern Hemisphere noncombatant countries where, if the nuclear winter wiped out a crop year (which it would unless the war was fought in late autumn or early winter), massive starvation could occur among the otherwise living and healthy populations. India, China, Indochina and northern Indonesia, which have all recently reached or approached self-sufficiency in grain production could, if they lost their entire crop, be thrown into a most catastrophic famine.

Results of the TTAPS Worst Case Scenarios

Unfortunately, most press coverage and, indeed, most of the public attention received by Sagan, Ehrlich, *et al.* have been concentrated upon their worst cases rather than their baseline scenario. This class of worst cases centers on a 10,000 MT exchange. Case 9 is typical.[94] It presupposes that three-quarters of each superpower's strategic arsenal is released upon the other more or less instantaneously. The authors admit that this kind of a war is unlikely. The National Research Council's study worked with a 6500 MT baseline case, closer to the TTAPS baseline case.[95] Indeed, the 10,000 MT case is most unlikely because of all the discounting factors we considered in discussing Schell's conception of nuclear war.

The results of such a "possible" exchange are indeed horrendous. In one 10,000 MT case, using the most severe assumptions about dust and smoke, ambient air temperatures would be lowered to -53°F (-47°C) for several months. Another 10,000 MT case would lower temperatures to -18°F (-28°C). After sixty days, under this scenario, temperatures would have returned to 1°F (-17°C), and after one hundred days to 18°F (-7°C). Obviously, the 10,000 MT cases are more consistent with the impression the public has been given of the severity of the nuclear winter. Still, there are even here a number of powerful ameliorating influences or conditions.

1. The oceans are a huge reservoir of heat and as a result would bring the temperatures back to normal within a reasonable time frame. The oceans would drop only a few degrees in temperature, if that.[96]

2. Even in the worst of the worst cases, almost all the temperature and sky-darkening effects will have worked their way out of the atmospheric system within approximately 400 days.[97]

3. The ameliorating effects of a three-dimensional model and coastal effects discussed above would still be present. The temperatures stated above are the products of a one-dimensional analysis and are for the continental interiors.

4. Under Case 17's assumptions, sunlight would become occluded enough to stop photosynthesis for only forty days and to bring sunlight under the compensation point for photosynthesis for approximately seventy days. (The compensation point for photosynthesis is the amount of sunlight such that the energy produced from photosynthesis exactly equals the energy used for plant respiration.)[98]

5. Although the authors make ominous references to the contamination of the Southern Hemisphere, they present no mechanisms for that. Among meteorologists a nearly universal consensus has been reached that the weather systems of the two hemispheres are almost completely independent. As a result, it is hard to credit this as anything more than scare talk.

6. Even less well-founded is such talk as this by Ehrlich: "In other words, we could not exclude the possibility of a full scale nuclear war entraining the extinction of *Homo sapiens.*"[99] If one follows Ehrlich's reasoning to this conclusion, it seems strained at best and perhaps something worse. First, he chooses the absolute worst case out of seventeen cases to use for a chapter entitled "The Biological Consequences of a Nuclear War," and then he goes on to systematically exaggerate even that case.

Problems with the Nuclear Winter Hypothesis

It is unfortunate that the public has not been made aware that almost everything that they have been told about the nuclear winter has been based upon the most severe and most implausible worst case scenario out of seventeen. What is even more unfortunate is that the public has been told by the media, with what appears to be the tacit assent of the scientists, that the nuclear winter simply *will* occur after a nuclear war. The implication is that it is as certain as that the sun will come up tomorrow or that a bowling ball dropped from a tower will fall. In short, it is a "scientific fact." The scientists know this to be completely false and say so explicitly in their scientific writings. They should say so explicitly in public.

It will take some time for the scientific community to digest the TTAPS claims and develop a careful, thorough response to them. This is due in part to the normal lag time in analysis and study. Unfortunately, it is also due to the intellectual intimidation of the "peace movement." Freeman Dyson has said of the TTAPS, "Frankly, I think its an atrocious piece of physics, but I quite despair of setting the record straight....Who wants to be accused of being in favor of nuclear war?"[100]

Perhaps the most searching criticism of the TTAPS study available in the scientific literature to date has come from Dr. Howard Maccabee, who is a physician specializing in nuclear medicine and who also holds a Ph.D. in nuclear engineering.[101] A good deal of my criticism of the TTAPS study will be based on his excellent article. In addition, a far more cautious study released in 1985 by the National Research Council, entitled "The Effects on the Atmosphere of a Major Nuclear Exchange," provides an invaluable list of caveats regarding this entire subject.[102] Finally, in March 1985 the Department of Defense released its own summary, "The Potential Effects of Nuclear War on the Climate," which, far from being a whitewash of the nuclear winter hypothesis, is a balanced and fair-minded evaluation.

The conclusion that I have reached from a study of these sources and from the original work by TTAPS is that the nuclear winter hypothesis, at least in the form advanced as the baseline case by the TTAPS authors, is highly uncertain at best and implausible at worst. The TTAPS worst case scenarios are even more dubious.

On the other hand, both the National Research Council and the Department of Defense studies agree that there is a threat.[103] The NRC study says:

> The general conclusion that the committee draws from this study is the following: a major nuclear exchange would insert significant amounts of smoke, fine dust, and undesirable chemical species into the atmosphere. These depositions could result in dramatic perturbations of the atmosphere lasting over a period of at least a few weeks. Estimation of the amounts, the vertical distributions, and the subsequent fates of these materials involves large uncertainties. Furthermore, accurate detailed accounts of the response of the atmosphere, the redistribution and removal of the depositions, and the duration of a greatly degraded environment lie beyond the present state of knowledge.
>
> Nevertheless, the committee finds that, unless one or more of the effects lie near the less severe end of their uncertainty ranges, or unless some mitigating effect has been overlooked, there is a clear possibility that great portions of the land areas of the northern temperate zone (and, perhaps, a larger segment of the planet) could be severely affected. Possible impacts include major temperature reductions (particularly for an exchange that occurs in the summer) lasting for weeks, with subnormal temperatures persisting for months. The impact of these temperature reductions and associated meteorological changes on the surviving population, and on the biosphere that supports the survivors, could be severe, and deserves careful independent study.
>
> *A more definitive statement can be made only when many of the uncertainties have been narrowed, when the smaller scale phenomena are better understood, and when atmospheric response models have been constructed and have acquired credibility for the parameter ranges of this phenomenology.*[104]

Climatology is very far from an exact science. At best, it can only use broad parameters within which climatological effects may with some probability fall. At worst, it is informed speculation. In the case of the nuclear winter it is especially close to the latter. The prediction of the climatological and ecological effects of a nuclear war is literally incalculably complex. To develop a feel for this, imagine the sorts of factors that would have to be considered in assessing the local and regional ecological effects of a single nuclear detonation:

A. The nature of the detonation:
  1. Yield in kilotons or megatons;
  2. Whether it is an air burst, surface burst, or a subsurface burst;
  3. If air, altitude; if subsurface, depth;
  4. Construction of bomb, amount of yield attributable to fission versus fusion, amount and composition of casing material.

B. Meteorological conditions which determine what happens to the energy released:
  1. Time of year;
  2. Time of day;
  3. Surface temperature at time of detonation;
  4. Temperature at various altitudes;
  5. Precipitation, cloud cover, humidity;
  6. Winds at surface, at various altitudes, jet stream velocity and direction.

C. The geographical, topological, geological features of the detonation site which determine what happens to the energy released and the nature and amount of dust produced:
  1. Proximity of detonation to water;
  2. Nature of soil and other surface material;
  3. Soil moisture, surface moisture;
  4. Soil temperature;
  5. Nature of plant life (likelihood of grass or forest fires);
  6. Topological features of the terrain. (Fire storms and conflagrations are less likely in a hilly city. Hilly terrain also provides greater "masking" from radioactivity.)

D. Features of human habitation (primarily for kind and amount of smoke):
  1. Does the detonation start fires? How many?
  2. What sorts of combustibles are available? What sorts of smoke do they make? What is the quantity of combustibles?
  3. What is the mean kindling temperature? What is the distribution of kindling temperatures?

All the possible answers to these and other questions make for millions of permutations of possible conditions. Moreover, many are synergistic, i.e., they causally influence and are influenced by each other, creating disproportionate effects. For example, a great deal of water vapor and liquid water droplets in the air (clouds or precipitation) dampen the initial heat effects of a blast (burns and spontaneous combustion) and also substantially lower the tendency of fires to spread. Another example: winds influence the spread of radioactivity, of dust, and of smoke, and also are crucial in spreading fires and starting firestorms.

Now imagine all the millions of possible sets of effects of a single nuclear detonation, then multiply those by ten thousand again (assume 10,000 detonations of an average one-half megaton for a 5000 MT nuclear war. One half of those detonations are on each side.) The number of possible nuclear wars is practically infinite. Not only are there literally millions of synergistically interacting parameters, most of which are unknown, but we also do not understand many of the physical laws by which they interact.

In addition to the overwhelmingly complex and uncertain nature of the task the TTAPS authors set for themselves, there are some very serious questions about their methodology and assumptions. The model they employed is one dimensional. That is, the interactions of smoke, dust, and sunlight are measured only vertically along a column. The movements of the air north, south, east, and west are ignored. The authors attribute their use of a one-dimensional model to the lack of a three-dimensional one.[105] Perhaps this is so, but, as we have seen, Sagan admits that a three-dimensional model permits tracking of general circulation which might moderate results by 30 percent.[106] Thus, the one-dimensional model automatically and very directly provides a worst case along at least one parameter (lateral circulation, which is implicitly held at 0).

But the one-dimensional model forces several other worst case assumptions indirectly. The inability to track the circulation laterally in space and time of dust and smoke leads the authors to make two crucial simplifying assumptions: first, that the cloud would be of totally uniform density and opacity over the entire Northern Hemisphere; and second, that it would appear instantaneously over that area. These are certainly simplifying assumptions, but they are also quite conveniently worst case assumptions. *Any* nonuniformity in the cloud will allow more solar energy to be transferred to the earth. *Any* time taken for the cloud to form will attenuate sun-occluding effects of the cloud and thus lessen the sudden temperature drop resulting in a smaller temperature decline.

These worst case assumptions are obviously false. There would be large areas of the Northern Hemisphere that would sustain few if any detonations—above 70° latitude north or below 30° north. In addition, the oceans would create huge "holes" in the cloud that would take some time to fill as they circled the earth.

The assumption of an instantaneous appearance by the cloud is also clearly false. Indeed, we have seen that the notion of an all out nuclear war, in which both superpowers release all their weapons at each other within minutes, is a myth. An actual nuclear war would last days, with detonations occurring thereafter for weeks or even months. The time taken to create the cloud is quite important in mitigating the effects on temperature. To keep in perspective the centrality of the time elapsed during a nuclear war, consider this: we dump into the air every year the same amount of smoke as would be produced by a nuclear war.[107] It does not have catastrophic effects precisely because it is spread over time.

In general, the TTAPS authors seem to have ignored the powerful ameliorating effects of the vast amount of water in the earth's ecosphere. We have already seen that the huge reservoirs of heat represented by the oceans would prevent a precipitous drop in temperature and would thus be indispensable to the recovery of the ecosphere. The combustion of the cities would also generate large amounts of water vapor. All this water vapor would either create immediate rain, a sort of dampening feedback system that would slow the very fires that generated it, or it would fall later downwind, thereby scrubbing the atmosphere of dust and smoke particles and bringing a more rapid end to the clouds occluding the sun. Atmospheric water follows a cycle from evaporation through precipitation and back to vapor in about one week. There is approximately 104 times more water vapor in the atmosphere than there is smoke assumed in the TTAPS model.[108] The cleansing effect of this water, which is essentially ignored by TTAPS, would in fact be of vast importance in producing an early end to the nuclear winter.

One important effect is mentioned by the TTAPS study. The clash of cold air from the continents and the relatively warm air from the seas will create highly unstable fronts and huge storms. Sagan points out that the storms themselves will be severe and that the "preferential rainout" would increase long term radiation deposits along coasts.[109] He totally neglects to mention the most important effect of the atmospheric instability: a vigorous scrubbing effect, purging the soot and dust particles and accelerating the atmospheric recovery by who knows how much.

Lastly, the hypothesis that forest and prairie fires will be ignited by the heat of detonations ignores the vast amount of water in plant life. Indeed, except for particular seasons and under specific conditions, the forests and grasslands of the world are simply not flammable because of the vast amounts of water that they contain through transpiration. Yet the smoke from these wild fires is crucial to the TTAPS hypothesis.

The TTAPS authors make a number of other unwarranted assumptions that tend to exaggerate the amount of smoke likely to be produced in a nuclear war. After all, it is the smoke or, more particularly, the carbon particles contained in soot, that disproportionately creates the opacity to the sun's rays. The authors assume that firestorms will occur in 5 percent of the cities struck. However, neither atomic bomb dropped during World War II created a firestorm of the intensity required by the TTAPS model; indeed, the great firestorms in Hamburg, Dresden, and Tokyo injected smoke and soot to no more than 10 kilometers into the atmosphere. The authors assume, however, that smoke and soot will rise to an altitude of nineteen kilometers and, for their hypothesis to work at all, the smoke must be injected above fifteen kilometers (into the stratosphere).[110] This absolutely crucial and highly dubious assumption is made without any justification whatsoever. In addition, we have seen that the authors ignore the evidence adduced by the OTA study that there are not sufficient pounds of combustibles per square foot in American or Soviet cities to create a firestorm.

The TTAPS study conducted no on-site analysis of possible targets to determine smoke quantities or characteristics. Instead, they used plausible values. This is certainly understandable in a path-breaking study such as theirs, but it must be considered when assessing the results. The Defense Department's analysis of the smoke situation cites an actual on-site analysis of a potential target area.[111] The results are quite astounding. It found that, with respect to their sample target area at least, the TTAPS study exaggerated smoke production by a factor of thirty in July to a factor of 300 in January.

The conclusion is overwhelming. We cannot now *predict* the climatological effects of a nuclear war; we can merely *speculate* about what it *might be like*. Just because a certain group of women and men hold advanced degrees from prestigious institutions and use computers and technical terms, this does not sanctify the enterprise in which they are engaged, nor does it constitute science. This is not to say that they ought not do what they are doing. Neither does it mean that their work is not useful. It is. Nor does it justify our ignoring it. We must not.

But there is one thing of which we can be relatively certain. Whatever a full-scale nuclear war would do to our environment, it would in all likelihood not be good. Just how bad it would be is quite another question. We have some reason to think that the TTAPS study as presented to the public errs heavily on the side of severity. Let us recall:

1. The TTAPS authors made certain that all of their "simplifying assumptions" exacerbated the climatological effects of nuclear war rather than mitigating them.

2. They chose their admittedly worst case scenario upon which to base their speculations about the biological effects.

3. They chose their worst case scenarios upon which to base their public statements.

4. The National Research Council's results indicated on balance considerably more modest effects.

Once we dispense with this type of grim prophecy, based on scant scientific evidence, of the extinction of human life on the planet, what is left? Ironically, the TTAPS authors themselves say it quite well:

> The long-term destruction of the environment and the disruption of the global ecosystem might in the end prove even more devastating for the human species than the awesome short-term destructive effects of nuclear explosions and their radioactive fallout.[112]

But we should keep in mind that even the TTAPS authors insert a cautious "might." It seems that the final statement on the long-term effects of a nuclear war by the OTA study are still quite true, even if it was written before the nuclear winter hypothesis was formulated:

> In contrast, the incalculable effects of damage to the Earth's ecological system might be on the same order of magnitude as the immediate effects, but it is not known how to calculate or even estimate their likelihood.[113]

G. *A Threshold of Conscionability*

Let us say that I have shown unlimited nuclear war to be conceivable, commensurable, and survivable by a relatively small, but not insignificant percentage, and a very large absolute number, of people in the combatant countries. So what? It would still be so huge a catastrophe, its cost in human terms so much higher than any other man-made event, that it is difficult to imagine what possible difference its commensurability in principle could mean to the formation of national policy. Is nuclear war not permanently beyond a threshold of conscionability, i.e., so bad that it is beyond possible moral and sane choice? Yes, it is! But that is not the end of the matter.

To argue that there will be survivors is surely not to argue that nuclear war is somehow a desirable or viable policy option, or that a free, unconstrained choice to wage it would not be thoroughly immoral. This point seems so obvious as to be trivial. But given the super-heated emotion that attends this subject, it is not. It is not that the death of "only" 50 percent to 80 percent of Americans makes nuclear war more acceptable. It most certainly does not! However, the likelihood of large numbers of survivors *changes* the moral problem profoundly and, thus, the policies and strategies we should pursue before and during a nuclear war.

What choices do we have? We shall soon see. However, I will argue first that we do not have any choice we might possibly want. The United States is not the only chooser on the planet, and in virtue of that our choices are constrained.

IV. Constraints on Policy Choices

A. *Prudential and Moral Considerations*

There is a fundamental distinction in moral philosophy that applies directly to the issue of war and war waging. That distinction is between the counsels or dictates of morality and the counsels or dictates of prudence. It is a counsel of prudence that you ought not to hit yourself on the head with a hammer. You are, after all, in charge of your own actions, and it is simply not prudent or wise to cause yourself pain. It is not immoral to hit yourself on the head because you are not hurting someone else. On the other hand, when you stop short of telling a hurtful lie about an acquaintance whom you dislike you are acting from a counsel of morality. It is simply wrong to lie and hurt another, even though you know (let us suppose) that the lie will never be traced to you, and you will never suffer for it. Your restraint is based on morality, rather than prudence.

Broadly, prudence has to do with you and your interests, morality with others' interests as you affect them.[1] Note also that certain actions can be both imprudent and immoral. Committing murder in front of witnesses, for example, violates the basic right to life of another human and causes him and his loved ones pain. However, the prospect of execution or imprisonment will cause you suffering, so that deciding not to commit murder could well be based on prudence as well as, or instead of, morality.

Now, let us make the somewhat simplistic, but here harmless assumption that nations can act in their own interests, including the interests of their citizens.[2] If a nation acted in this way, it would be acting from prudence. On the other hand, a nation can act in the interest of all nations and all people or, at least, all those affected by its actions. That would constitute acting from morality. Thus, nations, like individuals, can act from prudence or morality or both. Hitler's war in Eastern Europe was waged strictly in the interest of the German nation state, with no regard for the Slavic peoples. Churchill, on the other hand, waged a defensive war for the good of all mankind or, at least, of Western Civilization. His was a policy based upon moral grounds. However, he also waged war to defend England from invasion, and at least some of his actions—the defense of Suez for example—were intended to preserve the British Empire. Thus, his overall policy was based upon some mixture of prudence and morality.

Machiavelli taught that politics was always and only based upon prudence, and Clausewitz extended this Machiavellian notion to war. In *On War,* Clausewitz told us: "When whole communities go to war....the reason always lies in some political situation and the occasion is always some political object."[3] And later in the same work: "It is clear, consequently, that war is not a mere act of policy but a true political instrument, a continuation of political activity by other means."[4] But as we reject moral nihilism with regard to war, so we reject this view. We want our nation's policies to be moral as well as prudent. Indeed, our purpose is to construct a moral theory that justifies a nuclear defense policy, and that is *ipso facto* a moral enterprise. But if we are to work with a moral theory, we must accept boundary conditions which are morally relevant. One such boundary condition is limitation upon choice. One is imprudent or immoral only if one makes imprudent or immoral choices *from those available to be chosen.* One cannot be morally liable for not making choices which, through no fault of one's own, are not available.

What, then, are the limitations on the choices concerning war and peace that we as a nation can make?

B. *The Notion of Constraints Upon Choices*

Until now we have dealt with the rationality and morality of a free choice to wage war unconstrained by other limits. But, of course, this is wholly artificial. A nation does not choose to wage war, especially nuclear war, in a moral vacuum. Following just war theory, there exists a strong but rebuttable presumption against any war waging. Surely that presumption is all the stronger against nuclear war. War, especially nuclear war, could be justified, if at all, only in a situation of severely constrained choices.

We are all intuitively aware that constraints upon choices can modify, or even completely change, the moral judgments we make about certain acts. Most of us would agree that it is a *prima facie* wrong to destroy the property of another. It is wrong to break the glass in a storekeeper's window to steal something behind it, for example. It is also wrong to break the window because the storekeeper is a member of a minority you dislike or for the sheer thrill of doing it. It is not wrong or, more accurately, it is an *excused wrong,* to break it to fetch medicine for a dying person. Thus, the constraint upon choice—i.e., either break the window or let the person die—can excuse otherwise immoral (and often illegal) behavior. Various defenses in criminal law represent a recognition of the excusing nature of certain situations which pose severely constrained choices.[5] Some of these situations are the result of an especially cruel fate. The case of the window pane and the medicine would, for example, be called "duress of circumstance" in the law. Other excusing conditions such as compulsion by threat or the need to defend oneself, arise from the actions of other people.

One set of constraints imposed by other actors defines "strategic situations." Thomas Schelling defines a *game of strategy* as: "a behavior situation in which each player's best choice of action depends on the action he expects the other to take, which he knows depends, in turn on the other's expectations of his own."[6] Our choices of war or peace, armament or disarmament, alert status or relaxation, are constrained by the behavior or disposition to behave of potential adversaries. Choices which might be prudentially irrational or morally impermissible in a vacuum take on rational purpose and moral justification when they are seen as reactions to an adversary's actions or as precautions taken in anticipation of an adversary's actions based upon his proven disposition to act.

Some examples of these sorts of justifications for choices and subsequent actions seem almost trivial, but they bear repeating because they have important implications for the global situation in which we find ourselves. It is literally inexcusable for B to strike A with a baseball bat because she "doesn't like him" or because he "dresses strangely." It is clearly excusable if she strikes him when he is also carrying a baseball bat, has already struck her once, and continues to shout, "I'm going to kill you."

It would be an idiotic overreaction, outrageously provacative and, from a moral point of view, inexcusably intimidating, for two policemen to go into a peaceful neighborhood tavern wearing bullet-proof vests and carrying shotguns just to "check on things." However, it might be justifiable prudence if the tavern was a primary drug trafficking site frequented by armed thugs and the location of six recent murders, including those of two policemen.

One could multiply such examples *ad infinitum.* The point is merely that we cannot judge our military policy or strategic behavior without looking at the behavior of other players with whom we interact. Our "nuclear strategy," then, just *is* our nuclear defense policies including those constraints, both moral and prudential, and especially our rational anticipation of the behavior of other players.

C. *The Other Player*

There are many such "players" or actors on the stage of international relations; most, but not all, are nation states. The behavior of the United States is in some small degree conditioned by all of them. But there is only one other nation that mirrors our most strategically significant characteristics to such an extent as to create a nearly bipolar world, where that player's behavior and disposition to behave becomes central to our success, even survival, as a nation. Before naming the obvious, let us point out the characteristics that make *us* so central in the lives of so many other nations:

1. We are one of the largest countries in the world in both land area and population.

2. We have one of the world's largest economies (as measured by gross national product).

3. We have one of the world's largest armed forces.

4. We have one of only two large deep-water navies in the world.

5. We have one of two military establishments with significant capacity for global force projection.

6. We have one of only two large, modern nuclear arsenals and the means of delivery.

7. We are the political and ideological leader of one of two primary blocks of nations.

Now, it will not have escaped the attention of the reader that those six points are true only of the United States and one other nation on Earth. If you combine that unalterable fact with the simple observation that the two political systems and ideologies compete with one another in some important sense, you have an essentially bipolar world in which rivalry and adversarial relations are inevitable.[7] To most readers, this probably constitutes a protracted path to the obvious. But it should silence those who object to the mode of analysis that I will develop on the ground that the adversarial relationship is created by precisely this type of analysis: that the only adversary is one we invent. This is patent nonsense. The Soviet Union exists and it will not go away. Its existence constrains our choices and that reality must be reflected in the policies we adopt.

The constraints imposed on the United States by the existence of the Soviet Union are of several different kinds, two of which I will consider in detail. First, there are logical constraints which would exist regardless of the characteristics of the Soviet Union or the U.S. If two powers face each other, each armed with nuclear weapons, and each suspicious of the other, that very situation imposes certain logical boundary conditions upon the choices made by each.

Second, there are the actual characteristics of our primary potential adversary. I will not attempt to discern Soviet motives or intentions. Do they want to conquer the world for communism, or do they want an expansionary Soviet empire, or do they want to live in peace if only the United States would stop ascribing sinister motives to them? Are they messianic or opportunistic or benign? Such an inquiry would take us deep into the arcane field of Soviet studies (sometimes called "Kremlinology"). Instead, I shall focus upon two facets of the Soviet *perception* of the strategic situation about which there exists a fair amount of Soviet writing and considerable agreement in the West: the role of war as conceived in Marxist-Leninist ideology, and the role of nuclear war in Soviet military strategy. Our choices concerning nuclear war and peace and, thus, our moral problems in making those choices are thoroughly dependent upon how the Soviets perceive their options and upon what choices we can anticipate that they will make. In other words, one can hardly work out a practical moral theory of nuclear war without taking into account one's prospective opponent's moral theory of war and its strategic consequences.

Constraints of Logic

The application of formal analysis to conflict situations has produced a vast technical literature.[8] So vast and so technical is that literature that the essential message for the Soviet-United States relationship is easily lost. Even if we limit our attention to applications of game theory, there is still a massive literature; but some key notions do begin to emerge.[9] The basic lesson of all of game theory is just this simple: choices one player (one power in international conflict situations) makes influence the choices the other player(s) makes. Things we perceive, believe, do, and threaten to do influence what the Soviet Union does, and *vice versa*. Things the Soviet Union does or is capable of doing foreclose certain options we might otherwise have and force us to make choices between undesirable alternatives, because the desirable ones have been eliminated by Soviet action or threat of action or disposition to act. And similar option-foreclosing moves or attitudes on our part affect Soviet choices.

The chief problem posed by this reciprocal choice-constraining behavior (or option foreclosing) is the notorious Prisoner's Dilemma. Before proceeding to an examination of the Prisoner's Dilemma, a brief comment is in order about the theory of games of which the Prisoner's Dilemma is a part.

For some reason, members of the antinuclear movement attack with special relish game theorists who apply the theory to the nuclear question. E.P. Thompson raises *ad hominem* argument to truly silly heights by referring to nuclear strategists as "Monkish celebates," or "alchemists," and by labeling them "intellectually disreputable."[10] Many critics of "nuclear strategy," game theory, and deterrence theory (the distinctions among these are usually ignored) share Thompson's penchant for argument by insult.

Fred Kaplan, however, is an exception. He is one critic who is familiar with game theory. His criticism is close to what others less conversant seem to want to say.[11] Kaplan tells us that the application of game theory to international relations fosters international tensions and distrust, elevating both to the "status of an intellectual construct, a mathematical axiom."[12] But Kaplan is confused. Game theory makes no assumptions about tension or relaxation of tension, about trust or distrust, or about self-interest or altruism, for that matter. It *is* a mathematical axiom (or, more properly, an axiomatic system). It says, "tell me about the two (or more) agents who play the game, tell me the rules of the game, the stakes and the odds, and I'll tell you what will happen." Game theory by itself is morally neutral; it assumes no theory of human nature. Indeed, both philosophers[13] and game theorists[14] have discussed variants of the Prisoner's Dilemma involving unselfish and altruistic players.[15] Certainly, it is true that most game theorists who look at United States-Soviet relations (and many other especially interesting games) do assume a large amount of self-interest and a certain degree of distrust on the part of the two players. Any decision-theoretic treatment of diplomatic or military history certainly seems to make such assumptions sound.[16]

However, if Kaplan or anyone else does not like the results of applying the theory of games to international relations, they should look to the premises, not the formalism. Perhaps nations are altruistic, or should be and can become so, if only we wish hard enough. Perhaps nations are intrinsically trusting, or will be, if only each of us puts aside his personal distrust and makes a "leap of trust." Indeed, one can assume a certain amount of trust or even unselfish behavior by nation states and still use game theory and generate dilemmas. All one need assume to apply game theory is that nations have *some* self-interest and are not *completely* trusting. So one need not be a hopeless cynic to apply game theory to international relations. One need not reject morality in the realm of international behavior, either.

In fact, I believe strongly that nations are occasionally capable of predominantly unselfish acts, and I believe the United States has performed several significant ones throughout its history. I also believe that nations *do* trust the ostensible policies of other nations, often to their own detriment, but not always. But a nation never acts with strict and complete disregard of its own interests (at least as it perceives them), nor can it ever completely and without reservation trust another nation state. Jonathan Schell was surely right when he argued that to totally remove ourselves from the nuclear dilemma, and thus the domain of game theory, we must "reinvent politics,"[17] although it is not exactly clear what that means. Until we do so, however, game theory works quite well in describing the old politics.

A word of warning, though. If we make a "leap of trust" to overcome the game-theoretic constraints upon our action, we had best be sure that the other fellow does so as well. And therein lies the rub. It is called the Prisoner's Dilemma, and it constrains choices in an especially nasty way.[18] Because of a choice or possible choice by an adversary, you often find yourself required to make a choice which you would rather not make; that pair of choices (yours and your adversary's) combine to make both of you worse off than if you had made another choice—only you couldn't. Confusing?

It is really not so very complicated. The story, from whence comes the name *Prisoner's Dilemma,* is that two confederates in crime are apprehended and held in separate cells. Each is urged by the authorities to confess, and offered the following inducement. If both confess, they will be convicted of burglary with a recommendation of leniency and receive five years in prison. If one confesses and the other does not, the former (i.e., the one who confessed) will be let off and the latter will receive the full sentence of ten years. If neither confesses, both will be convicted only of possession of burglary tools and receive one year in prison.

Now consider Figure 1 (page 84), in which prisoner A's choices are set out in rows and prisoner B's in columns. The numbers in each cell represent years in prison and, since time in prison is a disutility, they are expressed as negative values. The numbers on the left in each pair represent A's years in prison, those on the right B's.

Figure 1

	B	
	Confess	Do not confess
Confess	-5, -5	0, -10
A		
Do not confess	-10, 0	-1, -1

Notice that each prisoner is better off confessing whether the other does so or not; by confessing he guarantees that he will spend a maximum of five years in prison, rather than a possible ten. However, each is worse off when both confess (they each get five years) than when both do not (they each get one year). The dilemma is that what it is individually rational for each of them to do is, when their actions are taken together, not optimal and, thus, collectively irrational. Prisoner's Dilemmas abound in possible Soviet-American confrontations.[19] I will examine only a few very simple and particularly relevant ones.

Let us begin by examining the nuclear freeze proposal (Figure 2). What are the various incentives and disincentives for the United States in choosing to freeze our nuclear weapons "build-up" (really, modernization) or continue it.

Figure 2

Nuclear Freeze

	U.S.S.R.	
	Build-up	Freeze
Build-up	A -5, -5	B 10, -10
U.S.		
Freeze	C -10, 10	D 5, 5

The numbers in each cell represent a very rough utility measure; they are important only for their order and relative magnitude. Consider cell D first. This clearly is where it is rational for us both to be. We both freeze. Thus, we reduce expenditures on arms compared to cell A and do not risk falling victim to nuclear blackmail (as we did in cell C and the Soviets did in cell B). Then why do we not freeze? "Can we count on the

Soviets to do so?'' we ask ourselves. We cannot because the Soviets would gain by letting us freeze while building up themselves (cell C). "Look at what they could do to us! Maybe we better build,'' we say. Meanwhile, the Soviets look at the situation as if in a mirror. Of course, they would like to be at D, although C is tempting. But they observe, "Look at B and look at the huge incentive those disreputable Yanks have to build while we freeze. Better not chance it. Let's build!'' And off we both go to A and the arms race.

Figure 2 suffices to demonstrate a strong tendency toward the arms race.[20] Note that our choice to freeze or build is strongly influenced by what the Soviets may do. With the Soviets out of the picture altogether, we would stop building nuclear weapons. So it is not as if we choose to build arms because we like them, or because the military-industrial complex is in it for the obscene profits, or because male hormones drive us to kill, or for whatever other extraneous causes we might dream up. Note that these causes might drive us to engage in a strategic buildup without the Soviets, although I, for one, am extremely skeptical of this. The point is that as long as the Prisoner's Dilemma exists, any other postulated cause is superfluous. We elect to build because we *cannot control the Soviets' choice* and we realize that *they have the same motive to build as we do,* i.e., they are prisoners of the same dilemma.

How can both parties escape the dilemma? Well, they could trust each other. Each could make a solemn commitment and proceed to freeze in the hope that the other party would honor its commitment. But ought the United States to make such an agreement? That raises two questions: First, will the Soviets simply lie and take advantage of our freezing to build in order to blackmail us (put us in cell C)? I personally believe the Soviets to be a rather untrustworthy lot, and I would be very dubious about such a course of action without some kind of verification. But let us suppose that, holding a high opinion of our fellow man, we elect to trust them and, low and behold, our trust is well-founded; the Soviets have no intention of breaching the agreement. Have we defeated the Prisoner's Dilemma? Not quite yet! For the Soviets, even though of good intention themselves, are terribly suspicious of us. They articulate their fears this way: "Sure we want to freeze, but those Yanks are deceitful. They'll cheat as soon as we freeze and have one up on us (put us in cell B). We'd better build to protect ourselves against their cheating.'' The next thing we know, we are in C without anyone intending us to be there. Of course, everything I have said about the Soviets could also be said about the United States. Thus, trust means trust not only that your adversary does not want to cheat, but also *trust that he will perceive you as not wanting to cheat.*

Another alternative is to create an independent and impartial entity capable of enforcing adherence to the freeze, a sort of world government, perhaps. A number of critics of present American (and, presumably, Soviet) policy see the elimination of national sovereignty as the way out.[21] This sounds like a nice solution, but it is not. For a number of Prisoner's Dilemmas lurk on the road to world government. One way or another, we must face this dilemma.

Thus, we see how the Prisoner's Dilemma can constrain our choices. Even if both parties have good intentions, they are constrained to choose courses of action which lead to less than optimum (and therefore objectively irrational) outcomes. How might this cause us to "have to" fight a nuclear war?

The most ominous Prisoner's Dilemma lurks in the willingness to launch a nuclear first strike (that is, a first strike that is not a response to *any* aggression, conventional or nuclear).[22] Since a large proportion of the strategic forces of both sides is (or is becoming) vulnerable to a first strike by the other, the nation launching first will considerably limit damage to its homeland. The premium to the first striker is great and growing greater. As of now, there is sufficient motive for each side to withhold a first strike. But at such time as either or both sides conclude that a confrontation will inevitably (or with a very high probability) lead to nuclear war, the Prisoner's Dilemma described by Figure 3 will unfold.

Figure 3

First Strike

		U.S.S.R.	
		Strikes	Waits
U.S.	Strikes	A $-10, -10$	B $-5, -20$
	Waits	C $-20, -5$	D $5, 5$

Again, the same logic holds. The United States strikes because we know we cannot trust the Soviets, and we cannot trust them to trust us. The Soviets strike for identical reasons.

Reciprocal Fear of Preemption and the Security of the Deterrent[23]

The situation described in Figure 3 poses the greatest danger of nuclear war for the foreseeable future. Its danger has increased most recently as a direct result of two technological developments that occurred in the 1970s. Our land-based ICBMs are rapidly becoming vulnerable to a Soviet ICBM strike for two reasons.[24] The most oft-cited but least important reason is that Soviet missiles are becoming accurate enough to score direct hits on our missile silos. However, in years past this alone would have caused no particular worry. For if the Soviets were to have wasted their fourteen hundred odd ICBMs on our one thousand ICBM silos, they would have had precious few left with which to attack our bomber and submarine bases, our command and control system, and, should they choose, our cities, transportation links, and industrial sites (countervalue targets). However, when the Soviets began to mount many warheads on each ICBM (called MIRVing), that limitation ended. Now, their giant SS-18 and SS-19 ICBMs carry from six to ten warheads each. The Soviets are not only *able* to destroy our silos, they can *afford* to. MIRVing changes the ratio of missiles expended to silos (and missiles) destroyed from 1:1 to 1:8 or 1:10. Thus, the Soviets could now attack our ICBM silos with approximately ten percent of their ICBM force. The rest they could hold in reserve, hoping to blackmail us into not retaliating. More likely, they would use their remaining force to smash our national economic and social structure.

This means that the Soviets have a huge incentive to strike first. If a confrontation arises and they believe war is imminent, they can attack our weapons, particularly our fixed, land-based ICBMs, before we strike them. If they do, and they catch our ICBMs still in their silos, they will mitigate enormously the damage to their homeland. This premium exists because our ICBMs are vulnerable to attack, i.e., their missiles are accurate enough to hit ours, and they can afford to spend the missiles to do it.

For a variety of technical reasons we do not have the same counterforce capability as the Soviets do (at least against ICBM sites), but we are obtaining it rapidly.[25] To the extent that our force of fixed, land-based ICBMs makes us capable of destroying theirs with a fraction of ours, the temptation *to us* to strike first also grows. For not using them early in a war risks losing them to a Soviet first strike and losing all the damage mitigating effect their hitting Soviet ICBMs represents.

In general, deterrence works precisely when neither party has a vulnerable strategic offensive force. An adversary will deem itself able to launch a nuclear strike only when we can no longer visit upon him nearly certain and unacceptably high damage, even after absorbing his first strike. Notice that the damage must be to whatever the adversary values, not necessarily cities and people. If the adversary values its military power, then retaliatory capacity to hit military power will deter.[26] Such certain and unacceptable damage can only come from a powerful, *secure* second-strike capability; that means a strategic force that is *invulnerable* to a first strike such as missile submarines on station, or bombers on airborne alert. A strong, secure nuclear force tends to defuse crises before they go nuclear. Why strike if you know you will pay an unacceptably high price, if the premium to you as first striker is negligible? It is far better in that case to delay, send signals to your opponent of your intention not to attack, even to negotiate.

But deterrence theory has another sinister side. It treats cruelly those who do not maintain a strong deterrent force, secure from attack. The temptation to preempt is nothing more than a measure of the lack of a secure deterrent. A vulnerable deterrent is no deterrent at all. Indeed its capacity to be used as a first strike force makes it a goad to attack, especially in a time of high tension.

Bernard Brodie, the father of modern deterrence theory, never ceased to warn of the absolute centrality of the security of the deterrent if deterrence was to work at all. He tells us:

> It should be obvious that what counts in basic deterrence is not so much the size and condition of one's striking force *before it is hit* as the size and condition to which the enemy thinks *he can reduce it* by a surprise attack... [emphasis added].[27]

This means that a commitment to a policy of deterrence

> dictates *primary concern* with the *survival* of a retaliatory force of adequate size following an enemy attack [emphasis added].[28]

History teaches this in dramatic fashion. In the late 1930s, the American Pacific Fleet was stationed at San Pedro Bay in California. In the face of growing Japanese naval power and truculence in foreign policy, American planners decided to move the fleet to Pearl Harbor. This was meant to deter Japanese naval adventures. But, of course, it had precisely the opposite effect.

At Pearl Harbor, the American fleet was a far greater offensive threat to Japan. It was much closer to the theater of their ambitions, e.g., Southeast Asia and the China coast. Thus, it was better able to intervene early and decisively in Japanese naval operations. In their minds, it also gave the United States a capacity to preemptively attack their fleet in home waters. At the same time, being at Pearl Harbor made the American fleet significantly more vulnerable to surprise attack by putting it within practical range of the Japanese fleet. (We compounded the problem by making ourselves even more vulnerable than we needed to be, with terrible reconnaissance and readiness, for example.) When based at San Pedro Bay, the fleet was far less vulnerable since it was approximately twice as far from Japanese bases. Thus, the move gave us a more potent offensive force that was at the same time more vulnerable. History will never let us forget the results.[29]

The invulnerability of a deterrent force spells safety. Vulnerability spells a very deep and frightening kind of instability, by inviting a preemptive attack. If one destroys an adversary's vulnerable offensive strategic forces, that mitigates potential damage to one's homeland. In the case of our ICBM force, such potential mitigation to the Soviets is huge. *Now comes a particularly vicious infinite regress.* The Soviets know we know our ICBMs are vulnerable. In their eyes, we are more prone to use them to strike first. Better to use them first than have them destroyed. The Soviets believe that, knowing of their knowledge of our intention, we would be tempted to strike preemptively. We know they know we know this. And they know we know....Thus, the regress turns in ever escalating spirals, each time inviting anew first one superpower then the other to strike preemptively. We may know that we never would. The Soviets do not.

So *one* vulnerable strategic offensive force tempts *both* adversaries to preempt. *Two* vulnerable strategic forces only compounds the danger further.

From this we can see that maintenance of an adequate and secure nuclear deterrent is a *condition of stability*. It does not insure peace, but it is an *absolute prerequisite* to it. Any measures taken to lessen the chances of war must take the maintenance of this stability into account. Certain disarmament proposals which increase vulnerability automatically decrease stability and thus directly increase the chances of nuclear war.

In a curious sort of way, the bilateral maintenance of adequate and secure deterrent forces by the United States and the Soviet Union constitutes a solution to the Prisoner's Dilemma, at least of the most dangerous type delineated in Figure 3. It is, of course, not without cost. Many members of the "peace movement" decry expenditures for deterrent forces as the most immoral sort of waste while human beings around the world go hungry. Yet those same people would most happily pay to maintain the police forces of a world government that maintained nuclear peace and order (unless they are the most naive and optimistic sort of pacifists). If the only way we can overcome the Prisoner's Dilemma is through coordinated bilateral measures, rather than unitary ones, exactly what is the difference?

Critics of American nuclear strategy often talk as if we are locked into an arms race, or will not disarm, or are willing to fight a nuclear war because we are immoral. If we would simply understand the terrible price of nuclear war and exercise moral decency, we would behave both rationally and morally. Occasionally, though less often, similar comments are made about the Soviet Union. As we shall see in the next chapter, there is much to ponder about the immorality of Soviet nuclear doctrine. However, it is not our immorality, nor even that of the Soviets, which is the primary cause of the arms race or the risk of nuclear war. The primary thrust toward nuclear antagonism grows from the *logic of the situation*. Our nuclear defense policies are not morally corrupt. They do not create the Prisoner's Dilemma; they are an attempt to cope with it.

It is easy and comforting to perpetuate the illusion of American omnipotence, that we could stop all this dangerous nonsense if only we were determined enough. But we are not omnipotent! There exists on the globe another world power with military forces as strong as (some would say stronger than) ours. We do not control their actions. The existence of that power, and particularly the onset of nuclear parity between it and ourselves, is a brutal, irreducible fact. Thus our constrained choices; thus our need to react as well as act.

Even so perceptive a philosopher as Bertrand Russell could be blinded to the game-theoretic forces that come into play. He once wrote: "We are not doomed to persist in the race towards disaster. Human volitions have caused it and human volitions can arrest it."[30] Of course, it is true in some sense that human volitions have caused the Prisoner's Dilemma of nuclear policy, but this is not the whole story. The Prisoner's Dilemma is what philosophers call an *emergent property* or, in this case, an *emergent relation*. That is, it is made up of human volitions, but it is also more. It arises only when two or more individual and independent human wills interact in a specific way. Out of the complexity of this interaction, something new and different emerges. Russell is wrong because we cannot merely *will away* the Prisoner's Dilemma of nuclear policy. We can escape the doom threatened by nuclear weapons, but not by ranting against wicked human nature or aggressive capitalism. The Prisoner's Dilemma must be painstakingly removed, piece by piece if you will; and to do that, we must first understand it.

It is not due to our immorality that we find ourselves in a Prisoner's Dilemma, and if we should ever conclude that we must fight a nuclear war, the fact that we are in that dilemma must be taken into account in the moral evaluation of our decision. That is, in large measure, *why* we would have to fight.

The Other Side of the Hill: Soviet Doctrine and Strategy as Constraint

We in the West are so used to assuming that any war must have a specific moral justification that we almost cannot think about wars without thinking of their justifications. America's experience in Vietnam is too familiar to require elaboration. Certainly part of what happened to us in that war was an erosion of the justifications with which we entered it. The British experience in the Boer War (1899-1902) and the French in Algeria (1954-1962) represent similar phenomena.

The Soviet-Marxist philosophy of war requires no such specific justification. It does, however, provide an elaborate classification system for wars.[31] The primary characteristic that distinguishes wars is, of course, the classes involved. In Marxist theory, it is antagonistic classes which drive the historical process. Therefore, the clash of nation states is only a manifestation of a deeper class struggle. Marxist doctrine provides an exhaustive analysis of the various kinds of wars. There are "imperialist wars" between capitalist, imperialist powers, such as World War I or World War II prior to the invasion of the Soviet Union. There are colonial wars between an imperialist power and a people who resist being colonized, such as the Opium War (1839-1842) between China and Britain. And there are "wars of national liberation," in which native peoples attempt to throw out the colonial power, such as the Algerian Revolt and the Vietminh's war against France.

For our purposes, the most important kind of war is one in which the Soviet Union, a "proletarian state," engages in (or contemplates) a war with the United States, a "capitalist-imperialist state." P.H. Vigor characterizes such wars in this way:

> But this communist notion of 'class struggle' is not confined to a struggle *within* a society; it also finds expression on the international scene in the shape of a struggle between countries....It can be waged between all the capitalist countries on the one hand...and all the socialist countries on the other.[32]

In such a clash, the proletarian state is *ipso facto* in the right, justified, and fighting a "defensive war," even if it struck first. "If a 'proletarian' government is involved in war, then that is a 'just' war so far as that government is concerned...."[33] Thus, there is no moral constraint preventing the Soviet Union from attacking the United States or the NATO alliance, even without provocation. Our existence is provocation enough. The only possible inhibitions on the Soviets are prudential ones.

In the Marxist scheme the issue of specific moral justification evaporates, and thus war becomes the pursuit of politics (in this case, allegedly revolutionary politics) by other means. If one detects echoes of Clausewitz in this attitude toward war, it is no accident. To some extent Marx, and even more Engels and Lenin, drew on Clausewitz's conception of war. For them, war and peace were merely gradations of class conflict, or different manifestations of the same struggle. Thus, the "war" of the proletariat upon capitalist society, whether literally violent or not, is always justified because it is on the side of history. For the Marxist, especially Lenin, there can be no coherent question about the permissibility (or justice) of a given war. If it is waged by the right class (or the right country representing the right class), it has the imprimatur of dialectical necessity as evinced in history, and that is all the moral sanction any act or policy can possibly have. Then the only question is a prudential (and Clausewitzian) one. Does the war *fit* the policy objective it seeks to achieve?

Just war theory, as we understand it, is not only irrelevant, it is perverse. For in a narrow legalistic way, it might condemn a war fought by a proletarian state against a reactionary power, and that is unthinkable. Indeed, it is clear that, had Lenin taken time to think about it, he would have found just war theory part of the legal and philosophic superstructure of the bourgeois state, to be discarded along with all else in that superstructure.

Clausewitz, of course, goes a great deal further than merely describing war as a tool of policy. Not only is the decision to go to war a pragmatic one based on furthering policy aims, the *strategy one adopts in making war* is determined by that policy. The Soviets unhesitatingly endorse this Clausewitzian point of view. Victory itself is defined as the attainment of a policy goal.

Most strategists in the West have departed from Clausewitz on one key point. Technology, especially weapons technology, can have crucial effects upon the strategy adopted. The American admiral, A.T. Mahan, believed that the advent of the armored battleship revolutionized naval warfare and, as a result, global power. An American general, Billy Mitchell, and an Italian general, Giulio Douhet, preached that the long-range bomber had changed military strategy forever. Similarly, between the World Wars Charles DeGaulle and the British strategists J.F.C. Fuller and B.H. Liddell Hart held that the tank had radically changed land warfare. Bernard Brodie was the first of many military theorists to argue that the nuclear bomb had changed warfare and military strategy forever.

We have so internalized this conception of the reliance of strategy upon weapons technology in general, and the utterly revolutionary character of nuclear weapons in particular, that the contrary point of view is difficult even to articulate. But the orthodox Clausewitzian refuses to admit that changes in weapons technology, even ones as profound as the nuclear bomb, change basic strategy. After all, strategy is set by *what* you *wish to accomplish,* your policy objectives, not *how you go about it,* which, to be sure, is affected by your choice of weapons. In the West, where we seem mesmerized by the awesome destructive power of nuclear weapons, it is hard to conceive that a rational school of thought would hold that nuclear weapons do not fundamentally change warfare. But this is what a strict Clausewitzian would hold, and today most of these are found in the Soviet military. Indeed, this is regnant Soviet military policy. The Soviets see no difference between the policy goals to be achieved by conventional war and those to be achieved by nuclear war; therefore, the strategies do not fundamentally differ.

Indeed, the most authoritative statement of Soviet strategy goes further. The greater capacity for violence created by nuclear weapons makes them *more* capable of accomplishing political ends.

> Therefore, the essence of war as a continuation of the politics by means of armed violence and the specific nature of war appear today more distinctly than in the past, and modern means of violence acquire ever-increasing importance.[34]

And:

> As a result of the rapid development of productive forces, science, and technology, the resources of waging war have become so powerful that from the military point of view the possibilities for attaining the most decisive political goals by the use of armed conflict have grown immensely.[35]

In the recently published "Lenin's Teachings on Peace, War, the Army and the Present," Colonel General G.U. Sredin explicitly applies the Clausewitz-Lenin instrumental conceptions to nuclear war:

> War always was and remains the continuation of politics by this or that class and state. This is fully applicable also to a possible missile-nuclear

war which, in the event it were to occur, would be the most "political" of all wars known in history....

A possible missile nuclear war would, in its genetic source, contain the general essence of war; the continuation of politics by other violent means.[36]

However, simply saying that strategic nuclear war can accomplish policy objectives is not very informative. Moreover, for those of us in the West who are used to thinking of nuclear war as the end of politics, if not the world, the notion of a nuclear war fought for policy objectives, and "political" objectives at that, seems anachronistic at best and monstrously perverse at worst. (What would be wrong with this notion according to just war theory will be considered below.)

What might be Soviet war aims in a nuclear war? For the answer to this question we must return to the Marxist classification of types of war. Soviet military theory, for all practical purposes, has considered only one possible type of war with the West.[37] It would be a world war. In all probability, it would also be a "coalition war," in that NATO and the Warsaw Pact would be involved. The crucial point is that it would be the final *class struggle*. As Vigor says, it would be "a war between two mutually antagonistic *classes* which happened to be fought on a worldwide scale rather than within the confines of one country."[38]

The overwhelming thrust of Soviet thinking is that any war between what we in the West call the "superpowers" would be an unlimited, thermonuclear war with no quarter given, and one in which one side would emerge victorious, albeit grievously damaged. Soviet military theorists have made quite clear that victory remains a meaningful concept in nuclear war. N. U. Karaborov, for example, writes that: "There is profound erroneousness and harm in the disorienting claims of bourgeois ideologies that there will be no victor in thermonuclear war."[39] Marshal Ogarkov, until very recently Chief of Staff of the Soviet Army (and thus the second highest defense official in the Soviet Union), said in a 1979 article in the *Soviet Military Encyclopedia*:

Soviet military strategy proceeds from the view that should the Soviet Union be thrust into a nuclear war then the Soviet people and their Armed Forces need to be prepared for the most severe and protracted trial....this creates for them the objective possibility of achieving victory.[40]

Is the Soviet Union preparing to fight a nuclear war? Would it ever actually launch a nuclear war to attain policy ends? We have seen that the Leninist philosophy of war would morally permit it, and that is of huge moment both in assessing the moral posture of our adversary and in measuring the degree of constraint upon our own choices. But, prudentially, would such a course of action make sense for the Soviets? There are two schools of thought regarding this aspect of Soviet nuclear strategy. Each view poses different but very real problems for the United States in formulating its own position on nuclear war.

Richard Pipes, a professor of Russian and European history at Harvard and a member of the National Security Council in the first Reagan Administration, believes that the Soviet Union would be willing to wage a nuclear war to attain policy ends.[41] Pipes believes that the Soviet military and, to a large extent, the civilian leadership as well, reject the Western conception of mutual assured destruction, i.e., the view that the only purpose of nuclear weapons is to deter war by threat of the unthinkable. He says: "In Soviet doctrine, nuclear weapons do not serve primarily deterrent purposes; they are the principal weapons of modern war....Should general war break out they are expected to determine the outcome."[42] Indeed, he goes even further. The Soviet Union is developing a capability to fight and win a nuclear war, not because that capability itself could deter war, but for the obvious reason that it might choose to use that capacity to achieve some policy end. Pipes tells us:

> Implicit in all this [Soviet strategy] is the idea that nuclear war is feasible and that the basic function of warfare, as defined by Clausewitz remains permanently valid, whatever breakthroughs might occur in technology....It spells the rejection of the whole basis on which U.S. strategy has come to rest: Thermonuclear war is not suicidal, it can be fought and won, and thus resort to war must not be ruled out.[43]

Thus, Pipes theorizes, the Soviet Union might well choose at some time in the future to engage in nuclear war with the United States in order to achieve some policy end: dominance of Western Europe and the eviction of the American presence, for example.

Having just reviewed the horrifying effects of an unlimited nuclear war, one is driven to ask: how could anyone who is rational treat nuclear war as a means to a policy goal, as Clausewitz did? One possibility, which we shall consider below, is limited nuclear war. The Soviets might believe that by limiting strikes by both sides to military targets only, one side might emerge victorious in some sense. But this is simply *not* what the Soviets believe, for there exists a consensus among experts on Soviet strategy that they reject the notion of limited nuclear war altogether.[44] Any nuclear war will necessarily be or become an unlimited one.

How can a rational person believe in using *unlimited* nuclear war as a means to some policy objective and that achieving it at the expense of an adversary would constitute victory? Pipes provides one plausible explanation, even if it is hard for Westerners to understand. We take for granted an ongoing (and largely public) dialogue among our scientific, political, and military leaders about defense policy. In such a dialogue, the obvious empirical facts about the terrible effects of nuclear war get aired, criticized, and, to the degree they stand up, accepted by all parties. The Soviets make a great pretense of doing the same thing. Analysts from the Institute for the Study of the United States and Canada appear on *Nightline* and *Meet the Press* to forswear recourse to nuclear weapons. Prominent Soviet scientists join panels with Carl Sagan and Paul Ehrlich to press the dangers of the nuclear winter. Soviet members of the Physicians for Social Responsibility appear to accept their share of the Nobel Peace Prize.

But the Soviet Union is not at all like the United States. Those Soviet spokespersons speak only to the West. They are not independent individuals representing independent groups within their society. Various groups representing various opinions do not argue issues out in public forums in the Soviet Union and arrive at rational positions after having considered all points of view. The Soviet military is hermetically sealed from other leadership groups in that society and its conception of nuclear strategy is a received dogma. If the historians of Soviet military thinking are correct, the "party line" on the use of nuclear weapons became fossilized as accepted political dogma in the 1950s or early 1960s. Accounts differ as to whether it was enshrined when Malenkov was sacked (1955)[45] or when Khrushchev was sacked (1964),[46] but it was the result of a *political* and *ideological* rejection of mutual assured destruction and the conscious acceptance of a *war-fighting* and *war-winning* doctrine.

We should remember that during the 1950s, Allied thinking went through a period in which strategists at least considered the possibility that nuclear war could be a policy instrument.[47] But such a view could not bear scrutiny as we learned more and more about the power and effects of these weapons. The Soviets may well have held a similar view of nuclear weapons in the late 1950s, and when those views became caught up in a leadership struggle, the winning side enforced its views as the "party line." In short, the Soviets possess an awesome 1980s nuclear arsenal while still holding a 1950s conception of its appropriate use. This is analogous to someone carrying a high velocity big-game rifle but believing it to be a BB gun: a dangerous person indeed.

Most Soviet analysts do not fully agree with Pipes. They do not believe that the Soviets would wage nuclear war to attain policy objectives. The view held by Sonnenfeldt, Hyland, Ermath, Gartoff, Lambeth, and most other authorities is that the Soviets do adopt a strategy of deterrence.[48] However, they agree with Pipes that the Soviets will start and fight a nuclear war if they perceive the machinery of deterrence to be breaking down. These same analysts see the Soviets as believing that if they are decisive enough and hit hard enough, victory in some sense is possible. Lambeth, for example, says: "Soviet military doctrine is...explicitly geared to a belief that should deterrence fail, some recognizable form of victory is theoretically attainable through the skillful exploitation of initiative, surprise and shock."[49] Thus, Pipes and the other Soviet experts agree that, given the appropriate incentive, the Soviet Union:

1. Is willing to fight a nuclear war.
2. Adopts a thoroughly articulated strategy for fighting it.
3. Would be the *first* to launch such a war.
4. Would do so with as much surprise as their technology would allow.
5. Believes that victory, in the form of attainment of war aims, is attainable.

Pipes disagrees with the regnant view only in his view of what constitutes a sufficient incentive for such a war. He believes that the Soviets might well choose to fight a nuclear war for purposes other than a belief that deterrence was failing and nuclear war was, therefore, inevitable. Lambeth, Sonnenfeldt, *et al.* believe that only the latter condition would constitute sufficient incentive. Without claiming expertise in this area, my own examination of primary sources (mainly Soviet military writings) leads me to agree with the regnant view. However, for our purposes, the difference between them is of little moment. The brute fact, one which can only be disputed by a Pollyanna, and an ignorant one at that, is that superpower relations could conceivably deteriorate to such a point that we would have visited upon us, in the *absence of any clear choice on our own part,* a preemptive first strike by the Soviet Union.

Indeed, it is this fact which frames my entire analysis. Circumstances beyond our immediate control, *viz.,* the logic of the situation and our adversary's predispositions, could well force us into a nuclear war where our only choices would be capitulation after receiving a first strike, or a second strike in self-defense. What would be our moral situation? What choices might we make if we were placed in that terrible predicament and how might they be justified? We cannot acquiesce to the temptation, as Schell and others do, of simplistically viewing nuclear war as the end of history and refusing to consider our alternatives. Schell concludes, as much of the popular thought on this subject has for a long time, that morality ceases to make sense at that point. Somehow our being in a nuclear war is already so illustrative of our moral baseness that there are no meaningful moral choices left. This implies that the lives of our surviving citizens are morally worthless. Schell wrongly believes that they will *all* be dead, or he presumes to judge them to be better off dead. Therefore, self-defense is a meaningless notion in this context, and nothing much matters. But this is a kind of moral nihilism which is not worthy of us. We do have choices, constrained though they may be, both as to what we do now and what we should do if a nuclear war were to occur. What are our choices, given the constraints we considered above? What, prudentially, can we do? What, morally, are we permitted to do? Among all the possible choices we have, are there any that are both prudent and moral? It is to these questions that I now turn.

V. Genuine Policy Choices

I have examined the constraints—physical, logical, strategic, and moral—which bear upon the choices we must make with regard to nuclear weapons and nuclear war. It is those constraints which prevent us from having a wide range of possible ideal choices. Anything we choose will be conditioned by the horrible nature of nuclear war, the Prisoner's Dilemma, the reality of Soviet strategy, and so forth. It is important that we honestly examine only genuine choices, i.e., those permitted within the constraints. Given this, what choices are left to us? *Prima facie,* there would seem to be three general classes of choices. The first would be to refuse to fight a nuclear war under any circumstances. I shall call this the "surrender option." The second class of choices would counsel a willingness to fight nuclear war, indeed to precipitate nuclear war if necessary. I shall call these "first-strike options." The third choice counsels defensive nuclear war waging, if such a thing is possible, and threatening same to deter nuclear aggression.

A. *The Surrender Option*

One of the most disarmingly simple responses to the catastrophic character of nuclear war and the logical puzzle of the Dilemma of Nuclear Weapons is simply, "Why not surrender?" It is so obvious and straightforward a limiting position that it would have to be answered even if no one seriously recommended it as policy. But, as we shall see, many do, a few candidly, many without quite admitting it.

Surrender could be defined as eschewing violent resistance (or, at least, nuclear resistance) and putting our fate in the hands of an armed adversary who appears willing to use nuclear weapons. In pursuing the surrender option, *when* might we surrender? There seem to be two possible junctures. First, we might surrender now, immediately. That is, we might examine the threat of nuclear war and decide that the world is too dangerous already, that since the nuclear arsenals exist and the consequent danger of their use does as well, the time to act is now. The second

view, a postattack surrender position, would hold that immediate surrender or unilateral disarmament in the face of nuclear threat is unnecessary. But if we should be victims of a nuclear first strike, we ought
to surrender rather than fight.

The first surrender option—surrender now—corresponds closely to a
version of nuclear pacifism. It is not identical, however, because nuclear
pacifism is a moral doctrine. The surrender option, on the other hand, is
a policy which flows from nuclear pacifism and additional counsels of
prudence. That is, it is morally owed by us to those innocent Soviet
citizens whom we would have to kill if we chose not to surrender and, instead, defended ourselves; and surrender is prudentially in our interest, as well.

Typically, nuclear pacifists hold that we should get rid of our nuclear
weapons completely, unilaterally, and immediately. The mere possession
of nuclear weapons is immoral and they should be done away with. Does
this version of nuclear pacifism imply surrender and the choice of the
surrender option? Yes, it does indeed, and we shall soon see why.

The second surrender option, i.e., surrender after absorbing a first
strike, follows from a nuclear pacifism quite like that of the American
Catholic Bishops. The Bishops hold that possessing nuclear weapons is
morally acceptable, but that we should never under any conditions use
them. Likewise, genuine threats, i.e., threats involving real, even if conditional intentions to use nuclear weapons, are morally wrong, although
a curious kind of bluffing seems morally acceptable.[1]

Arguments for Immediate Surrender

The argument for immediate surrender takes several different forms.
The first is based upon a moral cost/benefit assessment: whatever the
potential benefit to be derived from nuclear resistance, it could never
outweigh the horrible costs of nuclear war to every one involved. Germain G. Grisez has put this form of the argument as simply as anyone:

> When I say that the deterrent [i.e., nuclear weapons] is morally evil, I do
> not mean we ought to try to dismantle it if and when world amity is
> established. I mean we ought to dismantle the deterrent immediately,
> *regardless of consequences. The end simply does not justify the means!*
> [emphasis added][2]

George Kennan makes a very similar point when he says:

> There is no issue at stake in our political relations with the Soviet Union
> —no hope, no fear, nothing to which we aspire, nothing we would like
> to avoid—which could conceivably be worth a nuclear war.[3]

On this view, the costs *always* outweigh any benefit gained by the use of nuclear weapons, including defensive use. Indeed, the cost always outweighs even the *risk* of their use.

However, unless one believes all moral issues are only matters of cost and benefit, one is likely to believe that there exist rights and duties which transcend a utilitarian cost/benefit analysis. Arguments which invoke rights and duties cut both ways. One such, made by the philosopher Anthony Kenny, argues more strongly than the cost/benefit argument I considered above that we must never use nuclear weapons. Regardless of costs and benefits to us (regardless of prudence), we owe it to the population of an aggressor nation never to strike them with nuclear weapons even in our own defense. Kenny clearly formulates this duty not to resist. He says:

> But the nuclear strategy...is one which involves as an option, at one, or other stage, the use of weapons to destroy large centers of population and to bring an enemy society to an end.
> The exercise of this option is something which nothing could justify.[4]

And this is because:

> *it is better to be wronged than to wrong.* That principle holds good even when the wrongs in question are considered in isolation from the question of who perpetrates them, comparable in scale. But of course the wrong we would do, if we used nuclear weapons in a major way, would be incomparably greater than the wrong we would suffer if the worst came to worst after nuclear disarmament [emphasis added].[5]

It is the duty we have to the supposedly innocent people of a nuclear aggressor which prevents us from acting, whatever may be in our own interest.

But what of *our* interests and *our* rights? Are we as impotent to support them as both the cost/benefit argument of Grisez and the argument that we must do no wrong to others articulated by Kenny tells us we are?

There is yet another version of the surrender argument which attempts to take our interests into account. It is based upon the cost self-defense imposes upon the American people alone. It accepts the view that we are not forced to count the citizens of the aggressor state as moral equals in our choice, for they are partially responsible for our having to choose. It counsels surrender nonetheless, and it runs like this: We should surrender because no possible benefit *to us* of not surrendering can outweigh the costs *to us* of not surrendering and, therefore, possibly having to fight. Note, however, that as long as we are not told that we

somehow owe surrender in part to the population of the attacking country or to third parties, then the decision to resist or not resist is a purely
prudential one. It is a decision that says it is in *our own best interest* to
surrender. But that form of argument forces us to assume that we must
engage in a simple cost/benefit analysis for ourselves; it does not take
into account the existence of rights we have to resist and, more deeply,
the rights we have to be free.

It seems that we have a *prima facie* right to surrender if a legitimate
political decision procedure concludes that we should. (However, I shall
have reason to question even this.) It is equally true, however, that we
have a *right* to resist and not to surrender, however much it costs us. As a
free people, we have a *right* to continue to be free, a right against threat,
coercion, intimidation, and forceful interference in our lives and in life's
choices. Something is wrong with an argument which says, if only an aggressor is willing to heap *enough* harm on enough people, his own included, we lose our right to self-determination. We are free to value our
rights to life and liberty as we will. We may listen to all the cost/benefit
analyses and prudential considerations in favor of surrender and choose
nonetheless to resist. Nothing in the cost/benefit argument tells us we
should (morally) surrender, only that if we realize what we are doing we
will want to surrender. Perhaps, though I doubt it!

Nuclear Monopoly and Slavery in a Post-Surrender World

Why is it that, however rational the surrender option may be made to
sound, we (or most of us) find it so unpalatable? Is it only our national
machismo? Some demented ethos growing out of Rambo movies,
perhaps? Would the logical force of the argument for surrender be apparent if only we could shed the crude jingoism that forces us to insist
upon being "number one"? Hardly! To forswear resistance and put
ourselves into the hands of a nuclear-armed and aggressive adversary is
something very like selling ourselves into slavery. One must be careful in
drawing analogies between relations among individuals and relations
among states. But in the end, a decision by a polity to give up, without
qualification or limitation, its own sovereignty and autonomy directly
leads to its citizens doing the same. Thus, perhaps, availing ourselves of
the surrender option is not only *like* selling ourselves into slavery, but
simply *is* that. The price we receive for our freedom is, then, our lives
and safety (as the argument might go).

Before I launch into the consequences of a Soviet nuclear monopoly, I
must enter a caveat. In the real world, many defense authorities believe,

one likely outcome of unilateral disarmament by the United States would be very rapid and widespread nuclear proliferation, as other powers attempted to achieve their own deterrents against Soviet coercion. This proliferation would not only mean that many new powers would acquire nuclear weapons, but also that those which now have them would quickly and dramatically expand their arsenals (which, presently, are miniscule in comparison to those of the superpowers). Whether rapid proliferation or a Soviet nuclear monopoly would result from our disarmament would depend upon several variables: how fast we would disarm, how sincere and committed to disarmament the Soviets judged us to be, and how much risk they would be willing to incur by preempting the creation or expansion of other nations' arsenals by threat or nuclear strike.

If rapid and extensive proliferation were the outcome, we would have an absurd and highly dangerous situation. The risk of nuclear war would have increased dramatically, through proliferation, and *we,* who had completely disarmed, would be subject to nuclear blackmail, dependent for our ability to resist upon the good graces of nuclear-armed allies like Mexico and Italy. We must remember that for us to disarm is for the rest of the world to have to arm or face the Soviets as a nuclear monopolist. There is a deep lesson in this: unilateral disarmament does not necessarily decrease the likelihood of nuclear war. Indeed, it probably substantially increases it. Albert Wohlstetter makes a related point.[6] He points out that if the entire world fell under the domination of communist forms of government, very little by way of peace or stability would be insured. Communist states would almost certainly fall to fighting one another. Indeed, they already have. Communist Vietnam fights communist Kampuchea and the Peoples Republic of China. The latter and the Soviet Union engaged in brigade-sized border clashes in 1968 and 1969. "It is possible to be both red and dead," Wohlstetter tells us, and he is doubtless correct.

However, as moral theorists we need to perform a thought experiment. The thought experiment, even if not terribly close to the reality created by a unilaterally disarmed United States, will tell us a very great deal about the moral rights and duties that pertain in nuclear defense. Imagine a world in which all nuclear powers other than the Soviets were at once seized with a desire to unilaterally lay down their nuclear weapons. This would include Britain, France, Israel, and China. Moreover, no other countries would attempt to build a nuclear deterrent. In such a world, the Soviet Union would possess a true nuclear monopoly, and *what a monopoly.* Best estimates give them approximately twenty-five thousand nuclear warheads and devices.[7] These include perhaps eight thousand strategic warheads and another fifteen hundred intermediate or theater nuclear warheads (primarily SS-20s). In addition, they have a highly variegated and flexible tactical nuclear arsenal including artillery shells, battlefield rockets, land mines, anti-ship missiles, nuclear torpedos, and so on. Also, it must be remembered that this nuclear arsenal would be in the hands of the world's largest navy and air force with the world's most powerful army.[8]

Compare this world to an even more fanciful hypothetical case. In some Buck Rogers, twenty-fifth-century world, an evil ruler makes you wear a special collar which you cannot remove. By turning a blue dial, he can cause you ever more excruciating pain. By pushing a red button, he can instantly vaporize you. Now imagine that you are not alone, but are joined in your captivity by many of your fellow men and women—a nation perhaps. We surely know what it is for a ruler to hold a people in slavery. The Pharaoh so held the Jews, Hitler the Jews, Poles, and Ukrainians, Stalin the Volga Germans, Crimean Tatars, and Ukrainian Kulaks, and Pol Pot the Cambodians. However, the evil ruler's hold over your people in the twenty-fifth century is all the more clearly collective slavery because it is closer to omnipotence. Such power is just what a nuclear monopolist would possess.

With the United States Navy neutralized by a nuclear-armed Soviet Navy (already bigger than ours) and every city on the planet subject to obliteration within minutes without any defense, what we would have is simply global omnipotence. The analogy with the fiendish twenty-fifth-century ruler's collar is strict, for such unrestrained military power would allow the use of very refined gradations of violence against us, from harmless demonstrations of nuclear power through vaporization of most of us. It would allow for conventional conquest without any resistance possible. It would allow for stationing paramilitary or police forces anywhere in the world.

The reader might be tempted to say at this point, "Of course, surrender to a Soviet nuclear monopoly might have rather bad consequences, but *slavery*? Isn't that a bit hyperbolic?" The answer is simply, no. It is as accurate as language and the concept of slavery itself allows. A slave, in the purest sense of that notion, is a thing, an object of possession like an animal. Roman law so defined a slave, at least until the later years of the Empire.[9] A slave is not a person because he or she is not a locus of rights and duties as is a free person. *American Jurisprudence, 2nd* says:

> Under the system of slavery as it existed in this country prior to the Thirteenth Amendment of the Federal Constitution slaves were the property of their masters and had no civil rights. Legally they were not considered as persons, but as things....[10]

This lack of personhood represents one of the two most important ways of defining slavery in both law and political philosophy. The other speaks to the submission of the slave's will to that of the master. *Corpus Juris Secundum* cites the case of *U.S.v. Ingalls* and says:

> A slave has been defined as a person who is wholly subject to the will of another, one who has no freedom of action but whose person and services are wholly under the control of another.[11]

And later it says that a slave is held "subject to despotism."[12]

Thomas Hobbes believed that the slave bartered his liberty for his life and some security for that life.[13] We saw that the partisans of the surrender option seem to think that is what they are buying from a nuclear aggressor, using their freedom as coin. But as Montesquieu so powerfully argued against Hobbes, he is quite wrong.[14] For as soon as this transaction occurs, as soon as I attempt to trade my slavery for my life and safety, I have handed over my life and safety to the complete discretion of another. As a slave, I have lost any means of enforcing rights and as a thing, chattel property can possess no right of any kind. I may, at my master's discretion, be allowed to live, but I have no *right* to do so.

The despotic character of slavery follows from the definition of the slave as an object. Locke defined slavery as the complete dependence of one man upon the will of another, as did Rousseau.[15] Obviously, an individual totally without rights or legal personhood is deemed to be an object of personal property and is wholly subject to another's will, so that the two definitional strands come together in both law and political philosophy.[16]

Nuclear surrender and the nuclear pacifism that mandates it is, in the most accurate definition that law and political theory can provide, submission to slavery, for it is submission to the arbitrary, omnipotent power of another. There is no way to sugarcoat it.

We have seen that the introduction of nuclear weapons has given us the capacity to wreak havoc over much of the Earth's surface, if not to extinguish life on the planet. But power has many uses, and vast power can be used to vast *and diverse* effect. The age of large nuclear arsenals is also an age of potential global slavery, as well as potential global conflagration.

One can mount a strong natural rights argument that, in attempting to alienate an inalienable right, one is committing a moral wrong.[17] It may well be that we not only have a right but a *moral duty* to resist coercion and aggression the end of which is logically equivalent to slavery. But that argument need not be made to defeat the surrender option. It is enough that we have a *right* to resist, and that we surely do. While I believe we have such a duty and that surrender would be morally wrong, that claim depends upon strong natural law arguments that go well beyond this essay. My argument here requires only a *right* of resistance.

Does the massive cost to us of the preservation or exercise of that right abrogate it? Surely not! You cannot be said to lose a right because another threatens you with some massive harm. That threat may cause you to choose not to exercise the right, but it does not cause it to disappear. The last step in the argument is obvious. The American people have never been partial to the surrender option. Those who prudentially prefer it are free to campaign for it among their fellow citizens. (And it is crucial that they remain free to do so.) But so long as the American people choose to take the risks to defend their freedom (and so long as the political system truly reflects that choice), we have a powerful moral right to do so.

Policies Equivalent to Immediate Surrender

In a paper which is overly idealistic, Douglas P. Lackey has attempted to convince us that we can obtain the safety of surrender without its attendant costs.[18] His arcane decision-theoretic argument reduces to this: if we were to unilaterally disarm ourselves of nuclear weapons, the risk that the Soviet Union would attack us is less than the risk of nuclear war if we remain armed with nuclear weapons. He spends much of the time talking about different casualty levels, depending upon whether we are armed or not, different postures we might assume if we will not unilaterally disarm, and so forth, calculating various outcomes decision-theoretically. But all of that is really quite beside the point, for his argument rests on some very dubious empirical premises about possible Soviet behavior.

By our complete and unilateral *nuclear* disarmament (Lackey would have us keep our conventional weapons), we will remove a great threat to the Soviets. According to Lackey, the unilateral possession of nuclear weapons by the Soviets will not cause them either to launch a first strike against us or even to threaten to do so. He admits that there exists a small probability that they might do either, but he argues that it will actually be lower than the probability of nuclear war if we maintain possession of our nuclear weapons. Concerning the danger of a Soviet first strike, he says: "I believe the chance of a Soviet first strike is small even under the strategy of [*Unilateral*] Nuclear Disarmament."[19] Again, "We have already argued on a variety of grounds that the chances of a Soviet first strike under N.D. [*unilateral nuclear disarmament*] are small."[20] And a bit later, "The chance of war between the Soviet Union and the United States is small, even if the United States gave up its nuclear weapons."[21] And neither will the Soviets be more likely to threaten us with nuclear weapons: "If the chances of a Soviet first strike are slight, then the chances of successful blackmail will also be slight."[22]

What are Lackey's arguments for this conclusion? There are three that I can discern:

1. If we stop threatening the Soviets, they will stop threatening us.[23]

2. If the odds of a first strike are small, then one can not effectively use it for blackmail.

3. Nuclear weapons are not efficient weapons for blackmail.

The only argument for 1 seems to be 3. Obviously, 2 begs the question and really depends upon 3. In 2, he also misses the point that a first-strike option, assuming a nuclear monopoly, is a free choice of the monopolist's. In the argot of decision theory, it is a "choice node" not a "chance node," so Lackey's use of odds here is inappropriate.[24]

The crux of Lackey's argument thus reduces to 3. Let us consider what he says in support of his claim: "We will keep our conventional arms, thus we can always resist with these."[25] This is a naive argument. He seems to rest it upon the following insight: "nuclear weapons are not inherently more destructive than other sorts of weapons."[26] To support this, he informs us that: "the napalm [sic] raids on Tokyo in March, 1945 caused higher casualties than either atomic bomb."[27] Although the inference is correct (that conventional raids were more destructive), the implication of Lackey's statement is astounding. If a partisan of a strong defense were to make such a statement, he or she would be pilloried. Nuclear weapons constitute a revolution in weaponry.[28] Above, I argued that the near-term effects of nuclear war would be *commensurable* with World War II. But as I carefully pointed out, "for the overall consequences to be measurable on the same scale as" and "for the weapons to be no more destructive than" are radically different things. Indeed, for a three-week war (let us say) to be commensurable with but more destructive by many times than a six-year war implies a mighty revolution in weaponry.

Another author who argues for the use of conventional forces to deter nuclear threats is David Hoekema.[29] A quick examination of his proposed "conventional deterrent" illustrates the deep problems with this notion. Hoekema tells us: "A widely dispersed force of several thousand highly accurate conventional weapons can effectively threaten an enemy's cities and military bases."[30] Now, keep in mind that a one megaton warhead has, by definition, the explosive power of *one million* tons of TNT. If we imagine these "highly accurate conventional" missiles to be carrying a one ton payload (the throw weight of our Minuteman), a conventional arsenal would need 1,000,000 such missiles to equal the explosive power of a single one megaton warhead. The United States has a strategic arsenal of approximately 9,700 nuclear warheads. Those warheads combined equal 3,727 equivalent megatons of destructive power. Hoekema would need over three billion seven hundred and twenty-seven million of his missiles to make up the equivalent of our present nuclear arsenal.[31] He might counter that we have overkill. We do, although survivable second-strike overkill is just a measure of redundancy and redundancy increases the credibility of the threat and therefore the safety it confers. But we don't have *that* much overkill. If we assume 2,000 such conventional missiles, that would reduce our strategic arsenal by *six orders magnitude,* or to approximately one two-millionths of our present arsenal.

Hoekema would threaten to launch these missiles against cities. First, this is still a countervalue deterrent threat against innocents, so it is not clear that it is moral. Moreover, it would not be *effective.* Again, he seems to have no conception of the limitations of conventional arms. In World War II, the British Lancaster bomber carried maximum bomb loads of 20,000 lbs. Bombing raids carried out by a thousand bombers at a time over one target city were not unusual in 1944 and 1945. Hoekema's conventional missile force could inflict far less damage (20 percent, to be exact) on all of the Soviet Union than one raid on one night over one target by the RAF Bomber Command.

With respect to the "accuracy" of Hoekema's missile force, our present ICBM accuracy, which is very good, is not good enough to score a direct hit on a missile silo.[32] Cruise missiles might do a slightly better job but, simply put, we do not have the technological accuracy to do what Hoekema would require of us. Even if we did, a conventional warhead would not destroy—indeed, it would hardly scratch—a missile silo or other hardened target. (In fairness to Hoekema, he points the way to a partial solution to our problems, although one that is many years in the future. Smart and therefore extremely accurate delivery systems could someday replace nuclear warheads with conventional ones for many, though not all, targets. But more of this later.)

If conventional forces cannot mount a credible deterrent threat against a nuclear power, it is just as clear that they could not offer meaningful resistance to a nuclear force. A conventional force set against nuclear forces (especially today's highly accurate, mobile, and flexible nuclear forces) would be so overwhelmed that it is mind boggling to contemplate. There simply is *no defense* against nuclear weapons (the President's Strategic Defense Initiative excepted). Conventional forces would simply stand there and be obliterated. Imagine a Soviet army armed with tactical and intermediate nuclear weapons against a conventionally armed NATO force, or a naval battle between U.S. forces armed with conventional explosives and a Soviet force armed with nuclear weapons. The one-sided slaughter would be far worse than that visited upon native armies by nineteenth century European forces, whose superiority in firepower was nowhere near as overwhelming as that of nuclear-armed forces over conventional ones.

One other thinker has contemplated conventional versus nuclear forces and arrived at an important conclusion.[33] Jeff McMahan, a Cambridge philosopher, is an active member of the peace movement (the Committee for Nuclear Disarmament) and would certainly be no friend of most of the conclusions reached in this book. He is, however, a thinker of notable intellectual honesty, and in a searching examination of the notion of nuclear blackmail, he concludes that there are only two effective ways of preventing nuclear blackmail: developing an independent nuclear force or forming an alliance with a nuclear power.[34] Of course, his British perspective is apparent in his solution and, in fairness to him, he expresses skepticism as to the dangers of nuclear blackmail in the first place. What is of great moment, however, is that he concludes, in spite of himself, *that nuclear force alone deters nuclear force.* He is correct.

If we may put aside the recourse to conventional forces, what other arguments does Douglas Lackey have in favor of unilateral disarmament? Nuclear weapons are militarily and diplomatically awkward.[35] "The diplomatic losses a nation would incur upon using even tactical nuclear weapons would be immense."[36] Again, Lackey's complete misunderstanding of the nuclear revolution is striking. A nation having a nuclear monopoly, especially with so large and so refined an arsenal as the Soviets have today, is *answerable* to no one. Diplomacy is even more impotent than conventional forces. Diplomacy assumes a reasonable balance of power, some ability of one side to impose costs upon the other if its ends are not respected. Where one side would have a large, modern nuclear monopoly there would be none of this. What need does an omnipotent power have for diplomacy? The age of diplomacy would be dead.

At rock bottom, the basis of Lackey's argument is this: in the early postwar years (1945-1949) the U.S. had an atomic monopoly and we found it difficult to use it to control Soviet behavior. Hence, the Soviets would find it equally difficult to use their monopoly to coerce us and control our behavior. There are two crucial assumptions in this argument from history:

1. The nature of the monopoly, though reversed, would be roughly the same today as during the earlier period.

2. There exists no moral difference between the Soviet Union today and the United States in the 1945-1949 period.

Lackey's first assumption will not withstand scrutiny. We had very few atomic bombs, no hydrogen bombs, and very limited means of delivery (B-29s of what today would be considered medium range based in Europe and Japan).[37] There existed no vast nuclear forces such as the Soviets deploy today. There existed no capacity at all to use nuclear weapons on the battlefield, no plethora of types of nuclear ordnance and delivery vehicles. Compare Soviet nuclear forces today to several score of gravity bombs and a couple of hundred slow, limited-range bombers with which to deliver them!

Lackey's second assumption, implicit but logically necessary, is the most interesting: that there is no moral difference between the two states. That is, either we were not restrained in those years by anything but *Realpolitik,* or the Soviets possessed of a nuclear monopoly in the future would be restrained by the same morality that restrained us. Lackey never clearly says which alternative he endorses. This assumption in its undifferentiated form is common among adherents of the "peace" movement, often explicitly stated: the Soviet Union and the United States are moral equals.[38] It strikes me as sad indeed if we have so lost our moral compass that we cannot see the obvious flaw in this assumption: that an open society, the rule of law, civil liberties, and representative democracy count for nothing in the moral equation; that a higher standard of living and pluralism in belief and life style are without moral right or weight; that *what we are* counts for so much less than what we have allegedly *done* (e.g., the Vietnam War, the support of a Marcos or a Pinochet); and that what we have done is interpreted so one-sidedly as to emphasize our mistakes and ignore our moral triumphs (e.g., the Marshall Plan, the

Food for Peace Program, the Peace Corps, world leadership in medical and agricultural technology, and so on and so on).

But for the sake of argument, I shall try to ignore the unignorable. Let us play Lackey's game, and postulate that we and the Soviets are cut from exactly the same moral cloth. Let us assume that when we unilaterally disarm, they will not threaten us. As long as they do not disarm also, *we have still sold ourselves into slavery.* We have in all likelihood alienated our rights to life and liberty, or at the very least left these rights hostage to Soviet good intentions. For as long as the Soviet nuclear monopoly continues, the implicit threat is always there. We must not only bet with our lives that the Soviets are benign; we must bet that they *always will be.* We must bet that the regime which, in living memory, gave rise to Stalin and Yezhov and Beria (the latter two successive heads of the secret police who served Stalin as Himmler did Hitler) will *never* use its life-and-death power to force us to change our political system or in any way sacrifice what to this date, cliche or not, is our very precious birthright.

The counterargument to Lackey and all the advocates of unilateral nuclear disarmament is simple:

1. Unilateral nuclear disarmament just *is* the irrevocable alienation of our right to life and liberty. For given the Soviets' nuclear arsenal, their monopoly would, quite literally, be the power of life and death.

2. While the Soviets might not actually exercise that power now, they could do so at any time, under any new leadership, into the indefinite future.

Passive Resistance

Lackey and Hoekema would at least have us keep our conventional weapons in an effort to protect ourselves. Some other unilateralists go much further. They counsel passive resistance to Soviet nuclear threats.[39] Let us perform a short thought experiment. We disarm unilaterally. Suppose that the Soviets, having a nuclear monopoly, then tell us that we must repeal the Bill of Rights and outlaw any party not friendly to Soviet policy. Is this scenario merely the paranoid nightmare of a conservative hawk? Perhaps. However, this is equivalent to what the Soviets have done to every country that they have conquered, including many that are now part of their "Union." But George Kennan assures us: "Nor does anybody use this kind of blackmail. Great governments do not behave that way."[40] However, in a revealing addendum he says: "Of course,

Hitler did with Hacha, in the case of Czechoslovakia; but Hitler was an exception.''[41] Need one say more?

The simple truth is that we *don't know* what the Soviets would do should we unilaterally disarm. I do not, George Kennan does not, and Mikhail Gorbachev probably does not. But they surely *could* make these kinds of threats, and there would be nothing but their own sweet disposition to stop them. Suppose that the Soviets do try to coerce us and that a group of brave souls attempts passive resistance. "We won't obey," they say. "We'll go to jail first....Besides you can't put a whole country in jail," they add. "But we won't even try," say the Soviets. "We'll just strike New York, Chicago, and Los Angeles with a one megaton warhead each. If that isn't enough, we shall add Washington and Boston to the list. Just let us know when you've had enough." What would we do then? What *could* we do? We would have no moral choice. We would have to acquiesce. Would the Soviets really do this? Would Mikhail Gorbachev do it? I truly do not know. Would Nikita Khruschev have done it? Who knows? He made threats enough. Would Stalin have done it? In the wink of an eye! And George Kennan knows that!

There simply is no viable resistance of any kind to a nuclear monopolist equipped as the Soviet Union is. Slavery is slavery, pure and simple! It is sobering at moments like this to reflect that it is only the men and women of the Strategic Air Command and the United States Navy's ballistic missile submarine fleet who stand between us and slavery. Perhaps we should call them the "thin blue line." The equation is simple: the only deterrence in the nuclear age is nuclear deterrence. Life without a nuclear deterrent on the same planet with a well-armed nuclear monopolist is slavery.

On Knocking Down Some Straw Men

This is a volatile subject which generates much heated argument and even more vilification. A few words of caution are in order, lest what I am saying be taken for some hoary straw man that the "peace" movement loves to hate.

1. I am not here saying "Better dead than red." I shall look more deeply into that strange expression below. For now suffice it to say it is not clear what that slogan means. Although I am no friend of statist socialism, and even less of one-party dictatorship, I am not at all sure that that is even relevant. The issue is a Soviet monopoly of nuclear-tipped ballistic missiles—absolute, omnipotent power—not a system of government. Furthermore, I do not see that our maintenance of a force

to resist the alienation of our basic rights (i.e., a nuclear deterrent) is a choice to be dead, though it assuredly is a choice to run that risk.

However, there is much that we can do which will serve to maintain and stabilize deterrence. Some of this maintenance and stabilization would be all the more effectively done in concert with the Soviets; thus, there is a genuine place for arms control negotiations. The point, though, is that the probability of nuclear war is not an uncontrollable variable. There are concrete steps that we can take to substantially reduce the risks, steps far short of surrender, many of which would make us more rather than less well-armed, i.e., strong conventional forces and a strong, secure nuclear second-strike deterrent.

2. I use the term "slavery" in a technical sense. It has nothing to do with the, shall we say, rather broader use of the term by a well-known radical right-wing organization which boycotts East European products on the grounds that they are made with Communist "slave labor."

I use the term not exclusively with Marxist regimes in view, but because it is technically appropriate for a situation of complete omnipotence enforced by threats of violence. The definition I provided has deep roots in the history of Western law and political philosophy.

3. Nothing in my argument assumes the past or present moral superiority of the United States or its form of government over that of the Soviet Union, for the Soviets have all the same rights against any attempts we might make to practice nuclear aggression or coercion against them. It would be less than candid, however, if I did not admit to a very strong belief in such superiority. But admitting to such an orientation does not require the dehumanization of either the Soviet leaders or people. Nothing I have said implies (and I would explicitly reject) any view that makes monsters out of all Soviet leaders (although Stalin, like Hitler, was surely monstrous) or one which makes the Soviet people less than human or less valuable person-for-person than other people on earth. One can express moral preferences as to a nation's leadership structure, its behavior and disposition to behave, and its institutions and ideologies without dehumanizing its people.

B. *First-Strike Options*

If we must not surrender and must not undertake policies tantamount to surrender, we must be prepared to resist nuclear threats and nuclear aggression. Yet we have seen the staggering, ghastly human costs associated with unlimited nuclear war. It seems truly to be beyond *the threshold of the conscionable*. And we have seen that our choices in whether or not we face such aggression may not be our own, and our responses might therefore be severely constrained. Given that the world we live in is not entirely of our own making, could resort to nuclear weapons ever be justified? If so, to what purpose: tactical and limited, or strategic; for genuine military advantage; or for revenge? It is to these vexing questions that I now turn.

At the outset we should note that there need be nothing intrinsically more deadly about a nuclear explosion than about *a very large number* of conventional explosions. Efforts can be made to minimize radiation effects, efforts which could include the use of "clean" bombs and only high altitude blasts. The rule of least harm mandates that one is morally constrained to use the means creating the least unnecessary human cost. It is possible in principle that the rule of least harm would actually *mandate* the use of a nuclear weapon as opposed to the use of a large number of conventional weapons. Let us imagine a hypothetical case where this would be obvious.

The First Use of Nuclear Weapons: A Hypothetical Case

Imagine that a U.S.-Soviet confrontation occurs after the two countries have enacted a system of crisis controls and secure command and control links, so that reciprocally limited nuclear war seems feasible. The Soviets launch a lightning, conventional, armored strike directly at U.S. forces through the Fulda Gap in the Federal Republic of Germany. They do not, for their own strategic reasons, launch a front-wide attack; only one armored column is launched at U.S. forces in one sector. Perhaps the Soviets wish to impose a quick, clean defeat on U.S. forces to make a point or to test the resolve of our NATO partners, without committing all their forces. But their reasons are unimportant. The U.S. command has the choice of a massive conventional barrage using medium and heavy bombers and heavy artillery bombardment or a precision strike by one neutron warhead mounted on a "smart" weapon. Despite the hysterical talk of a few years ago about neutron weapons killing people and preserving property for capitalists, the salient feature of the neutron weapon is its highly *limited range of lethality*. It kills with intense radiation over a very limited radius, as short as one and one-half miles.[42] Its radiation also penetrates even thick steel plate; thus, it is an ideal anti-armor weapon. Now, if the armored column is not within two miles of a village or town when struck, it is almost certain that fewer civilians would be killed by the single neutron warhead than by the necessarily sustained and inaccurate series of conventional attacks, lasting over several hours and following the column as it progresses through the countryside. Thus, fewer civilian casualties would result from use of the nuclear device.

Suppose also that NATO Command has decided that if the Soviets break through, they must escalate to theater nuclear weapons or lose all of Western Europe. It is quite possible that the nuclear device would be more effective in stopping the armored thrust, while also better controlling escalation.

Let us review our assumptions:

1. U.S.-Soviet command and control systems can, with high probability, reciprocally control a highly limited tactical use of nuclear weapons. That is, we can tell the Soviets what we are doing and they will not escalate from panic or confusion.

2. The U.S. has neutron warheads on ultra-accurate smart weapons (at least a few).

3. One neutron weapon will stop the assault; the much larger, more protracted conventional strike might not.

4. Left initially unchecked, the Soviet armored assault will almost certainly trigger rapid NATO escalation, perhaps to unlimited nuclear war.

5. The neutron warhead will kill fewer noncombatants than a large number of conventional strikes.

The conclusions from just war theory seem overwhelming:

1. The neutron weapon constitutes the "least harm," compared to conventional means, with regard to noncombatant casualties in particular.

2. The Rule of Proportionality would dictate use of the neutron warhead since that would cause far less human cost than either the purposive escalation to theater nuclear weapons or the loss of all of Western Europe to Soviet aggression. (Remember: aggression is a war crime under just war theory and resistance to it is legitimate under the Standard of Permissible War Waging.)

It seems to follow that morality *dictates* the use of a neutron warhead. What is wrong with this hypothetical case? Well, we have made many assumptions, both normative and factual, and some are questionable. Why do the Soviets attack in a single column? Why don't the Americans have smart conventional weapons? Why has NATO Command decided that it must escalate to theater weapons immediately, if the Soviets break through? Are crisis controls involving such clear communication with the Soviets fanciful?

However, the somewhat dubious factual assumptions do not really matter. The hypothetical case shows us that it is *possible* that morality could *dictate,* not merely *allow,* the use of a nuclear weapon. If you are not a general pacifist, how could you, in this case, be a nuclear pacifist? Nuclear pacifists assert that nuclear weapons are *sui generis:* that they never can be used while conventional weapons often can be. But why is that so, especially in a case such as this one? If it is morally appropriate that Western Europe be defended against aggression and the facts obtain as outlined in the hypothetical case, then that is all one needs to know. One is then constrained to choose the nuclear device. It is surprising enough that one might be morally *allowed* to use a nuclear weapon and *use it* first. But here it seems to be *required.*

Of course, one could protest that the hypothetical case we examined is too fanciful. The world is just not like that. However, the rejoinder is dispositive. It easily could be! The facts assumed may be somewhat unlikely, but they are neither logically nor physically impossible. A moral theory must be able to hold up under any reasonably possible set of assumptions.

May we conclude from our example that the *first use* of nuclear weapons is justified in the world as we know it? Not yet. It does tell us that nuclear pacifism as an absolute ban on nuclear weapons is false. Now we can meaningfully ask the question, "Can the use of nuclear weapons be permissible in the real world, as opposed to the realm of thought experiments?"

Nuclear Response to Conventional Aggression: A Morally Viable Option?

Is the United States morally permitted to use nuclear weapons to resist conventional aggression, as present NATO strategy requires of us? This is the famous notion of 'extended deterrence'. Extended deterrence actually has two facets which are not always carefully distinguished:

1. the extension of our nuclear umbrella to alliance partners, by threatening to attack with nuclear weapons any country launching a *nuclear attack* on an alliance partner;

2. the extension of our nuclear umbrella to threaten nuclear attack upon any country attacking an alliance partner, even if that initial attack is solely with *conventional forces.*

Note that 1 does not commit us to a policy of first use, but 2 does. It is 2 that I shall discuss here because it is current NATO and, hence, U.S. policy.

Now, no one can deny that conventional aggression by one super-power upon the allies or armed forces of another is a very nasty business indeed. It is morally wrong for two reasons. First, any aggression is wrong. Second, and far worse, it risks escalation to unlimited nuclear war, so it violates the Rule of Proportionality. As we saw earlier, no policy end could be worth that. There may or may not exist so-called "firebreaks" (natural stopping points in the process of escalation) between limited and unlimited nuclear war. If there are none now, perhaps we could construct them in the future. But the most important firebreak of all is that we and the Soviets not shoot at each other in the first place. For forty years we have avoided this, as we must always.

Suppose, however, that a massive Soviet conventional assault *is* launched in Europe. Should we use nuclear weapons to stop it? In our hypothetical example we saw that given some very special conditions the answer might be yes. But given the facts as they exist today, the answer must be no—at least so long as we have reason to believe that nuclear war is, with high probability, uncontrollable and that escalation would run all the way to an unlimited exchange. Remember that this is a factually contingent assumption and perhaps we, or we and the Soviets working together, would be prudent and moral to consider trying to achieve controllability.

Would cooperative efforts to make limited nuclear war more controllable also make nuclear war more thinkable and therefore more probable? To get a grip on this question, let us look at the converse argument. Charles Krauthammer has argued that "No First Use" is immoral.[43] It would, he tells us, make nuclear war more probable in the long run by making conventional war more likely in the short run. His argument goes like this: if we and the Soviets both make a policy declaration to forswear first use, then conventional war becomes more likely. But a massive, stalemated conventional war, a "thirty years war" between the United States and the Soviet Union, is highly unlikely. Somebody would certainly use nuclear weapons. That would escalate, and we would be off to Armageddon.

There is a great deal of substance to Krauthammer's argument. The key "firebreak" is most definitely, as he says, the line between shooting at the Soviets and not shooting at them. However, it is prudent to build as many firebreaks as possible between ourselves and unlimited nuclear war. We need one at no use of conventional force, one at no use of nuclear force, and as many as possible on the way to an unlimited nuclear exchange once nuclear weapons have been used. Krauthammer's argument is based upon a premise deeply embedded in the conventional wisdom: that in making limited nuclear war possible we diminish the firebreak between conventional and nuclear war, thus making *some* sort of nuclear war more probable. To put the point simply, firebreaks are reciprocally related: widen one and you narrow another; create one and you eliminate another.

I believe this position to be profoundly mistaken. Perhaps, as Krauthammer argues, *a declaration* of no first use would have the effect of increasing Soviet consideration of conventional aggression. But declarations of this sort are certainly empty, in any case. The Soviets claim that the Warsaw Pact is a defensive alliance, then spend all their time arming for and practicing lightning offensive armored strikes. They forswear first use of strategic nuclear weapons, then build a vast, vulnerable, first-strike-oriented ICBM force.

However, remember that just war theory tells us that we must try all reasonable measures short of war to avoid war, and this is even more true for nuclear war than conventional war. One such measure is to avoid putting ourselves in a position where the choice of conventional defeat and conquest or first use of nuclear weapons are the only options. In short, we are under a *moral* as well as a prudential obligation to enhance our conventional forces to ensure that we will never have to face that grizzly choice.

The Russian army has been conceived by Western military leaders since before Napoleon as a massive juggernaut, unstoppable by mere mortal men. We still think of it in this way. But this is arrant nonsense. The Soviet Union's pool of manpower is not in fact a lot larger than our own. The NATO countries' combined population is greater than that of the Warsaw Pact countries, and NATO's combined GNP is more than twice as large as that of the Warsaw Pact. If we and our NATO allies have the force of will to protect ourselves against a Soviet conventional attack with conventional arms, we can. Both prudence and morality dictate that we must. It is a mistake not to arm ourselves in order to make conventional resistance to conventional aggression a genuine option. Whatever we decide to announce as policy should be calculated to minimize the eventual chance of nuclear war, and just what that announced policy should be I do not claim to know. But what we *do* should allow us not to have to respond to tanks with nuclear weapons. Actually having the conventional option, whatever we may say, simply *must* make us safer.

Krauthammer puts his finger on why we do not have adequate conventional forces. It ''derives ultimately from Western unwillingness to match Soviet conventional strength in Europe.'' Well, we should be willing. It is shortsighted, imprudent, and immoral not to. We owe it to ourselves and world peace to be able to practice credible conventional deterrence. We and, especially, our NATO allies have not done enough to make our conventional forces a credible deterrent. Far too often we are intimidated by fears of "massive conventional rearmament" and an exponential growth in military spending that would bankrupt Western economies and turn our societies into garrison states. A moment's reflection, however, shows these fears to be groundless. If the weak and inefficient economies of the Warsaw Pact countries can afford to threaten us with conventional forces, we can surely afford to defend ourselves with similar forces. However, dovish proponents of "no first use" who say that we would not need to increase defense spending at all are quite wrong. Additionally, conventional rearmament might necessitate a return to the draft for the United States and some other NATO countries which do not now have it.

The key point is simple. We have one important means to make nuclear war less likely already at hand, *viz.,* stronger conventional forces. Just war theory tells us that we must act now by all reasonable means to avoid nuclear war. The reason we have not strengthened our conventional forces is simple lack of political will, and that lack of will finds us morally wanting.

Constraints Upon the Option of Limited Nuclear War

The greatest objection to the use of tactical nuclear first strikes to arrest conventional aggression, however, is that limited nuclear war will not stay limited. Our previous thought experiment will fail precisely because we do not have, either alone or in concert with the Soviets, means to limit and control nuclear war with any degree of assurance.

There exists a huge technical literature discussing limited nuclear war and escalation which stretches back over the last two decades.[44] Again we must simplify in order to draw moral conclusions. Most analysts have concluded that the actual strategy of the United States has, at least since the advent of the ICBM, endeavored to give an American president a number of options in responding to a Soviet attack, some of which would be less than an all out counterattack.[45] Yet the doctrine of limited nuclear war is fraught with problems.

Two notions must be carefully distinguished. A single power can choose to unilaterally limit its nuclear war waging by type of weapon, by geographical area, or by type of target, although there exists a problem in maintaining communication with and control over field commanders, so that even such unilateral war limitation is not a foregone conclusion. But with care and attention, it could probably be executed. However, the kind of war limitation that represents a true alternative to an unlimited nuclear war involves the *mutual* and *reciprocal limitation,* that is, *control* of nuclear war. As with any attempt to control war, this kind of limited nuclear war depends upon communication between adversaries. This means either agreements—explicit or tacit—reached before a battle is fought, or agreements that occur after initial exchanges. Both depend in crucial ways upon knowing what your adversary is doing, what he intends to do, and to some degree, upon mutual trust. Indeed, most of the problems in mutual, reciprocal war limitation are just new instances of the Prisoner's Dilemma we met earlier.

Neither time nor space permit an extensive discussion of limited nuclear war. I will provide a very brief outline of arguments that show that nuclear war is not controllable, reach a tentative conclusion, and proceed. There are essentially five reasons why nuclear war in the present environment could not (or with high probability would not) be controlled:

1. The definitions of tactical weapons or use, theater weapons or use, and strategic weapons or use are notoriously fuzzy. Thus, you cannot know when your adversary has escalated and when he has restrained himself.

2. In war, merely properly ascertaining the facts on the battlefield is nearly impossible. Even if, under 1, we could adequately define each weapon type or use, one side could never be sure of where the other side stood on the path of escalation.

3. With today's weapons, quick response (by preemption or first use) provides a huge premium in damage limitation to the side that strikes first. Thus, each combatant is strongly tempted to strike first. In addition, when faced with 2, each combatant will assume the worst about what its adversary has done, i.e., that it has already escalated. The decision to escalate is a classic Prisoner's Dilemma: if I do not, he will, and then I will be worse off than if I do, whatever he does.

4. Knowing what the situation is and thus being able to make a rational decision is made even more difficult because command centers themselves, where sit the decision makers, will be hit. This is known as C^3 vulnerability (command, control, and communication).[46]

5. The loser at almost any level of escalation, having "nothing left to lose," will almost certainly escalate in hopes of winning at the next level of escalation. Years back, a great deal was made of so-called *escalation dominance,* that is, having so much more power at one level of escala-

tion that your adversary would never dare escalate to that level. We had escalation dominance at the strategic level in the 1950s. Thus, even if a tactical nuclear war had broken out along the East-West border in Europe and the Soviets were losing, they would most probably have stopped escalation before going to strategic weapons. (*We* might not have, and therein lies a lesson about limited nuclear war: victors, too, escalate.)[47] However, today, there is no escalation dominance for either side at any level. The age of "rough parity" is the age of easy recourse to escalation.

I will take 1 through 5 as dispositive and assume that nuclear war today could not, with high probability, be reciprocally limited.

There is an important qualification of this position. Limited nuclear war cannot be an option *at the present time.* But our inability to limit nuclear war is a highly contingent fact. It is possible that some combination of technological advance (e.g., greater accuracy of weapons, limited lethality) and mutual agreement and controls between the superpowers (e.g., hot lines, secure command and control links) could lower the risk of escalation, so that *for some ends* limited nuclear war might be a tolerable risk. What ends? Only the genuinely defensive ones of resisting large conventional invasion! Needless to say, this is a position that is fraught with moral and policy problems. But it is, *prima facie,* a viable one, if only the risk of escalation is low enough and the collateral damage is small enough.

For the moment, I assume that, at present stages of technology and superpower cooperation, the risk of escalation is very high. What does this mean? It means we have one more constraint upon our choice. We ought not to use nuclear force in the first instance to stop conventional aggression, because we cannot choose to wage limited nuclear war independently of incurring a very high risk of having to wage a practically unlimited nuclear war. We may limit our own war waging, for moral or strategic reasons, but it cannot be as part of any "bargain" with our adversary. The decision to use nuclear weapons, however limited in the first instance, is *ipso facto* a decision to take a very great risk of waging an uncontrolled and therefore unlimited nuclear war.[48] Could such a decision to wage unlimited nuclear war ever be justified?

Unlimited Nuclear War as a Political Instrument

War can be viewed as a policy instrument meant to bring about political goals, goals which are either desired (prudential), or right and good (moral), or both. I have discussed earlier the notion of the human cost that is always involved in war. Moreover, we have seen how the Rule of Proportionality as it applies to the decision to wage war (*jus ad bellum*) requires that we weigh the benefit to be gained against the human cost to be expended. At the prudential level, the Rule of Proportionality requires us to weigh cost and benefit as it affects our concerns (our nation and its people). At the prudential level, without invoking morality, we are free to ignore the interests of any other nation or people in deciding what is prudentially appropriate.

Would it ever be *prudent* to wage an unlimited nuclear war to achieve a political goal? We have seen that an unlimited nuclear war, while commensurable with the worst cataclysms in history, would be far worse than any mankind has yet experienced. If we were cold-blooded Machiavellians or Clausewitzians looking only to our nation's interests, would we ever decide that a particular policy end was worth an unlimited nuclear war?

Intuitively, the answer seems obvious. I have considered the horrible consequences of an unlimited nuclear war and have concluded that it transcends the "threshold of conscionability" as a policy instrument, considering only damage to our own country. This is what 'self-deterrence' means. However, let us go deeper than mere intuitive reactions and ask: Why can't unlimited nuclear war be a means to policy objectives? What exactly prohibits it?

Suppose, for example, we were to decide that the Soviet presence in Syria could no longer be tolerated. It threatens our friend and ally, Israel, and puts pressure on the flow of Persian Gulf oil. Does it make sense to unleash a nuclear war upon the Soviet Union to make them leave Syria? Of course not! The answer is so obvious it is trivial. But if we analyze how we arrive at that answer we will learn a great deal about nuclear defense strategies and policies.

We saw in our consideration of the effects of nuclear war that nuclear war is commensurable with the worst cataclysms of the past. That means that the human cost of nuclear war is finite, although very, very high. In that sense, the statement of MacNamara and Bethe, quoted earlier, that treated nuclear war as a truly *infinite* disaster (productive of infinite human cost) was wrong. However horrible, it is finite and measurable. Does that mean that we can weigh a nuclear war in the scales against the desirability of getting the Soviet Union out of Syria? Yes, by definition, because we can measure it. Does that mean that we might decide to use nuclear war as a policy means to get the Soviets out? No, we would never rationally reach that decision. Keep in mind that we are looking at the issue of prudence only; we are not considering anything but our own advantage. The Soviets have nuclear weapons, many of them, indeed, more than we do. They will surely use them against us if we attack them. Whatever the advantage may be in getting the Soviets out of Syria, it could never even approach the terribly high (even if finite) cost to us of an unlimited nuclear war.

Contemplate, if you will, the possible policy ends for which nations might go to war or those for which nations have gone to war in the past. Are there any worth an unlimited nuclear war? Allowing for some slight hyperbole about the consequences of a nuclear war, Gwynne Dyer has, nonetheless, said it quite well:

> The disproportion between ends and means in warfare has widened to an unbridgeable chasm: the causes and the various national war aims of this country's wars are no more profound a complex than those that sent Tuthmose III's army marching into Palestine three thousand years ago, but the means by which wars can now be fought have placed the whole human race on a permanent thirty minute schedule of extinction.[49]

There simply are no such national war aims, at least among the typical kinds of ends normally pursued by nations seeking their own interest. Thus, while MacNamara and Bethe were wrong to describe nuclear war as an infinitely negative cost, they were right in what else they said. Nuclear war can never be a "final arbiter of disputes" between nations. The arbitration is far more costly than any policy end which could be in dispute.

Nuclear war (at least against a nuclear-armed opponent) simply will not work in the way that Clausewitz told us war works. It is not a political instrument. Even leaving morality aside, it is far too expensive in human cost ever to be prudentially worthwhile. Add the moral value of what would be destroyed and we can see clearly that the choice to wage unlimited nuclear war transcends the threshold of the conscionable.

When we hear, as we often do, that nuclear war would be madness, it is just this lesson the speaker usually has in mind. It is irrational to trade a small benefit for a huge cost. Similarly, it is this small benefit and huge cost that is referred to when we hear, as we often do, that a nuclear war can never be won. You do not win if you fail to achieve your policy end or pay so high a price that obtaining it ceases to be meaningful.

Recall, for a moment, our attempt to remove the Soviet presence from Syria by visiting unlimited nuclear war upon the Soviets' homeland, prompting full-scale retaliation upon us. Would it work, would it make the Soviets leave Syria? The answer is not at all clear. Perhaps Soviet troops and technicians would leave so as to help rebuild their stricken homeland. Perhaps they would stay for lack of means to leave. (Would there be any functioning airfields in the Soviet Union?) Perhaps a theater nuclear war would break out between Syria and the Soviet forces in Syria, on the one side, and Israel and the U.S. Sixth Fleet on the other. The possibilities are endless. What is very clear, however, is that it would no longer make a particle of difference to anyone in the United States whether the Soviets were in Syria or not. The background assumptions which prompted the initial attack, of strategic balance and advantage, would be rendered irrelevant. Who in a blasted United States or Soviet Union would care what was happening in Syria? Indeed, who would even know? There can be no doubt: nuclear weapons have made war as it is normally conceived meaningless, something no sane person would resort to for the purpose of achieving normal policy ends.

Beyond War as an Instrument

Note, however, that there are certain sorts of presuppositions built into the very notion of a nation state or, more broadly, a polity, which might give rise to deeper kinds of goals nations might have. We saw above, for example, that the right of a nation to exist is taken for granted by international law. A nation could have as its goal insuring its own continued existence. Or a nation could seek to protect the lives or the liberty of its own citizens on their soil. Such things cannot be described as merely "policy goals." They are too fundamental for that. They are what a nation *is about*: a nation must be able to do those sorts of things or it fails to be a nation. Indeed, the Standard of Permissible War Waging, derived in Chapter II, allowed states and their governments recourse to war *only* in those cases in which they acted in defense of their citizens in their homeland (or in defense of alliance partners doing the same thing for their citizens). Thus, the kind of very restricted area in which my theory of permissible resort to war allows war waging tends to preclude wars fought for lesser policy ends. It tends to preselect as candidates for permissible war waging those cases which exhibit the purest form of self-defense. To be sure, I have not yet demonstrated that nuclear war waging ever can be justified, even for those very basic ends. I only wish to point out that rejecting nuclear war as an instrument of policy is not *ipso facto* to reject it in all cases for all possible purposes.

We saw previously that popular writers like Jonathon Schell and Gwynne Dyer make national sovereignty out to be the villian of the piece, the source of the thrust toward nuclear conflict. If only we could be rid of this bugaboo, they tell us, then the risk of nuclear war and, indeed, of all war would evaporate. If Dyer and Schell mean by national sovereignty the notion that a given people delineated by race or language have a certain historical mission, then I can only agree with them and say good riddance. But unfortunately that is not all they mean. National sovereignty or, more generically, political sovereignty is a conceptual tool, rather like the legal notion of a contract, for example. It is a means to an end, not an end in itself. It is the mechanism by which a group of people get together to arrange for their common defense (among other things). Moreover, that defense is necessary if those people are to be free from attack or coercion from outside their polity. And if they are to be free to plan their own lives, projects, and goals, in short, to be secure in their life, liberty, and property, they must have this sort of protection. That is all that "national sovereignty" means or ought to mean.

Gwynne Dyer seems to grasp this, and tells us that we cannot have both "peace and independence" and that to avoid nuclear war "we will have to let all sorts of foreigners who think in strange ways have a say in what we do."[50] Obviously, there is a backhanded implication of xenophobia directed at partisans of national sovereignty here. But we can ignore that as a mere debating point. The real question is this: does Dyer mean that the era of the free, self-determined (sovereign) political community died with the birth of nuclear weapons? Does this mean that there is no permissible resort to war for such a polity or, at least, to war having a significant probability of going nuclear? Is this true even if that resort to war is solely for the purpose of protecting citizens' lives, liberty, and property? For if it does mean this, it also means that we no longer have a *right* to be free in our own polity and, therefore, no right to defend our own personal freedom or allow our government to defend it for us.

Let us hope that this is not the case. Indeed, one way of conceiving of my enterprise here is as an exploration into precisely what rights we still have to protect our lives and our freedom in the face of nuclear threats.

The Morality of Waging Nuclear War

If nuclear war never makes sense as a prudential instrument of policy, can it ever be moral? The obvious answer again seems to be no. After all, if you cannot justify nuclear war considering only your own interests, how could you justify it when you add the interests of your adversary and its peoples, which you must devastate in the pursuit of your interests? In addition, there are third-party nations which might well suffer some of the horrible consequences of a nuclear war, e.g., radioactivity or some form of the nuclear winter. This is, of course, the conventional wisdom: waging nuclear war can never be justified. Indeed, there are powerful arguments in behalf of this view.

Let us review the prerequisites of a just war (or of permissible war waging) and see how nuclear war would fare. Nuclear war seems of necessity to violate the Rule of Proportionality (rule 4 in Chapter II), at least for any ordinary political objective. It simply is not worth it when one takes into account not only the cost to one's own nation and people but the interests of others as well.

Nuclear war waged to obtain a policy goal must also violate rule 5 in Chapter II, which states: the purposes or ends sought must be practicable and achievable. After all, the destructive power of nuclear war would negate any political end sought (as we saw it do with our effort to strengthen our position in the Middle East by kicking the Soviets out of Syria by using unlimited nuclear war). The traditional criteria for just (permissible) war waging cannot be met by unlimited nuclear war.

There is yet a third way in which nuclear war seems to be impermissible: nuclear weapons do not allow us to discriminate between combatants and noncombatants. But I shall defer consideration of this very difficult problem until later. Let us first analyze the notion of *nuclear threats*. Nuclear war cannot be used to achieve traditional ends of policy. But what of threats to wage nuclear war? What about nuclear coercion, rather than nuclear force actually applied? After all, threatening to do something is not the same as doing it. If I threaten to murder you if you do not pay me protection money, let us say, that may well be both morally wrong and legally criminal. But it is clearly not the same as murder, in law or morals. What about coercive threats to use nuclear weapons? Are they prudent? Are they moral?

Nuclear Threats to Achieve Policy Objectives

Nuclear weapons, like other weapons, can be instruments of coercion through the threat of their use. In 1948, President Truman considered threatening the then nonnuclear Soviet Union with atomic bombing when it stopped traffic into West Berlin. He decided against it and mobilized an airlift instead. A few years later, President Eisenhower did threaten the People's Republic of China with nuclear weapons in order to end the Korean War. It worked or, at least, it appeared to work. The Chinese came to the peace table. But note, in both of these cases the nation threatened was nonnuclear. Whether such threats are moral or not, they are surely prudentially rational. They are also probably effective.

But what of threatening the use of nuclear weapons as a means of obtaining policy objectives against another nuclear power, particularly one of equal or near equal strength. Krushchev did it in 1956 over Suez with some success. (By threatening to wage nuclear war against France and the United Kingdom, he was implicitly threatening general nuclear war, because the NATO Treaty would have brought in the United States.) He also directly threatened the United States over Berlin in 1959 and again in 1961, although we ignored him and his coercion failed.

Keep in mind that threats need not be explicit, as in "I'll bomb you if you don't." One can do things that are implicitly threatening. In 1973, during the Yom Kippur War, Nixon and Kissinger practiced nuclear threat by putting our nuclear forces on alert to prevent the Soviet Union from landing their airborne troops in Egypt to save the Egyptian Third Army, which was surrounded and trapped by the Israelis.

If the risk of escalation to unlimited war is so great that it would be immoral to use nuclear weapons, is it immoral to threaten their use? Consider two divergent views on the subject. Colin Gray and Keith Payne tell us:

> Strategic forces do not exist solely for the purpose of deterring a Soviet nuclear threat. Instead, they are intended to support a U.S. foreign policy....Such a function requires American strategic forces that would enable a president to initiate strategic nuclear use for coercive, though politically defensive, purposes.[51]

In commenting specifically on the U.S. nuclear alert in 1973 over the prospect of Soviet troops in Egypt, Jeff McMahan says:

> To prevent this adverse effect on the 'American position' (a shift in the balance of power in the Mid-East), the American government deliberately aggravated the threat of all-out nuclear war, thereby putting at greater risk not only the lives of the people the world over but also the very existence of future generations. The arrogant parochialism of the assessment of importance of the American position is astonishing.[52]

Who is right? What would just war theory tell us? The most obvious candidate for application is the Rule of Proportionality. Is the gain achieved by the threat, the prevention of the installation of Soviet troops, worth the cost paid, the risk of all-out nuclear war? McMahan clearly thinks not. But before answering this question, we must assess the level of risk. If the risk was miniscule (approaching zero), perhaps it was justified. After all, a fundamental change in the balance of power in the Mid-East is not quite so parochial an interest as McMahan thinks. It is a position from which great leverage could be exerted upon the vital interests of the power which was disadvantaged.

However, threatening nuclear war poses more than a near-zero risk of nuclear war. We have seen the large (and, unfortunately, still growing) premium upon a first strike which vulnerable counterforce weapons create. So great is this premium that some analysts have concluded that once both powers reach maximum alert status, nuclear war is almost inevitable. In addition, alert status significantly increases the risk of accidental war. All in all, one must come down on the side of McMahan. The Rule of Proportionality makes immoral the use of nuclear threats to obtain policy objectives short of preventing an adversary's use of nuclear weapons, precisely because nuclear coercion involves nonnegligible risks of nuclear war.

Does this mean that we are impotent to protect our legitimate interests in the world? Does this mean, as McMahan's quote might imply, that our concerns with political objectives are always parochial and based in arrogance? Are they never "politically defensive," to use Gray's and Payne's criterion? Of course, we must be able to carry out foreign policy objectives. Of course, some (I would say most) of our foreign policy objectives are legitimate. Indeed, keeping Soviet troops out of the Yom Kippur War was a perfectly legitimate, "politically defensive" policy objective. My concern lies entirely in *how* we do it. Another rule of just war theory, the Rule of Least Harm, tells us exactly what was appropriate here. What would have been the least harmful means (in terms of the risk of escalation and thus of vast human cost) of stopping the Soviet move? The answer is obvious: adequate conventional forces. In this case that meant a powerful rapid deployment force conjoined with naval and aerial domination of the Eastern Mediterranean. Such conventional force would have been at least as effective as nuclear threats, and much safer.

But, one might object, we did not have such ability to project conventional force. That is not clear, but if we did not, we should have had. In a world in which the risk of nuclear war is made dramatically higher by nuclear threats, explicit or implicit (e.g., calling alerts), we simply must have conventional forces to meet conventional threats. The alternatives are undertaking immoral risks or the weakening of our capacity to carry out our moral duties as leader of the free world. If one believes, as I do, that the United States is predominately a force for good in the world, to weaken that capacity is itself immoral. Nuclear forces must not be used as a cheap but risky substitute for conventional force. They are for nuclear deterrence only. For the United States, the possession of adequate conventional forces is *a moral obligation*.

Nuclear war simply is not a viable instrument to secure policy objectives, nor is the threat of it. It is not even analogous to using the proverbial hammer to kill a fly. It is more analogous to using dynamite to kill a fly in your immediate vicinity. It is always more destructive and costly than the objective (being rid of the fly) is desirable. Indeed, it is so destructive as to make the enjoyment of being rid of the fly nugatory. And, we must not forget, it is very likely to destroy the user. It appears that waging unlimited nuclear war can never be prudentially rational or morally permissible. This demonstrates the revolutionary character of the combination of nuclear weapons and strategic delivery vehicles (long-range bombers, cruise missiles, and ballistic missiles), and it is profoundly important for the ways in which states can relate to each other and military power can be used.

Still, the undeniably great importance of these truths is sometimes overstated. For all they really tell us is that it is both irrational and immoral to *start* a strategic nuclear war for the typical ends of national interest. As we saw, however, this tells us nothing about rationality or moral right when life and death issues of national survival and the protection of citizens in their homeland are at stake. On the other hand, we certainly have not shown that it is permissible to use nuclear weapons in defense of national survival or the lives of citizens. However, the limitations upon traditional notions of national interest and national policy do not rule it out.

What if we are genuinely faced with a threat to our freedom and either threats of use or actual use of nuclear weapons are the only ways in which we can defend ourselves? What if we are faced with that dichotomous cliche: red or dead?

Better Dead than Red? Another Hypothetical Case

Suppose that there is a very small country, Whiteland, which is threatened by a much larger and militarily stronger country, Blackland. Blackland has an overwhelming superiority in conventional forces. However, both countries possess roughly equal nuclear arsenals. Blackland informs Whiteland that it must unconditionally surrender or be conquered by conventional force. Blackland will not use nuclear weapons unless Whiteland does, for it does not need to.

Whiteland is a representative democracy, and in the meeting of its assembly it weighs the following facts. If it surrenders to Blackland, its political system will be changed from a free democracy to a one-party dictatorship like Blackland's. It also knows that it will have Blackland's army and paramilitary forces stationed on its soil. But beyond that, it knows very little. Blackland is at present ruled by an oppressive collective leadership which brutally crushes all dissent and discourages personal freedom and self-fulfillment as "individualistic and selfish," requiring instead a kind of tiresome, "public-spirited" participation in party or state activities. It discourages privacy and individual initiative to the best of its ability. However, Blackland is neither Hitler's Germany nor Orwell's Oceania. The regime is neither ambitious nor efficient enough for that. But a generation ago it was a true totalitarian nightmare state, and it is the opinion of Whiteland's experts that it might be so again some day.

Whiteland is convinced that its future will be no better than that of Blackland's natives if Whiteland chooses surrender, but it has no idea how much worse it might be. It might end up like an Eastern European state today, say Hungary or Romania. On the other hand, it might end up like Russia under Stalin or, worse, Poland under Hitler or Cambodia under Pol Pot. The leaders simply do not know. Note that this is not just an issue of which political system Whiteland will have imposed upon it, the term "red" to the contrary notwithstanding. It is conquest and subjugation by an omnipotent, alien power, the kind of open-ended slavery we examined above.

The other path is nuclear resistance. Whiteland's generals are convinced that they can stop Blackland's threatened conventional conquest by using nuclear weapons, but in the process they will trigger an unlimited nuclear war with Blackland. The best estimates are that 65 percent of Whitelanders will die as a direct effect of the war and, perhaps, another 15 percent as the result of subsequent temporary climatic changes. The longer-term future for the 20 percent who survive is one of a rude, fourteenth-century existence of cold, disease, and grinding poverty lasting for an indefinite time. Approximately the same percentage of casualties will result in Blackland, and there will be similar, although not equal casualties in nearby neutral countries as well.

Should Whiteland fight or surrender? Think about it very carefully. There is no dearth of those who think the answer easy and obvious. The problem is that among them they disagree, and that is frightening. For myself, I cannot say what is the correct course. Either horn of the dilemma is so completely ghastly that the mind recoils from the choice.

The absolutely crucial point, however, is this: we do not face that choice. *We are not Whiteland.* We never will be, unless we heedlessly fritter away our conventional defenses because we would rather spend money on microwave ovens and publicly-supported ballet companies.

For economically and technologically we are the strongest nation on earth, and the leader of virtually all of the other economically strong, industrialized nations of the world. We can resist conventional threats with conventional force, if only we have the strength of character and force of will to do it. Indeed, to allow ourselves to become a Whiteland would be a sort of immoral negligence that would trap us in a moral *cul de sac,* either red or dead. We must never do that to ourselves. Now is the time to act as morality dictates: to be certain that we are adequately defended by both nuclear and conventional forces. If we undertake a morally proper course of action, we should never have to choose to initiate a nuclear war. Thus, we can label the parable of Blackland and Whiteland as a philosopher's curiosity and conclude that it will never be moral for the United States to be first to choose the path to nuclear war.

C. *Defensive Nuclear War*

It would seem that the only possible use of nuclear weapons left to us which is not demonstrably immoral and imprudent is a strictly defensive one, in which we *use nuclear weapons only after we have been attacked by nuclear weapons.* But this also seems to be precisely when nuclear weapons become their most useless. After all, we have already been attacked; once we launch a counterattack we are finished as a nation, and most of us are probably dead. Anthony Kenny puts the putative dilemma as well as anyone:

> But would it, in fact, be the rational thing to launch a retaliatory strike if one had suffered the unimaginable horrors of a full-scale nuclear attack? ...Otherwise than an act of revenge, a retaliatory strike would seem to be at best pointless....A second strike would have no deterrent effect. It would by this time be too late for deterrence to have any force.[53]

Since nuclear weapons can only deter *before* a war starts and cannot be morally used *after* a war has started, George Kennan can say:

> To my mind, the nuclear bomb is the *most useless weapon ever invented.* It can be employed to no rational purpose. It is not even an effective defense against itself [emphasis added].[54]

This notion grows out of the antiquated doctrine of Mutual Assured Destruction: "If you hit my cities ("countervalue targets" is the term), I'll hit yours." If this ever was U.S. strategy, it certainly has not been for some time.[55] However, it has long since become part of the conventional wisdom. Indeed, this belief is a key part of the Paradox of Nuclear Weapons: to possess strategic nuclear weapons is ultimately to have a weapon which is capable only of the mass murder of innocent civilians after it is too late to serve any useful or morally permissible purpose.

In different ways Anthony Kenny, Jonathan Schell, George Kennan, the American Catholic Bishops, and many others subscribe to this portion of the Paradox of Nuclear Weapons. However, it is pure myth and a pernicious myth at that. First, it assumes that the only possible targets of nuclear missiles are cities and "innocent civilians." But with the emergence ten years ago of a counterforce capability, i.e., a capability to destroy hardened targets such as missile silos, this is simply no longer true. Indeed, since nuclear weapons have always been able to destroy submarine and bomber bases, they have always been "counterforce capable," to use the jargon. Second, the Paradox assumes that nuclear war is the end of history or the end of man. Again, this is part of the myth that Schell and others propagate. It grossly oversimplifies the problem. Remember, I argued earlier that the survival of large numbers of people (even if relatively small percentages) in the combatant countries certainly *does not* make nuclear war any more acceptable as policy. But we also saw that it *changes* the moral situation and complicates it considerably. If some people will survive, then there may be things that we could do to save more people or to improve the long-term prospects for those who do survive. In short, maybe we could do something to mitigate damage to our society and our citizens, even if that damage remains grievous. If we can somehow use our nuclear weapons defensively to mitigate damage to our people, then perhaps defensive nuclear war waging makes sense and is legitimate as an instance of the right of self-defense.

Nuclear weapons today, since they are much more accurate than those of the past, can be used effectively against *other weapons* and offensive military forces threatening to destroy or conquer our people or the people of allied nations. Their much greater power, when compared to conventional weapons, makes them very effective for counterforce use. Perhaps the Principle of Discrimination, or the Rule of Proportionality, morally prohibit us from using them, because of the vast collateral cost in civilian lives. We shall have to see. But one thing is clear: Kennan is simply in error. Nuclear weapons today have a rational use: saving lives and preventing conquest.

Contrary to the popular wisdom, a nuclear war cannot be fought in a few minutes. There are a number of reasons for this. Different sorts of delivery systems take different amounts of time to hit their targets. More important, nuclear explosions will throw enough debris into the air to destroy incoming warheads, a phenomenon called 'fratricide'. Thus, a nuclear targeting plan must hit the outmost targets first, so that later warheads will not have to travel through explosions. In an attack on the United States, this would give rise to a targeting strategy known as a "walk" from south to north (since missiles coming over the pole and aimed at southern targets would not be able to penetrate the clouds of debris over northern targets, if the latter were hit first). This means that even a first strike could take some hours.

By a targeting policy known as *prompt counterforce targeting,* a series of second strikes could actually succeed in destroying a large number of the enemy's nuclear weapons *that were earmarked for a first strike.* This would save the lives of millions of Americans and Europeans. How many lives would be saved when a missile destroys another that has yet to be launched? It is, of course, impossible to say in advance. If the latter was targeted on Minot, South Dakota, perhaps 50,000; if New York City, perhaps ten million.[56] But the point—that targeting weapons will save lives—is beyond question.

However, the defensive use of counterforce weapons goes far beyond resistance to a first strike in progress, for important counterforce targets would remain after a first strike was complete. 'Prompt counterforce targeting' spells out what these targets would be. The Soviets would hold a large portion of their warheads in a 'strategic reserve', for two reasons. First, a number of those warheads *could not* be used. Missile-carrying submarines not on station, missiles to be fired from reloadable silos, and systems that were not operable during a first strike but that could be put in working order quickly thereafter would all fit in this class. Second, regnant Soviet strategy and simple prudence would require a reserve held for coercive negotiation or use after the damage from a first strike could be assessed.[57]

An attack on either or both of these classes of targets would save the lives of many millions of Americans and citizens of allied nations. If the Soviets reserved 3,000 strategic warheads (approximately 40 percent of their arsenal) by intent or inability to use them and we destroyed two-thirds of those reserved, between ten and one hundred million American lives could be saved, depending upon the nature of the Soviet first strike and the effectiveness of our relatiatory strike. Similar numbers of Western European lives could be saved by promptly striking intermediate and medium-range nuclear weapons. Very simply: *Prompt counterforce targeting saves lives.* It is from this undeniable fact that a theory of defensive nuclear war waging emerges.

Let us consider an American President's situation, taking account of these facts, and consider the options posed to him. Assume that the Soviets have launched a practically unlimited strategic attack of five thousand warheads (reserving 50 percent of their strategic warheads). The American president knows that the remainder of their warheads will either be launched as soon as they can be readied, e.g., when missile submarines in port reach station, when cold launch tubes are reloaded, and so forth, or used in the nuclear coercion of a devastated and prostrate America.

Let us consider this first class of weapons, those which have not been launched due to logistical limitations and which will be launched as soon as they are readied. Here the President faces a simple choice. To launch against these targets will save a large number of American lives. We have already been attacked. He has every reason to believe that as soon as these weapons are readied, they will be launched as well. An attack upon those weapons constitutes self-defense in the strictest sense of the term. It is attacking your attacker's weapons to save yourself or people for whose safety you are directly charged.

Of course, Soviet civilian casualties would occur. But the relatively isolated positions of most Soviet ICBM and submarine bases would hold such casualties to a minimum. The Rule of Proportionality is strictly upheld. The Principle of Discrimination is not violated because the doctrine of double effect would justify a defensive strike that might cost hundreds of thousands of Soviet citizens' lives to save tens of millions of American lives. This conclusion is based upon an equal weighing of the value of Soviet and American lives and as such is a pure utilitarian calculation that nonetheless proceeds under the *right* of self-defense. I can understand no argument other than the strictest form of pacifism that could dispute the right of the American president to launch such a minimal, prompt, counterforce second strike.

One might recall that in Chapter II, I formulated a Principle of Justified Defensive Counterfire that follows directly from just war theory. That is, a nation has a right to return fire over its borders, if its neighbor is attacking its citizens in their homes. We saw that such counterfire was subject to the Principle of Discrimination. That is, the defending nation cannot be wanton or reckless in its lack of concern for the number of innocent bystanders it kills. But with this constraint, defensive counterfire is permissible. For defense of its citizens' lives in their homes (and therefore on its own soil) is at the very heart of what a legitimate government is all about. Therefore, such defensive counterfire is acceptable under the very severe Standard of Permissible War Waging that I formulated in Chapter II.

Now, I formulated the Principle of Justified Defensive Counterfire in local situations such as the Israeli-Palestinian border clashes. But what difference does it make whether we are talking about 105 mm howitzers or SS-18's with one megaton warheads. It is and must be legitimate to destroy weapons that are killing citizens in their homes.

Extending the List of Prompt Counterforce Targets

Thus, the notion of self-defense using nuclear weapons can make sense. It has an application in nuclear war. However, the list of possible targets grows beyond the very narrow class of strategic nuclear forces being readied for another strike. It might include the nuclear forces held in reserve for coercion, conventional forces, Soviet war industry, Soviet political leadership, the whole of the Soviet economy, even social institutions which would aid in postwar recovery. This seems to be a long list. Indeed, it seems to be growing toward all targets and all people in the Soviet Union. Yet that is not at all what I have heretofore justified. Let us take these classes of targets one at a time. The preceding argument justified only a very narrow strike at targets such as ballistic missile submarines in base or reloadable silos, both of which could be presumed to be used for further strikes as soon as they became available.

How might we justify extending a prompt counterforce retaliatory strike? What about those strategic nuclear forces withheld for the purpose of postattack nuclear coercion? It seems that once it has been attacked, the United States is under no moral duty to endure nuclear coercion with forces not used in the first attack. There are two arguments for this conclusion.

First, the U.S. command is not in a position to know which forces are for coercion and which are for immediate use. It seems to put an unfair burden upon the nation that has been attacked to require that after a first attack, it must discriminate between forces to be used for additional strikes and forces to be held as a threat and used in an attack only if the threat fails. Indeed, the Soviets know we cannot know which of their forces they are intentionally withholding for purposes of threat, and that knowledge shifts the burden to them. It is they who expose their reserve forces to nuclear attack, knowing we cannot discriminate.

Second, even if we could know, are we obligated not to strike nuclear forces to be used to threaten us even after we have been attacked by other nuclear forces? If our domestic law is any guide, then the answer is no. The legal notion of self-defense permits the use of such force as is necessary to remove the threat to the lives of those threatened. One is not under an obligation to guess the further intentions of the attacker beyond his intention, conditional or otherwise, to inflict life-threatening violence —a situation which in this case unquestionably obtains. We have already been attacked. Indeed, our criminal law shifts the presumption strongly against an assailant who has initiated an attack with deadly force and with malice aforethought.[58] He is legitimately subject to continuing counterattack using deadly force, if this reasonably appears to be necessary. The attacker carries the burden of communicating the cessation of hostilities so as to "remove any just apprehension from his adversary."[59] In international terms, this can only mean a successfully communicated offer of truce.

Although one must be careful in moving from domestic law to international morality, there seems to be no fundamental disanalogy here. Thus, the right of self-defense against forces to be used for coercion proceeds upon two principles, one epistemic and one moral:

> *Epistemic Principle:* As a practical matter we can never know what an attacker intends to do with his reserve nuclear forces. Thus, we cannot discriminate between those forces he would use to strike us and those he would withhold for purposes of coercion. Since he has attacked us, we are entitled to the presumption that most enables us to defend ourselves, *viz.,* that all his remaining strategic nuclear forces are being readied for immediate attack and, therefore, are legitimate targets.

> *Moral Principle:* Even if we know that our attacker intends to use all nuclear forces that he has withheld for coercion and to strike us again only if we prove intransigent, we are not required to acquiesce. We may counterattack to disarm him and prevent his coercion.

We have seen that the legal notion of self-defense, to the extent that it is analogous, would support both principles. However, there is a deeper philosophical argument that underlies this position. Recall that slavery, complete omnipotence over another, includes the power to kill. From this fact John Locke draws a powerful presumption:

> And hence it is that he who attempts to get another man into his absolute power does thereby put himself in a state of war with him; it being to be understood as a declaration of a design upon his life.[60]

That is, an absolute power to coerce *is* a power to kill, and one is just as entitled to resist being put under such a power as one is to resist being killed. What is true for one person is true for many organized as a nation-state for their own protection. (Note that Locke's principle could be used to make a much stronger claim: since nuclear coercion in an attempt to obtain surrender before an attack constitutes an attempt to gain absolute power, that justifies a preemptive nuclear attack. I do not make that much stronger claim, but only that defensive attacks are justified after a first strike is launched.)

There are two important qualifications to the use of the epistemic and moral principles formulated above. First, they provide only a *presumptive* right to attack enemy forces. The Rule of Discrimination (modified by double effect) and the Rule of Proportionality would limit this right. Thus, the argument above cannot be construed as a blanket approval for any sort of attack against Soviet nuclear forces set aside for purposes of coercion, regardless of how much collateral damage would result. This limitation grows directly out of a similar limitation on justified defensive counterfire. In other words, we still must make efforts to honor noncombatant immunity. Second, only strategic *nuclear* forces have thus far been shown to be legitimate targets. But this last seems to be a very stringent limitation upon a country that has already been attacked and is acting in self-defense. Let us consider a possible extension of these two principles regarding forces to be used as coercive threats, an extension to *conventional* forces.

Might not we acquire a right in a postattack environment to counterattack all of the attacker's military forces which he could conceivably use to coerce us or our allies? If we can reasonably conclude that Soviet armies would be used, after a strategic nuclear attack upon the United States, to conquer our allies in Europe or even, conceivably, to launch amphibious operations against the continental United States, then they are legitimate targets in a retaliatory strike. (The latter, which seems fanciful today, might not be so in a postattack situation.)

So the Principle of Justified Defensive Counterfire could, thus, be extended to a *Principle of Justified Counterattack,* which would read as follows:

> Once it has been attacked, a nation acquires the right to counterattack any of the attacker's military forces which the latter could plausibly use against the victim or its allies.

However, such a rule seems in danger of broadening the scope of a retaliatory strike too far. Here, "military forces" begin to shade into war making capability. A tactical air base in Byelorussia would be a legitimate target under this rule, for it would with high probability play a role in either a nuclear or conventional attack upon Western Europe. But what about a refinery that makes jet fuel exclusively for military purposes? What about the technicians who work there? Are they *noncombatants* or *combatants?*

Noncombatant Immunity

The question of noncombatant immunity is absolutely central to this issue because the principal argument against the doctrine of prompt counterforce second strikes turns on it. The argument goes like this: the vast majority of Soviet citizens are innocent. One cannot meaningfully attack all the military targets in the Soviet Union without killing millions of these innocents, and that would be monstrously immoral. Perhaps the doctrine of prompt counterforce strikes does make prudential sense, argues the critic, but it can never be morally permissible. This argument must be taken very seriously for, if it is correct, nuclear weapons still have no morally legitimate defensive purpose, even though they may have a practical defensive use, i.e., prompt counterforce strikes.

Several recent papers by philosophers have provided us with an invaluable analysis of the distinction between innocence and noncombatant status in war, and I shall adopt this distinction without change.[61] It is generally accepted that there exist no cogent moral arguments, at least not within just war theory, which justify attacks which have as their objective the killing of noncombatants.[62] Most of us believe World War II to have been a just war, viewed from the allies' perspective. However, most of us would also hold that the massive firebombing raids carried out by the RAF Bomber Command with the sole purpose of killing civilians in Europe or by the U.S. Twentieth Air Force over Japan, or the two atomic bomb raids carried out by the latter, were morally wrong—a failure of *jus in bello* even while the allies genuinely stood for *jus ad bellum*.

I use the technical term "noncombatant" because that term must not be confused with the notion of innocence. In the context of the theory of just war, these two notions are clearly distinct. To use Jeffrie Murphy's example, the octogenarian Nazi who helped promote the policy of aggression and who delighted in his country's aggressive war waging is not liable to one's counterattack, for he is not part of the attack and he does not threaten the person attacked.[63] He is not innocent, but that is irrelevant. The anti-Nazi German conscript is liable to attack because he is bearing arms and, thus, one is acting to protect oneself under a right of self-defense when one attacks him. He may well be morally innocent, but that is irrelevant. As we shall see, the thesis I propose changes the octogenarian's status somewhat. But Jeffrie Murphy, Robert Fullinwider, and Thomas Nagel seem to be correct in saying that we possess no right to kill the octogenarian as a matter of purpose, purely as punishment or in retribution for his country's aggressive war waging.

If the purposive killing of noncombatants in urban saturation raids was morally wrong, what about the daylight "precision bombing" carried out by the U.S. Eighth Air Force over Germany? The Eighth Air Force employed a doctrine and practice totally different from that of the RAF Bomber Command or the Twentieth Air Force. The only targets bombed were military or military-industrial in nature. Considerable photoreconnaissance and analysis was done to choose targets, and substantial efforts were made, sometimes at grave risk to bomber crews, to minimize civilian casualties.[64]

Nonetheless, the Eighth Air Force caused thousands of noncombatant casualties by collateral damage. Despite considerable effort, even daylight bombing with the famed Norden bombsight was far from precise. Was the United States morally wrong in carrying out these kinds of raids, knowing that large numbers of civilian casualties would result?

We have already examined the notion of double effect, i.e., civilian casualties are acceptable if they are the genuinely unintended results of otherwise morally legitimate war waging. However, double effect cannot be stretched to include examples like either of the above. Double effect simply will not work when, as in the example of the Eighth Air Force, the level of accuracy in targeting is so gross that you know that regardless of the care you exercise, the probability that you will kill noncombatants in large numbers is somewhat greater than that you will destroy your target at all, let alone without killing many noncombatants. Similarly, traditional double effect will not work with nuclear weapons, since the destructive power is so massive that civilian casualties will result on a scale that might be far greater than the military value of the target. We must not so quickly gloss over justifications of noncombatant deaths by double effect without at least acknowledging that this notion has been at the center of the controversy over noncombatant immunity. Paul Ramsey, especially, used a very broad notion of double effect to justify the threat of countervalue strikes.[65] But I take this approach to be a blind alley. Elizabeth Anscombe's general analysis of the weakness of the double effect arguments in these cases and Michael Walzer's specific refutation of Ramsey are both compelling.[66]

If double effect arguments fail, is there any other argument which could justify attacks upon such targets? If not, then nuclear weapons, because of their failure to discriminate, have no role in a morally permissible defense. They are, as the critics claim, merely instruments of revenge. And we are back to the dilemma of nuclear weapons. I believe, however, that there is such an argument.

Limited Noncombatant Liability: A Hypothetical Case

Imagine two nations A and B. Both are armed with long-range conventional missiles, rather like the German V-2. A's long range missiles are based at the center of A-ville, A's capital. It is irrelevant where B's are based. In addition, both A and B possess armies, artillery, and short-range missiles based near their common border.

I assume that A is a direct democracy. Its leaders call its citizens to the popular assembly to propose war against B. The leaders of A neither have, nor even claim to have, any moral justification for attacking B. It is an aggressive war, plain and simple. Part of the policy proposed is the explicit authorization to launch A's long-range missiles at B City, B's capital. The citizens of A vote, not unanimously, to make war. A then proceeds to launch missiles at B City, as well as to commence an invasion of B. A has reloadable launchers for its long-range missiles, and it has missiles in reserve. A's missile commanders intend, B has strong reason to believe, to continue launching missiles from A-ville upon B City.

The members of B's government, being philosophically inclined, ask: "Do we have a moral right to attack A's long-range missile launchers in the middle of A-ville?" We know that if we do so, we will kill many noncombatant citizens in the process. We do not *want* to kill them. Killing them will not shorten the war nor serve any other military purpose. We do not believe that we have a right to punish them. But surely we have a right to protect our citizens by attacking those long-range missile launchers before they can reload and attack us again.

We can recognize the moral rule on which B is preparing to act; it is the Principle of Justified Defensive Counterfire. But we saw that that principle is limited by the requirement that we discriminate between noncombatants and combatants. Here, with the rockets located directly in the center of A-ville, we cannot easily discriminate. Does a government's right to protect its citizens in their homes extend to causing large, perhaps disproportionately large, noncombatant casualties by collateral damage? The answer seems to me to be yes, and that positive answer stems from the fact that the citizens of A are somehow morally liable for their government's action.

Note, I do *not* claim that they are liable to direct attack in retribution or as punishment, or even following some gross and dubious application of the Rule of Proportionality which might encourage us to "break their will" and shorten the war. The notion articulated by Murphy, *et al.* seems quite correct here. One justifies attacks upon combatants on the basis of self-defense only. Here, those noncombatant citizens cannot be directly and purposively attacked in self-defense, since they do not threaten B's citizens. But those missiles and launchers certainly do! Attacking them and their crews is a straightforward exercise of the right of self-defense. Thus, surely B can put A's citizens at risk—even a great many of them at great risk—as it attempts to defend its citizens from subsequent attacks it knows to be coming.

However, there is a further limit to this right of risk-imposing counterattacks. Not only must B *not try* to kill noncombatants of A, B must *try not* to insofar as this is possible with the means at its disposal. Assume that B can only knock out the launchers with rather inaccurate missiles. If it is that or leave A's missiles unattacked, can B attack? If B could have made its missiles more accurate and, with reckless disregard for A's noncombatant civilians, failed to do so, then no. But if B could not, due to the limits of technology, make its missiles more accurate, and if B has no other effective way of defending itself, then it seems that, given the argument above, B has the right to so defend itself, a right based upon B's citizens' right to life.

Moreover, if A knew B's missiles to be inaccurate and knew it had no other way of defending itself, then it seems that it is A rather than B which disregarded the safety of its own noncombatant citizens, and it is thus A which bears the primary moral responsibility. (It is worth noting in passing that B does have a duty to see that A knows of the inaccuracy of its missiles. This might also help prudentially, as a deterrent. The communication of all kinds of capacities and incapacities takes on a moral as well as strategic status in such situations.[67])

However, within its capacities, B must take reasonable care to minimize noncombatant deaths, as the Eighth Air Force did. This is a familiar concept to lawyers. B must *not be negligent* and especially not *wanton* or *reckless* in how it attacks A's weapons. That is what it means to say that B must *try not* to kill noncombatants. But given this limitation, B does seem clearly to have a right to counterattack in self-defense.

How might one justify this intuition that B has a right to attack A's missile launchers? I abjure traditional double effect for the reasons stated above. Certainly, the mere fact that there is a legitimate military target in the area does not totally remove B's duty not to kill noncombatants and open the gates to unlimited slaughter. But recall that A took a plebiscite. All citizens of A who voted for the attack certainly seem to be culpable. They actively approved. They are not completely innocent in Nagel's and Murphy's sense of that term. Surely, one acquires some degree of responsibility for the actions of one's government when one, through the political machinery of a democracy, votes before the fact for what one's government does. The legal notion of agency operates here as a strong guide to our moral intuitions. You are legally (and presumably morally) responsible when your agent acts in ways that you have *explicitly authorized*.[68]

What if A's government had only asked for and received an open-ended authorization to wage war upon B, rather than explicit permission to launch its long-range missiles against B City? Again, the law of agency seems an excellent guide to our moral intuitions. A principal is liable for the acts of an agent that are reasonably within the scope of the agent's authority, even if not explicitly authorized by the principal.[69] The citizens of A who voted for the referendum are still morally liable for their government's action, in the sense that they can be put at risk.

What of the citizens of A who voted against the aggressive war upon B? It seems to me that, absent other stronger dissenting action on their part, they are as liable to being put at risk by B's counterattacks as are their compatriots who voted in favor of the aggressive war. Let us again move to the law for an analogous situation, but now to the law of corporations. A company is considering engaging in some massively immoral and illegal activity—pouring large quantities of arsenic into the public water supply as a matter of ongoing operations, let us say. A member of the board of directors of the company, when the policy is before the board, votes no but does nothing else. Later, when sued in tort (or charged in crime) with these transgressions of duty, she pleads that she voted no. What would our reaction be? The answer is obvious! We would say, you are responsible as much, or nearly as much, as your fellow board members who voted yes. You should have blown the whistle, gone public or to regulatory authorities, or, at the very least, resigned from the board of so despicable a company. Mere formal dissent in this case does almost nothing to relieve her liability, legal or moral.

Similar liability exists, it would seem, for the dissenting citizens of A. There exists a range of activities which tend to relieve liability. Strong vocal dissent, continuing attempts to get the issue back before the assembly and to defeat it, civil disobedience, even emigration in protest, or warning B of the attack, all present themselves. (Note the similarity to the range of activities open to the opposing member of the board of directors.) At some point, the dissenting citizen's actions become strong and sustained enough to absolve him or her of responsibility or liability. Exactly where on the spectrum of dissident activity this occurs need not now detain us. It is sufficient merely to observe that in most polities and over most issues, the number of such dedicated dissidents will be very few.

In the case of the citizens of *A* who voted for the war, it was something they did, an act of commission, which made them liable to the risk imposed by a defensive counterattack. In the case of the citizens who voted nay and did no more, it was an omission. Indeed, we impose a negligence-like standard on the latter for *failing* to do something that they *should have* done.

Before I change the example by changing the political system of *A*, let us consider two other sorts of people living in *A*. What of the apathetic person who did not attend the assembly, who did not know the issue of the war with *B* would be considered, and in general does not much care what his government does. He is too busy watching television quiz shows, perhaps. The strong temptation is to say: "Well fellow, you *should have* cared." You should have skipped the quiz show on the day of the meeting. Your government claims to act for you, as well as those who participated in the assembly, and it is your business to know what it is up to and to act as best you can to influence it. Indeed, I would go on to say to the apathetic citizen, do not blame *B*'s citizens if their missiles, in a desperate effort to destroy your country's missile launchers, kill or maim you. There is something you should have done and failed to do, and that failure in some small way contributed to the dilemma in which *B* found itself. That failure stops you from assigning to *B* responsibility for harm to you.

What of the children of *A*-ville? They are true innocents and their plight is a heart-wrenching situation that is faced in any war by any warring nation, no matter how just its cause. If there is any justification for putting them at risk, it is by traditional double effect. One is tempted to say to the government and citizens of *A*, however, "*you* brought death and injury upon your children. The citizens of *B* are defending *their* children from your rockets, and however terrible the collateral killing of children, it is you, not the citizens of *B*, who must bear the primary moral responsibility."[70] This is not to say that it is not morally wrong for *B* to kill *A*'s children. It is, and nothing can right it. But *A*'s behavior and *B*'s right to defend its citizens can *excuse* the wrong.

I will gloss over the application of these standards to a representative democracy like our own, rather than a direct democracy like *A*. Suffice it to say that there is nothing in the somewhat more gross controls we have over our government's behavior that would obviate our responsibility should our government launch an aggressive nuclear war. It is we who elect or defeat warmongers, whether for Congress or the White House, and it is we who are answerable.

Now, let us bring the example of *A* and *B* a bit closer to the problem we face. Suppose that *A* is a dictatorship. It has no assembly, or perhaps it has a sham assembly which rubber-stamps decisions made by an oligarchic elite. The citizens of *A* have no say at all in the decision of its leaders to wage war upon *B* or, more specifically, to launch its long-range missiles against *B* City. Are the citizens of *A* immune from being put at risk by *B*'s defensive counterattacks because of their political system? Does their inability to participate preserve their absolute noncombatant immunity? Consider the question from *B*'s perspective. Are *A*'s citizens innocent in so strong a sense that *B* cannot even put them at risk as it seeks to destroy *A*'s missiles and launchers? Is *B* now morally prevented from taking action in its own defense solely because of *A*'s arrangements for political decision making?

There is one extreme case in which we might feel compelled to answer yes. Suppose *A* is ruled not by "its leaders" in any sense of that word but, instead, by an outlaw band who recently have seized power, and who are not even citizens of *A*. Suppose they are quite literally (the literalness is important) holding the citizens hostage or, even more accurately, using them as shields. This is a desperate moral dilemma for the citizens of *B* and one to which there may be no morally "right" answer.[71]

But let us not become too enthralled with this special case. Most dictatorships are not of this unusual sort. Indeed, they differ in ways quite important to the assessment of the culpability of *A*'s citizens for their leaders' action:

1. Most dictatorships are ethnically and nationally *of* their own people. Furthermore, in some broad sense of "social institutions," most dictators acquire power through preexisting institutions, procedures, and traditions, even if not by democratic vote. Stalin and all of his successors have done that. Hitler did that. True revolutionaries, such as Lenin and Mao, do not.

2. More important, the government of *A* will almost certainly make *claims to legitimacy*. Whatever else political legitimacy means, it means in part that the government can act for and in the name of its people. In this sense the notion of agency taken from the law is more than analogous, it is morally homologous.

   For many of us in the West, political legitimacy requires popular sovereignty, the rule of law, and some limitations upon the government's use of coercive force (these last two may be the same). A dictatorship, almost by definition, would fail on each of these three counts. But legitimate or illegitimate, it would certainly *claim* legitimacy, and thus claim to be the agent of its people in the arena of international politics.

3. Closely connected is the *acquiescence* of the citizens to the claims their government makes to act for them. No government can endure

long without at least the passive acquiescence of most of its people. That acquiescence may come in part from political intimidation or even terror, but in the real world (as compared to anti-utopian visions) it must also grow from a profound apathy on the part of much of its citizenry and the positive support of at least a significant number. Surely Hitler's Germany between 1933 and 1945 or the Soviet Union today exemplify such gradations from opposition through passive acquiescence to positive support.[72]

4. A government's claims of legitimacy must be given more credence if it has been in power for a long time. This point is closely connected to 1, in that preexistence for some time seems important in "legitimizing" both the government itself and the social institutions and procedures which gave rise to it. It is also connected to 3, in that sustained acquiescence is more legitimizing than brief or temporary acquiescence.

It is no accident that 1 through 4 are very close to the traditional criteria for the recognition of states and governments in international law.[73] That is the arena wherein governments act for and in the name of their people.

Surely, 1 through 4 do not tell the whole story of legitimacy, nor, perhaps, even of the legitimacy of a government's representation of its people in the forum of international politics. But they are just as surely highly relevant. Understanding now the deep relationship between the concepts of agency and legitimacy, let us return to the law of agency as a guide to our moral intuitions. If a person claims to represent you for some period of time and it is within your knowledge that she does so, and it is within your power to disclose to her and third parties her lack of authority, and you do not, then you will become liable for her actions within the reasonable scope in which she claims to be acting.[74] The primary reason for this is that others, knowing that you can object and do not, can reasonably conclude that she represents you.[75]

In other words, you acquire an affirmative duty to act to prevent her further representations as your agent. But what can the citizens of a dictatorship do to prevent this putative "agent" (the government) from acting in their name? First, citizens having any shred of political influence are responsible to exercise it against policies of aggressive war and attack upon the homelands of others. There exists a small but influential body of public opinion in the Soviet Union, or so Soviet experts claim.[76] To the extent that peaceful means of political influence are open to significant portions of the public, they are morally bound to exercise them.

Second, a people can go into the streets. They can protest violently. They can organize rebellion. These are desperate options, but desperate moral issues call for desperate solutions. Surely we intuitively feel that Hitler represented the German people or that Gorbachev represents the Russian people in ways that Jaruzelski does not represent the Polish people or Karmal the Afghan people (or Pinochet the Chilean people, for that matter). These intuitions are morally justified, for the Polish and Afghan people have given us *notice* in the most graphic way possible of their government's lack of legitimacy.

One of the central issues in Western political philosophy has been the rights and duties of states to people and people to states—what they are, how they arise, and how they are justified. Yet there is another, equally important question. What duties do people have to third parties to control the actions of their nation's government? John Locke taught that when a government violates the natural rights of its citizens they have a right, and perhaps a duty, to rebel. Our founding fathers agreed. Is any less required of us should our government threaten a massive assault upon the rights of another people? The question of exactly what these duties to control our government require of us or how they arise are topics that go beyond this discussion. But let us return to the war of *A* against *B* to try to discern answers to these questions in the specific context of noncombatant immunity.

Suppose for a moment that the dictatorship of *A* is of a rather unusual kind. Suppose that it permits open and ample sources of information about the doings of government; it merely excludes all but the elite from participation or control. (Whether such a system is practically possible or not is irrelevant here.) Thus, the citizens of *A* know that their government intends to wage aggressive war on *B*. They know that their government claims no justification for doing so. They even know that their government intends to attack *B* City with missiles and purposively inflict many noncombatant casualties in the process. They just "cannot" do anything about it under their present system of government. Are the citizens in this case more like the innocent child in a democracy, or more like an apathetic citizen? Recall, I concluded that the child was truly innocent in the strongest sense, while the apathetic citizen was morally liable to be put at risk by *B*'s efforts to defend itself.

The child, because of physical and mental limitations, is constrained by physical impossibility from doing anything. The apathetic citizen is constrained by the cost of participation which, in his preference scheme, is too high; he prefers television quiz shows. And I found his preference scheme to be morally wanting. It strikes me that the citizen of the dictatorship is far more like the apathetic citizen than the child. He or she can resist, as the citizens of Poland and Afghanistan have so nobly shown. To be sure, the cost of resistance might, at the hands of the state security apparatus, be high indeed. But sometimes we are morally required to pay high costs to carry out our duties to third parties. That this duty demands a great deal is manifest. But before we are tempted to say it demands too much, let us remember that the sanction for failure to discharge it is of a curious type. To fail to discharge my duty to third parties to try very hard to control my government *does not* entitle those third parties to kill me on purpose, or punish me in any way. But I lose one very special, and very strong, right I had against those third parties; that is my absolute immunity as a noncombatant from even being put at risk. (The regnant view in rights theory is that immunities are special kinds of rights.[77])

Let us change the example once again. The dictatorship of A is now of a more conventional kind. It controls the media, and the citizens of A are more or less in the dark about the specific war plans of A's leadership. I say "more or less" because outside of an Orwellian thought experiment, the grapevine, reading between the lines of official publications and announcements, and direct or secondhand contacts from outside (BBC or Voice of America, in the Soviet Union, for example), combine to give people a better view of what is going on than one might think. This is especially true if the citizens are willing to make the effort and take the risk to find out. Are they obligated to make that effort and take the risk? I believe so. There is a doctrine in law and morals known as "culpable ignorance." If you need to know something in order to do something, and a reasonable person would know they needed to know, then your ignorance is part of your culpability in not doing it.[78] You are very much like the apathetic citizen in our first example who preferred TV quiz shows to politics. Thus, the mere lack of knowledge does not absolve the citizen of A of the kind of moral liability that he incurs as a result of the actions of his government.

In an era when weapons of mass destruction enable nation states to wreak havoc upon whole continents, citizens simply must be held responsible for how their governments behave in regard to the use of those weapons. They are accountable to know and to act upon that knowledge. Any lesser standard rewards people who do not take responsibility for their own political destiny and penalizes most cruelly those who do. It penalizes them by obviating their right of self-defense at the hands of aggressive dictatorships.

Indeed, the consequences of my argument may well be that to allow a dictatorship to command your nation's policies and actions is by itself to fail a negligence-like moral standard. That, in turn, might well imply that a duty exists for any polity and the citizens thereof to rule themselves with a free and open democracy. Such a consequence would neither surprise nor trouble me.[79]

It is quite likely that bombs dropped by the Eighth Air Force killed some of those wonderfully brave men who tried to kill Hitler in 1944. That was a tragedy, as were the deaths of innocent children in those raids. Those deaths can only be justified by double effect, and the ratio of moral benefit gained to moral cost paid must be high indeed to justify them. But there are always a minority of these true innocents. For the death of the average German killed collaterally when the Eighth Air Force attacked the Schweinfurt ball bearing works, for example, there seems to me at least a good deal less blood on our hands. There seems to be a morally significant sense in which we can say to his shade, "Had you done something you should have done but failed to do, and had enough of your compatriots joined you in doing what they should have done, we would not have had to destroy the ball bearing plant, and we would not have killed you in the process. Of course, you could not have controlled what your compatriots did, but that does not matter. Not doing what you should have done (regardless of what they did) is what caused you to lose your absolute immunity to attack at our hands."

Similarly, when we consider the morality of prompt counterforce second strikes today, we can morally threaten to destroy the Soviet Union's remaining military forces should they attack us first. We can do this knowing full well that such attacks would produce millions of collateral noncombatant casualties. For it is the duty of the Soviet people that they restrain their government from such an attack and the fact that they are living in a dictatorship does not absolve them of that duty.

We might conclude with the following rule:

> Citizens have a duty to prevent their government from launching a nuclear war, and if they fail in that duty they are legitimately at risk as the attacked nation attempts by counterforce strikes to defend its people (or its allies' people) from subsequent attacks.

It is not necessary to show that a clear and immediate net savings of American lives will outweigh the number of Soviet citizens killed. Of course, there must be some limits of proportionality. We cannot kill 10,000 Soviets to save 3 Americans. Just what the balance should be is very difficult to say, but the moral presumption is *against* the Soviet citizens, whose country has attacked first, and *with* the American citizens, who are defending themselves. This rule presents another slippery slope, and we must be careful not to use it as a rationalization for unrestrained slaughter of civilians. This argument simply does not justify that. It is also sobering to remember that the same argument would hold *against* the United States and its people should we launch an aggressive nuclear war. We must never do so.

With that important caveat in mind, I conclude:

1. A retaliatory strike could legitimately strike all military targets of an attacking nation which might be used either in subsequent attacks upon ourselves or our allies, or to coercively threaten us or our allies with subsequent attacks.

2. The doctrine of noncombatant immunity allows extensive civilian casualties so long as legitimate military facilities are the intended target and a reasonable proportionality exists between civilian casualties and military objectives.

3. We can only operate under 1 and 2 if we take the greatest pains that are reasonable to limit civilian casualties. This would include all aspects of planning and staging the counterattacks.

Some Corollaries on Weapons Technology

It follows from 3 above that we must try very hard to use the weapons we presently have in such a way as to minimize noncombatant deaths. It also follows that we must try very hard to develop new weapons and new means of waging war generally which will limit lethality and minimize collateral damage. This is a *moral* duty.

This duty fits very well with the real world, for we are in the beginnings of a weapons revolution which will allow for a dramatic decrease in civilian casualties. This includes a new generation of nuclear weapons[80] and, potentially even more significant, the development of ultrasmart strategic weapons that might allow for a return to conventional explosives in missile warheads, for some purposes at least.[81] Indeed, the end of the threat of nuclear war might come as we develop tiny computers to guide missiles so accurately that conventional warheads are adequate for most purposes and nuclear detonations are needed only for a few sorts of hardened targets. Visionary? Yes. Totally absurd? No!

What about President Reagan's much heralded Strategic Defense Initiative (sometimes derisively called "Star Wars")?[82] For our purposes, the most important point is that SDI is not a near-term panacea. It does not remove the need for offensive nuclear weapons for, at the very least, a decade, and it probably never will. Thus, the task that I set myself here, the formulation of a moral policy for nuclear defense using offensive nuclear weapons remains pressing. SDI in no way nullifies that project.

What more can be said about SDI? First, if it is technologically feasible (and we certainly do not *know* that it is not), it does represent a passive way of protecting human lives. It is self-defense in the purest and most innocuous sense. Alone or in conjunction with much smaller invulnerable, second-strike strategic deterrents, it may help create a safer world.

The critics make one good and one very silly point about SDI, and each requires a rejoinder. First, the good point: critics point out that SDI can be destabilizing and, thus, increase the chances of war, at least while it is being installed. If it is implemented alone, without adjustment to our offensive forces and without coordination with the Soviets, this is true. For the Soviets could come to believe that their deterrent was becoming ineffective and that soon we might preemptively strike them. But President Reagan has made a staggering offer to cooperate with the Soviets in *the joint erection* of such a defense shield. This is surely the most innovative and boldest offer since the Baruch-Lillienthal Plan in 1945 to submit nuclear weapons to international control. One cannot help but observe that if a liberal dove had made such a proposal, it would be greeted as the beginning of a new age.

The second, silly point made by critics of SDI is this: hawks and conservatives are always looking for "technological fixes" to the danger of nuclear war and, of course, there cannot be any. Indeed, the application of new technology always increases the danger of nuclear war. SDI is new technology, and it therefore increases the danger of nuclear war. Thus, we must not pursue it. But technology is inherently neutral; neither good nor bad, it neither automatically increases nor decreases the risk of nuclear war. Surely the technology which allowed us to mount many independently targeted warheads (MIRVs) on a single missile was terribly destabilizing. It made the world more dangerous. But the technology that allows us to build ballistic missile submarines and to communicate with them at sea makes us manifestly safer. It does so because it provides us with an invulnerable, and therefore very stable, deterrent.

It is true that there are not any technological 'fixes' for the risk of nuclear war, not if we mean by that a magic wand that we can wave and make it all go away. But it is the mentality of the Luddite which says that no new technology can ever even *help* in the process of making the world safer. That achieving a safer world requires more than technology is implicitly recognized by President Reagan in his offer to share technology. Increasing safety requires new institutions, new strategies, new practices and procedures, and perhaps even new ways of thinking. But technology, if it is managed properly, can enhance our safety. Certainly, it is very hard to see what is wrong with researching and studying a purely defensive system.

Let us not forget, however, that for some long time to come our safety rests on offensive nuclear weapons. Deciding what policies concerning their use are both effective and moral is just as pressing now as it was before the advent of the idea of SDI.

The Nuclear Winter: Strategic and Moral Implications[83]

We saw in Chapter III that the nuclear winter hypothesis, at least the extreme version offered by the TTAPS group, is dubious at best and propagandistic at worst. Still, there is undeniably some risk of lesser climatic effects from an unlimited nuclear war. What might this entail for the morality of defensive nuclear war?

For those who would still treat a practically unlimited nuclear war as a policy option wherein victory is possible, any increase in the possibility of the nuclear winter is damning indeed. But who espouses such a view? Some Soviet generals, perhaps the Soviet heirarchy, maybe, though probably not, Colin Gray. In the West, this view is largely a convenient straw man for members of the "peace" movement, who need the position that nuclear war is desirable to attack.

Certainly, I have explicitly adopted the position that offensive nuclear war is both immoral and irrational. Nuclear war is already so undesirable an outcome that merely amassing more human cost in the scales, as the nuclear winter hypothesis does, changes nothing. The real issue is that the nuclear winter does not change what we morally *may* or what we prudentially *should* do if we are attacked with nuclear weapons. Therefore, it does not change what we may morally threaten to do to deter nuclear attack. Let us see why this is so.

In an effort to develop a lower threshold to the nuclear winter phenomenon, TTAPS created a scenario using only 100 megatons (approximately 1 percent of the strategic arsenal of either superpower).[84] They were able to show that, upon their very questionable assumptions, this exchange could trigger a nuclear winter. However, as with much else in the TTAPS study, there is something highly artificial (an unkinder word would be "rigged") in this particular scenario. They assume that all 100 megatons would strike cities and, of course, that all those cities will burn in firestorms. Now, such an attack as this would be manifest suicide, even without the nuclear winter. For it would leave intact *the whole of the enemy's retaliatory force* and, therefore, the aggressor nation would be devastated in a retaliatory strike. There could be no *reason* for such a crazy strike.

A pure counterforce strike, on the other hand, since it hits no cities and starts no firestorms, might be of several thousand megatons and still not trigger a nuclear winter (on TTAPS's own assumptions). Thus, the 100 megaton attack in no way establishes an invariable lower threshold of a nuclear winter. However, in much of their writings, the TTAPS authors act as if it does. Let us, then, do a thought experiment. Let us ignore all the very dubious assumptions involved in the nuclear winter hypothesis that I examined in Chapter III. Let us also ignore the artificiality of the 100 megaton threshold. Let us assume, with TTAPS, that this really does represent a meaningful lower threshold for the nuclear winter. Indeed, for the sake of argument, I shall adopt the strongest assumption of the TTAPS authors, *viz.,* that any strike of 100 megatons on a highly flammable target will trigger the nuclear winter.[85] What we shall find is that, even with this highly artificial assumption, very little of either morality or strategy is affected by the possibility of the nuclear winter. Indeed, some of the arguments which arise from this assumption cut directly *against* the TTAPS's strategic conclusions.

Thus, I assume that one nation's nuclear arsenal capable of launching a 100 megaton attack upon its adversary's cities constitutes a doomsday machine. That is, one power need not even threaten to attack the other; it need only detonate 100 megatons on its own soil in such a way as to produce sufficient smoke and dust. This might be done without incinerating one's own cities, e.g., by bombing forests or grasslands. Thus, assuming for the moment that the risk of escalation with the use of a single nuclear weapon approaches certainty, the use of nuclear weapons is, strictly speaking, national suicide and omnicide (or, at least, for the Northern hemisphere). We are automatically deterred, and nuclear war as a policy ceases to make sense. (So what else is new? It never did!)

Note, however, that the one thing we dare not do is to unilaterally disarm. For a single nuclear power need not even approach the crucial 100 megaton threshold to coerce the rest of the world. A nuclear monopolist needs only a few megatons to blackmail very effectively. As we have seen, 15 megatons deposited on two, three, or fifteen American cities is powerful cocercion indeed. The ability to deter nuclear threats becomes *more important* under the nuclear winter hypothesis. A would be attacker must continually be aware that he must attack the other side's nuclear weapons, and many of them, so many in fact that the victim of the attack no longer has 100 megatons to use on cities or other highly flammable targets. Keep in mind that it is the soot from burning cities and other flammable targets that creates by far the most occlusion of the sunlight. A nation could use far more than 100 megatons in a carefully targeted counterforce attack. The alternative is to run the risk that the adversary will use enough megatons to trigger a nuclear winter. The nuclear winter makes deterrence an even more effective policy compared to unilateral disarmament because it increases the cost/risk to the first striker, while it does nothing to increase the costs or dangers of nuclear blackmail against unilaterally disarmed opponents. Ironically, the nuclear winter hypothesis increases the moral mandate for deterrence and makes unilateral disarmament even more immoral than it initially seemed to be.

As we saw, there is emerging a new technology of highly accurate, low-yield weapons. Some of these could be designed with earth-penetrating warheads expressly for the purpose of minimizing the occluding effects of dust and smoke. They would nonetheless be quite suited to waging effective counterforce war. Because of their characteristics there would be almost no limit (certainly not 100 megatons) to their use. Indeed, Sagan cites these weapons as one way out of the risk of nuclear winter.[86] However, he rejects them because they would make first-strike warfare seem too attractive.

The nuclear winter hypothesis does, if further evidence bears it out at all, increase the possibility that the Soviets will launch pure counterforce strikes of much lower than the 100 megaton threshold. And we must be prepared to respond in kind, i.e., to respond to a 30 megaton attack with a 30 or a 10 megaton attack, but *not* a 2000 megaton attack. Thus, under the nuclear winter hypothesis, targeting accuracy and minimal explosive yield (and perhaps earth-penetrating capability) take on even more moral force than they already have.

Of course, the nuclear winter is not and never will be a certain or even a near-certain outcome. We simply cannot obtain that sort of knowledge of so vast and complex a set of interactive phenomena. But suppose that we could put a meaningful probability on its occurrence and that that probability was better than fifty-fifty. If that were the case, *and it is not,* what consequences would that piece of probabilistic knowledge have for the moral conclusions I have reached about defensive nuclear war?

Surprisingly, almost none. Remember, my argument turned upon the moral legitimacy of extended counterforce retaliatory strikes in the defense of human lives in our own or allied countries. Let us assume, for the sake of example, that there is a .55 probability that the nuclear winter hypothesis is true just as the TTAPS group formulated it, and a .45 probability that it is false. Suppose also that the Soviets launch a practically unlimited first strike of 3000 megatons. If the probability of our really being able to save millions of American lives by attacking reloadable

missile silos or ballistic missile submarines in port goes from near one to
.45 (the probability that the nuclear winter hypothesis is false), it is still
the moral and rational thing to do. Remember, by hypothesis, the
Soviets have ignored the nuclear winter threat and already put all of us,
themselves included, at a .55 risk of freezing or starving in a nuclear
winter. Anything we do won't change that. A .45 probability of survival
has, by definition, nearly half as much utility (for "utility" here read
"moral value" or "moral worth") as does a 100% chance. There is no
other countervailing interest not already considered before the introduction of the nuclear winter hypothesis. It changes nothing.

We have already seen that the possibility of limited strikes by the
Soviets clearly below the nuclear winter threshold requires an ability on
our part to respond in a highly limited and controlled way. That means
we must work hard at the technology of accuracy, limitation of lethality,
and intrawar command and control. But even this is not a new moral imperative. We saw above that regardless of the truth of the nuclear winter
hypothesis, we are under a strict obligation to minimize collateral
damage and noncombatant deaths. We must develop the technology,
deploy the weapons, and adopt the strategy of accuracy and limited
lethality in any case.

The nuclear winter hypothesis changes nothing about my conclusions.
Nuclear war is so horrible that more horror (or a probability of more
horror) makes little difference. Once the threshold of conscionability is
crossed, it is crossed. Yet self-defense and defensive nuclear war are still
coherent, moral, and prudentially rational. We must take care to use as
few megatons as possible, but we ought to do that anyway to minimize
noncombatant casualties. That is, if the nuclear winter hypothesis is true,
we must minimize blast effect on the Soviet Union for our own sakes as
well as for that of Soviet noncombatants.

While the nuclear winter hypothesis changes our strategy little, it
might change the Soviets' strategy from their present terribly immoral
one so chillingly described by Benjamin Lambeth. If you hit first with a
large percentage of your arsenal at the full range of targets, including
population centers, you risk reaping a whirlwind, a very cold, dark whirlwind.

Legitimate Targets of a Retaliatory Strike

We have seen that the notion of defensive nuclear war is coherent, and
that under the right conditions it might be morally permissible. We have
also seen that, if we make appropriate efforts to minimize noncombatant
casualties, including our choice of weapons, the risk of killing noncom-

batants alone does not prohibit us from waging defensive nuclear war. For the Soviet people, if their government launches a nuclear war, have given up their right to absolute immunity from risk. We have also seen that the risk of nuclear winter does not extinguish our right to use nuclear weapons in our own defense.

How, then, can we wage defensive nuclear war. What sorts of targets are legitimate in our efforts to defend ourselves? We have already seen that prompt counterforce strikes against military forces are morally justified. How far beyond military forces may we go? What are the moral limits of a second strike? We have seen that there are helpful analogies with the domestic law of self-defense. In the law of self-defense, when may a defender counterattack? *Perkins on Criminal Law,* a standard text, tells us:

> The danger must be, or appear to be, *pressing and urgent.* A fear of danger at some future time is not sufficient [emphasis added].[87]

LaFave and Scott, in another text, provide a similar standard:

> Case law and legislation concerning self defense require that the defendant reasonably believe his adversary's unlawful violence to be "imminent" or "immediate". If the threatened violence is scheduled to arrive in the more distant future, there may be avenues open to the defendant to prevent it other than to kill or injure the prospective attacker.[88]

Knowing what we do about the philosophical foundations of the notion of self-defense, we can see why this must be so. Obviously, the presumption against visiting violence upon one's fellow human beings must be strong, even if it is to be rebuttable. For that presumption protects *their* lives. If the danger is not immediate in both time and space, one is more likely to be in error about the probability and nature of the attack. If waiting will more fully confirm one's belief that an attack is imminent, it will more fully justify a violent defensive response.

There is another reason as well. As LaFave and Scott point out, the time allowed between apprehension of the danger and its becoming "pressing and urgent" allows for *nonviolent countermeasures.*[89] If a potential assailant calls on the telephone to tell you that he is coming to attack you, you can call the police, lock the door on him, or even leave the location in which he expects to find you.

When this standard is applied to nations at war the following rule emerges:

> A nation can counterattack when the attack to be launched against it is so pressing and urgent that it is virtually certain to be launched and there

is no time to implement nonviolent countermeasures to forestall or frustrate it.

A corollary with regard to target classification would follow as well:

> Those targets which themselves or in combination with others pose a pressing and urgent threat to the citizens (combatants and noncombatants alike) of an attacked country or its allies can be legitimately struck.

The philosopher Thomas Nagel, in his classic paper, "War and Massacre," provides a criterion very close to that which the law yields. Nagel says:

> the prosecution of the conflict must direct itself to *the cause of danger* and not to what is peripheral. The threat presented by an army and its members does not consist merely in the fact that they are men, but in the fact that they are armed and using their arms in the pursuit of certain objectives. Contributions to their arms and logistics are *contributions to the threat*; contributions to their mere existence as men are not [emphasis added].[90]

Let us list possible targets in the Soviet Union and see how either the criterion drawn from my extrapolation of the legal notion of self-defense or Nagel's criterion would treat them:

1. Nuclear forces to be used against us or our allies when readied, or in a planned second strike.

2. Nuclear forces purposefully held in reserve for coercion.

3. Conventional forces which threaten attack upon our forces abroad.

4. Conventional forces that might be used to attack or coerce allies.

5. Conventional forces, primarily naval and air, that might threaten our ability to supply or communicate with either our forces abroad or our allies.

6. Forces that would threaten our satellite warning and communication systems.

7. Conventional forces that might be used to attack the continental United States. This would include naval, air, and amphibious forces. (An amphibious assault on the United States seems fanciful today, but it is certainly a genuine threat in a postattack environment.)

8. Soviet military command, communications, and control structures.

9. Combat forces of Soviet allies.

10. Soviet industry which directly supports its war-making capacity.

11. Soviet political command, communication, and control structures.

12. The economic infrastructure that supports the society's continued functioning, but not its war effort directly.

13. Targets that enhance the postwar recovery potential of the Soviet society, but otherwise do not contribute to its war-making capacity.

I argued earlier that prompt counterforce defensive nuclear war—attacks on any military forces of the Soviets or their allies which threaten our citizens or those of our allies with attack in an urgent or pressing manner—is morally legitimate. Indeed, permissible targets would include virtually all Soviet and allied military forces. After all, such forces exist for the purpose of threatening enemies, *viz.,* us. Thus, all target classes 1-9 would be legitimate.

On the other hand, the Soviet economy (12, excepting war industry) threatens no one. The economic infrastructure may be a necessary condition to war making but, following Nagel, it does not *per se* contribute to war making. Also, it poses only threats several removes from actuality, and thus it is not a pressing and urgent threat. To be sure, the economic infrastructure (13) creates the potential for a political and economic recovery; that recovery might be devoted toward acquisition of more war-making capacity and that capacity might be turned upon us anew. If all of these contingencies occur, then at some time in the indefinite future self-defense may justify a subsequent attack. But this could only be much later: the threat posed by 12 and 13 is just not pressing and urgent enough to justify immediate attack. They do not *now* constitute a threat to us. At the same time it is clearly justifiable to attack military/industrial targets in an effort to retard or prevent the recovery of Soviet military power.

The concern so often expressed in recent writings on nuclear strategy for attacking economic (as opposed to military) recovery potential[91] would be better directed at the maintenance of adequate, *secure* deterrent forces in the first place. Our possession of such forces *after* a series of strikes upon us will guarantee that we are able to contend with a recovered economy which is developing a new war-making capability, if and when this becomes morally appropriate, i.e., if and when it becomes clear that it will be employed aggressively.

This point is especially relevant, both morally and strategically, to the Soviet Union. For one crucial objective of counterattacks must be to loosen the control of the Communist Party and its attendant security apparatus. Another is to weaken the grip of the ethnic Russians upon the captive peoples of the "Union." (These are almost the same thing, but more of this later.) That objective will require us to refrain from attacking many economic and population centers, precisely to encourage their resistance. Thus, on this point morality and a prudentially effective strategy run along the same course.

There remain two classes of targets that are difficult to assess: Soviet war industry, and Soviet political command and control structures. Soviet war industry must be treated as "pressing and urgent." The fighter assembly plant? That seems fairly obvious, for clearly a jet fighter can only be turned to war-like purposes. The jet fuel refinery cited above seems fairly urgent. That fuel will go directly and soon into jet fighters and bombers, if it is not destroyed. The aluminum for the fighter seems further away in time and process, and more apt to be put to other nonthreatening uses. Thus, the aluminum smelter is a less legitimate target. Here we come up against an inherently fuzzy line.[92] But for our purposes, the contours are clear enough.

The Soviet political command and control structure has been the focus of much discussion by nuclear strategists in recent years. These are the so-called C[3] targets: communication, command, and control (sometimes including intelligence as IC[3]). At issue here is the *civilian,* political IC[3] structure. The military IC[3] is an integral part of their capacity to kill our citizens and, as such, an unproblematically legitimate target. This, of course, assumes that we are no further along the road to being able to fight a mutually controlled and limited nuclear war. If we have that capacity, then it is mandated by both morality and prudence that we fight such a limited and controlled nuclear war (if we must fight at all). Military (and probably political) IC[3] centers are crucial to maintaining that war limitation and, as such, must be immune. Without this capacity, military IC[3] centers are prime targets.

In recent years one nuclear theorist, Colin Gray, has argued that Soviet IC[3] civilian political facilities should be the highest priority targets in any nuclear war.[93] This includes Soviet governmental institutions, the party control apparatus, and the state security system. This latter would especially include the command and control apparatus of the KGB. The Soviet government, Colin Gray believes, puts a very high premium upon central control and the maintenance of party domination. Surely he is correct, for almost all observers of the Soviet Union agree that they have a near obsession with party control, and party and ethnic Russian domination.[94]

But why does that make IC[3] targets so tempting for us? First, Gray argues that in a protracted nuclear war, the destruction of the Soviet IC[3] apparatus would be a major step toward victory. A properly staged attack by the United States might very well, as Gray believes, destroy Communist Party control, break up central, Great Russian control of the national republics and nationalities, and in general end the Soviet state. Thus, any possible war aims the Soviets might have would be frustrated. Second, since this price would be more than any Soviet leadership would dare to pay, the deterrent effect of credibly threatening to destroy the control apparatus ought to be the primary method for deterring nuclear war.

Gray is a subtle and deep thinker and it is important not to oversimplify his views. He points out, for example, that accomplishing this is not so easy.[95] It cannot be done, he believes, without a capacity to destroy Soviet military strength at the same time.

There is much that is objectionable about Gray's views. First, he sometimes intimates that he would be willing to strike the Soviet Union first, certainly in response to Soviet conventional aggression, but perhaps even to attain lesser policy goals. Second, his notion of victory seems to be simplistic. The mere denial of Soviet war aims (sometimes called "victory denial"), or even destruction of the Soviet state, do not constitute victory for us if we are sufficiently devastated. Third, Gray is so impressed with his new deterrent threat that he encourages using it for nuclear coercion to obtain policy objectives, and we have seen that to be gratuitously dangerous and consequently immoral.[96]

Despite these profound objections to Gray's position, there is much of value in what he says. Certainly, the Soviets' obsession with centralization and control makes them terribly fragile in a nuclear war. Certainly, that must appear to them as a great weakness and one that Western deterrent threats should play upon—*second*-strike threats, but not first-strike threats as Gray would have it.

Can we really meaningfully talk of specifically targeting IC³ targets without devastating whole regions where they exist? Two decades ago, such refinement in targeting would have appeared ludicrous. We simply could not have hit a KGB headquarters, for example, without vast collateral casualties. But as accuracy improves, we acquire the capacity to significantly refine our targeting. Political targets are often in or near cities, and numerous civilian casualties would result even with the new-found accuracy. I shall consider the justification for these casualties shortly, but it is important to note one important trend. As we continue to improve the accuracy of our weapons (which we are morally bound to try to do), the number of potential collateral casualties will continue to fall, while the effectiveness of attacks on IC³ targets will rise.

Let us for the moment assume that we are able (or soon will be) to strike Soviet civilian IC³ targets without an unreasonable number of collateral casualties. Would we ever be *morally* justified in intentionally targeting political IC³ centers in a *second* strike? There would be collateral damage, as with any purely military target, and the limitations of proportionality would hold. Double effect would justify some collateral damage, and the political responsibility of Soviet citizens would justify more (as I argued above), but not such as would be wanton or heedless of noncombatants. In this sense, there would be no difference between civilian IC³ targets and military targets.

But what of the morality of *intentionally* striking these civilian, political IC³ targets? A moment's reflection will show that Soviet political command and control centers are morally legitimate targets, more legitimate perhaps than any but reserve nuclear forces being readied for launch. First, the individuals at these centers are crucial to sustaining a protracted nuclear war effort. After they have launched a first strike, we have good reason to believe that they will be central to subsequent nuclear attacks upon the United States, or threats of same. Some of them may be central to conventional attacks upon our allies. Others may be *directly* (and, following Nagel, "direct" is the operative word) involved in the support of the war effort. Indeed, the highly structured, highly centralized social control exercised by the Soviet leadership apparatus can be seen as contributing to a *mobilized* state and society, one on a permanent war footing. Remember: targets which constitute a "pressing and urgent" threat are legitimate. I would argue that the nature of the Soviet state is directed toward mobilization and conflict with external enemies. Indeed, some thinkers hold that that is and has been its *raison d'etre* and the source of its claim to legitimacy.[97] Thus, when it goes to war, the entire governmental and party apparatus becomes, under either Nagel's criterion or the "pressing and urgent" legal standard, a legitimate target. It seems to me that on any reasonable criterion of direct support for a war, the Soviet leadership apparatus is a legitimate target. Keep in mind, however, that this is only true if we are acting in legitimate self-defense, i.e., if we have already been attacked.

There is, however, a separate argument for the legitimacy of targeting the leadership apparatus. Throughout this essay, I have rejected retributivist theories as justification for any acts of war. A nation has no rights to intentionally "punish" other nations or whole peoples. Such punishment could only be based upon notions of collective guilt which are repugnant to the Western moral, legal, and political traditions of individual accountability and dignity. But the Soviet leadership poses an interesting problem. By hypothesis, the United States is waging a defensive war; it has been attacked. When we consider the Soviet leadership apparatus as a target, we are looking directly at those *individuals* who made the decision to initiate a nuclear war and who are already responsible for the intentional, purposeful killing of scores of millions of our innocent countrymen and, indirectly, of millions of their own people. It must be morally relevant that they did so act. Indeed, it is difficult not to believe that in some sense the leadership *deserves* what it would get in such an attack. Retribution has always been accepted, even by those who require additional reasons to punish, as a method of determining *who* should be punished.[98] Here, it seems that civilian political IC[3] targets perfectly delineate the area of responsibility.

I find it convincing when Nagel, Murphy, and Fullinwider argue that war ought not be the purposeful punishment of the guilty, where guilt is collective. But here, guilt (and that is now the correct term, not just "responsibility") is so specific, so direct, and so manifest that it seems to be at least a supplementary justification for targeting the leadership—supplementary to their prospective role in the prosecution of the war, which is the primary justification.

There is yet a third justification for attacking civilian political IC[3] targets. We saw that attacking recovery potential *per se* was morally wrong. We should not attack an economy which is rebuilding its capacity to feed its people, for example, or to provide them with medical care. But certainly we can attack those social institutions which would allow for a recovery of a particular sort of society, *viz.,* a society *of the same bellicose nature as that which started the war in the first place.* Attacking political IC[3] targets would frustrate the recovery of the Soviet Union *qua* war-making society, rather than just some economic and social structure which would provide for its people's basic needs. Frustrating the recovery of the former is morally legitimate; frustrating the recovery of the latter is not.

In any case, with or without retribution, there seems to be ample moral justification for targeting the Soviet leadership and control apparatus. And note that if this is so, then it is perfectly moral to threaten their destruction as a deterrent to war; for if it is moral to wage a certain kind of war, then it is moral to threaten to do so in order to prevent a war.

Of Preemption and Temptation

We have already seen that the very nature of self-defense precludes preemptive first strikes where any of the following conditions exist:

1. Uncertainty about whether or not the attack is coming.

2. Any considerable time lag between the realization of the danger of an attack and its actual occurrence.

3. The existence of options short of preemption which could, with reasonable probability, forestall the attack.

These three conditions grow out of the "urgent and pressing" requirement for attack which I formulated in the last section. For example, if we were to conclude on the basis of political events in the Soviet Union that the Soviets are moving toward launching a nuclear war within several years to obtain certain policy objectives, we would *not* be justified in preempting. All three conditions above would deprive us of such justification.

The horrible cost of nuclear war requires a much higher degree of certainty of 1 than we could ever have for such a strike. (Note, however, where there is any reasonable threat of a nuclear attack some *years* hence, we are *morally obligated* to take action under 3, *viz.,* building and maintaining strong deterrent forces.)

If preemption in this sort of case is morally precluded, is all preemption precluded? Not exactly. The nature of modern nuclear war is such that in final preparation for a nuclear attack, an aggressor must make almost irrevocable steps within days or weeks of the intended launch. As many ballistic missile submarines as possible must go on station. The Soviets keep only about 10 percent on station at any given time. If that number began to climb toward 100 percent, for example, an attack would surely be imminent. Similarly, if ICBM crews were all put on alert, attack would be imminent. (The Soviets keep only about 10 percent of their crews on alert, an interesting sign of their faith in the West *not* to attack them despite their own essentially first-strike posture.) Attack on our reconnaissance satellites would be an even more "pressing and urgent" indication. We have seen that the preparations to launch a nuclear strike are so irrevocable that John Steinbrunner, a defense analyst at the Brookings Institute, believes that maximum alert by both powers makes war virtually inevitable.[99] In such cases, the United States might be the first actually to launch nuclear weapons, but we should not be the first *irrevocably to decide to initiate the use of nuclear weapons.* It is the latter which must always be beyond the moral pale.

If, indeed, waging defensive nuclear war is rendered moral because it would save the lives of a nation's citizens and those of its allies, then, where virtual certainty of a first strike exists, it would seem to be moral to preempt. Indeed, as we approach certainty, preemption may not only be a moral right, but also a moral duty.

There seems to be something wrong with this argument, and there is! Remember, we are under an obligation to take all measures short of war to prevent war. And note also that the situation described by Steinbrunner could be ameliorated, if not avoided, by our possession of a far more secure deterrent force (i.e., one that could absorb a first strike and still respond with force sufficient to protect our people from subsequent attack). Airborne bombers or ballistic missile submarines on station constitute such secure deterrent forces, as do mobile, land-based ICBMs or ICBM silos protected by effective anti-ballistic-missile systems. Secure deterrents dampen the very uncontrollable escalation to which Steinbrunner refers, for such escalation turns on fear of a preemptive first strike against vulnerable offensive missiles. So it is clear that we are under a moral obligation to build (or rebuild) as secure a deterrent force as possible, for we must take all reasonable measures to avoid war, and that is surely one.

We may also be under an obligation to take other measures unilaterally or, if possible, bilaterally with the Soviets, such as establishing the permissive action links and crisis control centers recommended by Senators Warner and Nunn.[100] I believe that we are. Nonetheless, it is sobering to consider, and should be sobering to the Soviets, that under present strategic conditions, preemption in the face of a virtually certain attack is our moral right and perhaps our moral duty.

Some thinkers, who believe in countervalue rather than counterforce threats, have argued that the possession of highly accurate, counterforce-capable weapons makes it too tempting to preempt *too early,* i.e., at a time when it is morally illegitimate to do so.[101] The argument for counterforce capability in the face of that objection has been made with thoroughgoing cogency by Albert Wohlstetter.[102]

Suffice it to point out here that it is a strange argument which holds that one ought to deny oneself a capacity to do the morally appropriate thing (attack weapons in a retaliatory strike) because it provides us with a capacity to do the morally inappropriate thing (attack weapons in a premature and unnecessary first strike). Ought we to refuse to arm policemen because they may use their weapons in ways we consider inappropriate? Is it not better to choose persons capable of exercising judgment and restraint, instruct them carefully, and implement a system of disciplinary procedures to be sure they follow the rules? This argument becomes especially convoluted when the only alternative is the maintenance of inaccurate strategic arsenals (countervalue-capable only), the only purpose of which is mass murder after the fact.

There is a second way to blunt this criticism, however. If the Soviet Union were to take our lead and convert to a more invulnerable deterrent, e.g., more submarine-based missiles and fewer fixed, land-based ICBMs, our temptation to illegitimately preempt would go down precisely because our *ability* to successfully disable their retaliatory force would decrease. The most stable possible situation is one in which each side has invulnerable deterrents, and thus we both have a moral obligation to move in that direction.

It should be noted that the Soviets have recently begun to develop a mobile, land-based ICBM, the SS-24. A mobile missile is less vulnerable and, therefore, more secure than a fixed one. Indeed, the Scowcroft Commission recognized this and recommended that the United States develop such a missile.[103] The Reagan Administration has shown its confusion (or its double standard) by calling the new Soviet missile "destabilizing." It is certainly not that, if it is planned as a replacement for the fixed, land-based ICBMs. However, it is a violation of SALT II. This illustrates, among other things, how some arms control treaties can perpetuate a dangerous situation and prevent progress toward a safer world by freezing the present composition of arsenals or making research and development a violation of the rules even if it is directed toward safer, more stable weapons.

Perhaps the strongest argument against those who fear a too ready resort to nuclear war when missiles are targeted in a counterforce mode is simply this: nuclear war, however it is fought and from whatever posture, remains too horrible to wage as a matter of whim. Wohlstetter believes that combatants would unilaterally restrain themselves. However, even he would have to admit that the risk of escalation to unlimited nuclear war is too great and *nearly impossible to measure*. In addition, there would be huge collateral damage at best, even from a largely counterforce war. Even if it is greatly exaggerated, there is clearly some risk of climatic catastrophe. There is simply too much that is unknown, and too much danger from those consequences which are known. This is what McGeorge Bundy (himself ironically a countervalue theorist) calls "existential deterrence," i.e., the nearly total uncertainty of the consequences of using even a few nuclear weapons.[104]

All that counterforce theorists (including myself) argue for is an attempt to plan weapons choice, control mechanisms, and strategies that would ameliorate the cataclysm if it comes. Existential deterrence should be adequate to prevent its coming even if we succeed in dampening its worst effects somewhat. Nuclear war is so dreadful in its potential consequences and so uncertain in the course it might take that plans which might lessen its effects somewhat would encourage only the truly insane to wage it as a means of achieving policy goals. It remains irretrievably beyond the threshold of conscionability.

D. *The Moral Status of Deterrent Threats*

For many years now, both the public and the academy have internalized the moral component of the Dilemma of Nuclear Weapons. The dilemma runs roughly like this: (1) nuclear war would be a massive catastrophe and thus a great evil; (2) in order to avoid nuclear war, we must threaten to kill many innocent civilians in the Soviet Union; (3) to kill many innocent civilians in the Soviet Union is morally wrong. Therefore: (4) we must threaten to do a moral wrong to prevent a great evil. The American Catholic Bishops have further elaborated on the dilemma:

> Specifically, it is not morally acceptable to intend to kill the innocent as part of a strategy of deterring nuclear war.[105]

The doctrine of nuclear deterrence is morally wrong, the Bishops contend, but a necessary wrong until disarmament can be achieved. Michael Walzer anticipated the Catholic Bishops' position almost exactly:

> Nuclear war is and will remain morally unacceptable, and there is no case for its rehabilitation. Because it is unacceptable, we must seek out ways to prevent it and because deterrence is a bad way, we must seek out others....deterrence, for all its criminality, falls or may fall for the moment under the standard of necessity.[106]

This notion grows more logically complex, however, when we realize that the moral inadmissibility of an intention to use nuclear weapons precludes the planning of or preparation for nuclear war, even defensive war. The Bishops explicitly say this. They also hold that having a capacity to fight counterforce war is wrong, for having it implies at least a conditional willingness to use it, and waging nuclear war is always irredeemably wrong. But that leaves only countervalue deterrence, that is, the threat to kill millions of innocent civilians on purpose. And this we may threaten to do, as long as we do not mean it. Confusing? Indeed! Albert Wohlstetter believes that the Bishops' position is logically incoherent. He claims that they hold at once the following:

> (A) We should not get or keep an ability to attack combatants. (B) We may maintain an ability to attack noncombatants while waiting for nuclear disarmament, and (C) We may use that ability implicitly (though not explicitly) to threaten retaliation against noncombatants. (D) Indeed, to deter nuclear attack, we must convince other nations that our "determination to use nuclear weapons is beyond question." (E) We should never intend to use nuclear weapons. (F) Nor (to make

the deception harder) declare an intent to use them even in reply to a nuclear attack. (G) We should never actually use them; that is to say, we shouldn't retaliate at all.[107]

I believe Wohlstetter's analysis of the Bishops' position is correct and that their position is incoherent.

The ultimate logical refinement of these seemingly contradictory imperatives was presented by Gregory Kavka some years ago when he argued that the premises of nuclear deterrence give rise to several moral paradoxes.[108] As we have seen, there are certain very real strategic dilemmas inherent in the U.S.-Soviet confrontation, e.g., the Prisoner's Dilemma. If we conjoin these with the kind of moral knots Wohlstetter ties the Bishops in and Kavka or Walzer tie themselves in, it is easy to see why the simplistic solutions of the "peace" movement and the unilateralists seem so attractive to so many. What are we to make of so bizzare a moral landscape? How can a democracy that wishes to be both moral and free from the coercion of a potential nuclear aggressor make meaningful public policy when trained logicians admit to rational bankruptcy?[109]

Quite simply. If things have gotten to this extremity, something must be wrong with the premises. After carefully analyzing the morality of nuclear war waging, a task few others seem willing to undertake, we can see a very simple way out. *It is moral to threaten what it is moral to do.* It is moral to wage defensive, counterforce nuclear war. In order to deter the Soviet Union we need not threaten to destroy vast numbers of innocent Soviet citizens, surely not intentionally and I hope not even inadvertently. If we can credibly threaten to leave the Soviet Union as close as possible to a headless, defenseless, but otherwise largely whole country, especially one in which Communist Party control is ended, we can deter. We do not need to kill tens of millions of Soviet citizens. Indeed, even if we were not constrained by morality, such threats of mass murder would probably not be particularly effective in any case. It is not at all clear that the Soviet leadership places sufficient value on the lives of its civilian population. Yet, given the Soviet leadership's obsession with control and the consequent high value it places upon its party, military, and security apparatus, it is highly probable that we will deter with this more limited and morally defensible threat.

Moreover, the attribution of total innocence to those Soviet citizens we do inadvertently kill, and there unavoidably will be many, is mistaken. While not so guilty as to justify retribution against them, they have enough responsibility for their nation's policies that we have every right to put them at risk by attacking their country's military forces and political and military leadership as we endeavor to defend our own people's lives.

No paradox! No dilemma! To wage defensive, counterforce nuclear war is moral. To threaten to wage it is also moral. To threaten it effectively, that is, to *be able* to wage it, will also genuinely deter. We have a moral *right* to defend ourselves by a moral and effective means. For all the sound and fury, it is really that simple.

VI. Conclusion

A. *Toward a Moral Defense Policy*

What have we learned from all this? What are we now able to say about our present nuclear defense policy? Well, our policy to date is not wildly off course. It is not the work of "moral idiots" as Jonathan Schell has said,[1] nor the product of aggressive male hormones, as Helen Caldicott would have it.[2] Considering the severe constraints upon our choices, we have not done so badly.

Where do we go from here? That is far more difficult to say and a detailed formulation of a future nuclear defense policy is beyond the scope of this work in any case.[3] But we can lay out some parameters within which future policy must fit, if it is to be both rational and moral.

1. *We have an overwhelming moral duty to avoid nuclear war.* While that duty need not be discharged at *any* cost, namely slavery, we must be prepared to pay a high price to avoid nuclear war, for it is truly beyond the threshold of the conscionable. We must never be the first to initiate that nearly irrevocable series of steps that would lead to nuclear war. It would be worth no conceivable policy end.

2. *We must take all reasonable steps which can now be taken to avoid nuclear war.* Ironically, the two most important such steps might, to those who have not followed the argument herein or otherwise thought hard about it, seem to be bellicose and dangerous. First, we must be certain that our strategic nuclear deterrent forces are adequate to deter and secure enough to survive an attack. This does not require more missiles, but it may well require new and different ones. Second, we must have strong, effective conventional forces to deter conventional Soviet aggression. We must not try to do this on the cheap with nuclear threats when only conventional forces can do it safely and effectively.

These two forces, a strong, secure deterrent force and strong conventional forces, will not by themselves guarantee peace. As many in the "peace" movement rightly point out, the world is far too complex to insure that every new rocket or bomb will make us more secure. Indeed, as we have seen, our own vulnerable offensive nuclear forces can become an invitation for an adversary's attack and actually make us less safe. A strong, secure, strategic force, and a strong, effective, conventional force are *prerequisites of stability*. We do not necessarily have a safe world with them, for we can do other things to make ourselves unsafe, and so can the Soviets. *But we cannot have a safe world without them.*

There is, to be sure, an appropriate place for arms control and, more importantly, for what we might call *mutual safety measures*. There are overlapping areas of interest between ourselves and the Soviets, and we must not be so stiff-necked as to refuse to see this. Neither of us, nor anyone else, has an interest in accidental nuclear war. Any measures that we can work out between ourselves in this area can only make us all safer. Similarly, we both have strong incentives to improve crisis control and crisis management tools, e.g., expansion of the hotline. What might be called "inadvertent war"—not a computer malfunction or a general gone mad, but a confrontation spiraling upward in tension with both powers tempted to launch a damage-limiting first strike—is probably the greatest danger we face. What a horror, a nuclear war starting in the way World War I began,[4] a war that no one wants yet no one can avoid. Techniques of mutual crisis management are not terribly well-refined, but we must try to implement those we have and to develop better ones. And here we can trust the Soviets, for we have only to trust their self-interest.

Although it takes us too far afield to discuss in any detail, the super-powers have a similar joint interest in stemming nuclear proliferation and should work actively together in this area. Arms control has its place, as well, though it seems far less important than measures against accidental and inadvertent war. And the emphasis in arms control must be on the composition of arsenals and their stability (more secure forces and less vulnerable ones). It should not be on numbers of weapons. The fixation on numbers manifests a deeper problem. We must work very hard not to grab for symbolic measures that only make us feel safer. We must not give in to the naive and possibly even dangerous view that any arms control measure is better than none. That is false. Removing in-vulnerable weapons, for example, while leaving vulnerable ones in place makes the world far more dangerous.

In addition, we must demand thorough mutual verification of any arms control measures. For we must not by panic or naivete give away at the negotiating table what we would never yield if it were demanded as a threat. We must remember that there is no clock running towards doomsday. If we maintain a strong, secure deterrent force and strong conventional forces, and take both unilateral and, if possible, bilateral steps to lower the risk of accidental war, the probability of a nuclear war can actually *go down* (perhaps a lot) without any progress on what is usually called "arms control," i.e., arms reduction. We must be patient and even obdurate: meaningful concessions only for meaningful concessions, not withstanding Soviet media campaigns in the Western press. We must act to truly lower the probability of nuclear war without increasing the probability of slavery. Measures offering less must receive a resounding no. We must be willing to expend effort and ingenuity in "getting to yes," as one expert on negotiation has put it. But as any good negotiator knows, you never get to yes if you are not willing to say no, and no again, and, if necessary, to make that no stick.

3. Perhaps the most surprising result we have reached is that, while it is to be avoided if possible, *we have a moral right to fight a nuclear war if we are attacked by nuclear weapons.* Nuclear defense against nuclear attack makes sense and is possible. Defensive, counterforce warfare could save the lives of millions of Americans and of citizens of allied countries. Moreover, we have a moral right that grows out of our right to self-defense to use nuclear weapons in that way. Indeed, if we as citizens chose to be so defended, as I believe we have, our government has not only a right but a duty to wage retaliatory counterforce warfare in our defense.

Once we have been attacked, we can legitimately counterattack all Soviet military targets and all industrial sites that directly support the military. Moreover, the civilian government, party, and internal security apparatus is a morally justifiable target of counterforce defensive warfare. The conclusion is irrefragable: *we have a moral right of self-defense which entitles us to destroy the Soviet Union's ability to make war or command war making.*

4. In any such attacks, *we have a duty to take great pains to minimize noncombatant casualties.* At no time is the purposeful, unrestrained slaughter of millions of civilians justified, regardless of what sort of attack the Soviets have launched at us. This duty requires that we take maximum care in the targeting and planning of any defensive attack. Moreover, we must work very hard to develop newer weapons which will further reduce possible civilian casualties. However, within the constraint of this strong duty of care adumbrated above, *we have a right to put Soviet noncombatants at risk, even large numbers at great risk, as we seek to save the lives of our own and allied citizens.* For people have a duty to restrain their government from committing nuclear aggression, and if they fail in that duty, their absolute immunity as noncombatants is

undermined. We must remember that if we are ever tempted to become a nuclear aggressor, the Soviet Union has exactly reciprocal rights against us.

5. Within the bounds set out above, we have a moral right to use nuclear weapons in our own defense in order to extinguish the war-making capacity of any nuclear aggressor. *It is surely moral to threaten to do what it is moral to do. Thus we can morally make these sorts of deterrent threats. Deterrence of this counterforce kind is moral.* We have a right to use it to keep the peace. It is not a "necessary evil," as the American Catholic Bishops would have it. It is morally justifiable. To be sure, once something safer comes along, such as workable, bilaterial disarmament, for example, we would be irrational and immoral not to replace the former with the latter. But until then, we need not feel guilty, nor allow ourselves to be made to feel guilty by those long on moral indignation but short on genuine alternatives.

How do we get from where our policy has been to where it is going? We have had a few missteps. The MX based in old Minuteman silos is a destabilizing offensive weapon, and we should not deploy it. But it has become so much of a political football that it surely will not be deployed in great numbers, if at all. At a more serious level, we should build and maintain a more credible conventional deterrent for NATO and adopt the strategy, though not necessarily the rhetoric, of no first use. We should be shifting our nuclear deterrent more rapidly than we are from fixed, land-based ICBMs to submarine-based missiles (the Trident) and mobile missiles (the Midgetman). Excepting these changes, though, our direction is more or less correct.

If you look at what we have *done* over the years, rather than all the nonsense that has been *said* about what was being done, we have gotten it nearly right. We have continued to move away from reliance on "city busting" countervalue strikes as technology has allowed. We have led in shrinking megatonnage and improving accuracy. Soviet propaganda, and even our declared NATO strategy to the contrary, we have evolved a largely retaliatory nuclear force maintained in a second-strike posture. (The Soviets have not.)

Our problem is not what we have done so much as what we have come to believe about what we have done. The *reductio ad absurdum* of the Bishops' controversy with Wohlstetter, Walzer's self-imposed self-contradictions, and Kavka's formal paradoxes arises only because we think less of ourselves than we merit. If we hear ourselves called would-be mass murderers often enough, and if we fail to understand the moral foundation of what we do, we come to see ourselves as would-be mass murderers and struggle with the moral consequences of that misconception.

We must stop the moral self-condemnation and remove the guilt. We have a right to protect ourselves and preserve our society and its traditions. No matter the enormity of harm a potential aggressor could heap upon us and the rest of the planet, that right is not expunged. It is morally correct to put any such aggressor on notice. We know our rights to defend ourselves and we shall exercise them. Knowing what we believe about our moral rights, any potential aggressor will know what course prudence dictates. So in the end, this deeper moral understanding of our position might help to prevent the most colossal of all catastrophes.

B. *Nuclear War and the Human Condition*

We have seen that our biggest problem in putting nuclear war in historical and global context lay not in exaggerating its effects, though there is a tendency to do that, but in ignoring the cruel lot our fellow humans have always faced at the hands of war makers. The prospect of nuclear war, more than anything else, has returned us to the perilous existence of our ancestors. But perhaps we never really departed from it or, at least, not as completely as we thought.

Nuclear war offers us the likely prospect of pain and death, not only for ourselves and our loved ones, but for most (although definitely not all) of our fellow countrymen and for many, many others. But everyone of us faces the likely prospect of pain and the certain prospect of death, in any case. The boundary conditions of human existence and consciousness determine that, without the help of the bomb.

Ernest Becker, in the *Denial of Death,* tells us:

> Man emerged from the instinctive thoughtless action of lower animals and came to reflect on his condition. He was given a consciousness of his individuality and his part-divinity in creation, the beauty and uniqueness of his face and name. At the same time he was given the consciousness and the terror of the world and of his own death and decay.[5]

Why, then, do we find nuclear war uniquely terrifying? There are two reasons. First, it threatens to destroy not only us, but our familiar world as well. It erodes a sense of permanence we feel beyond ourselves in our lives and our everyday surroundings. Yet, we all know permanence to be an illusion. For time and the universe will soon enough tear down every aspect of our all too transitory world. The bomb threatens to do in a shocking, compacted way what will happen to us and our familiar world anyway, given enough time. It dramatizes this aspect of the human condition, but does not profoundly change it.

What, then, is the second reason for the mind-numbing terror inspired by nuclear war? The answer is to be found, I believe, in a fascinating piece of cultural history. Our ancestors in the Western world through at least the Thirty Years War met war and marching armies, attended as they always were by rape and pillage and followed by economic chaos, hunger, and disease, firmly in the grip of a religious world view. They could face the terrible insecurity of their lives precisely because they were so certain of the transience of this life and the permanence and assurance of the next.

As the hold on us of this religious world view weakened and we moved on to a more secular and humanistic view, we also gained great faith in the notion of progress. Human culture, at least in the "civilized" West, would never again present us with horrors like the Thirty Years War. But it did. In our century it gave us Verdun and Auschwitz, the siege of Leningrad, and the fire raid on Dresden. And finally it gave us Hiroshima and fifty thousand nuclear weapons. To face the prospect of nuclear war is to face the cold and terrifying human dilemma of pain and death without the comfort of a religious world view. Nuclear war has become a symbolic, even mythic, but nonetheless very concrete, representation of the human condition.

Does this mean that, reconciling ourselves to our grim fate, we should stoically await nuclear Armageddon? No. Yet that is what tempts us if we yield to hysterical visions like Jonathan Schell's. Nuclear weapons are not God's tools, nor Satan's. They are man's. They will not exterminate all life on the planet nor consign all future generations of mankind to the world of what might have been. This part of the nuclear mythology paralyzes us by its enormity. But it is false. We face instead all too human weapons that pose an all too human threat. Death for many of us, injury, sickness, and grinding poverty for the rest. This is a fate faced by our forebearers at the hands of far weaker weapons. They lived such a precarious existence that the siege and sack of cities and attendant epidemics were an almost ordinary occurrence, making every small step toward progress ephemeral. We in the West have left such an existence far, far behind. Thus, it takes such an awesomely destructive weapon to hurl us back again. We have more to lose, but the bomb is quite capable of imposing that loss.

We must find ways never to use these weapons. However, that takes a great deal of a virtue that has been much abused in the West—courage.

And I am not speaking of the surrogate type of courage often represented in the popular media. We need no Rambos, nor Dirty Harrys. What we need is something very close to what the theologian Paul Tillich meant by "the courage to be." Human life and the human soul are defined in the struggle for meaning and value, the struggle with what Tillich calls "non-being": fate, death, hopelessness, moral ambiguity, and nihilism.

The nuclear bomb, as much as the death and meaninglessness it has come to be the mythic symbol for, can be seen as expressing Tillich's notion of non-being. To face a world in which the bomb threatens everything we value requires Tillich's kind of courage. He tells us:

> Courage is the self affirmation of being in spite of the fact of non-being. It is the act of the individual self in taking the anxiety of non-being upon itself by affirming itself...Courage always includes a risk, it is always threatened by non-being...Courage needs the power of being, a power transcending the non-being which is experienced in the anxiety of fate and death.[6]

Tillich goes on to say that: "Courage is the power of life to affirm itself,..."[7] while "the negation of life because of its negativity is an expression of cowardice."[8]

It takes a steady nerve and a strong resolve to look coldly and logically at the prospect of a nuclear war and try to reason out what to do. It is far easier to celebrate its power to paralyze the mind, to trumpet the infinite human cost it would exact, to lapse into hysterics, or to launch vitriolic attacks upon assorted straw men. Feelings of fear, panic, anger, or moral outrage, are quite understandable, indeed perhaps unavoidable, when one is confronted with the propsect of nuclear war. In the poignant and sensitive film "Testament," a mother buries her child, a victim of radiation sickness following a nuclear war. As she does so, she crys out in anguish, "Who did this?" And each of us wants to cry out with her, for it could be our child.

But even as we ask the question, we know the answer: everyone and no one, technology and the Prisoner's Dilemma, life. Even if one thinks as I do, that the greatest source of danger in the world today is the Soviet Union and its policies, that is not a complete answer, for Soviet leaders are themselves the products of a culture and a system which they did not make. The truth is that there is no one to blame. To invent someone is a kind of emotional self-indulgence. If we fail to confront the hard moral choices, we will have failed ourselves and our children. We must overcome our fears and get on with the job. There are problems to solve, solutions to try, *things to think about,* and *things to do.* Nuclear war is a special case of omnipresent death, and as L.C. Knights, the great Shakespearean scholar, observed:

> I think it is obvious that strong, unfrightened and affirmative attitudes about death can only exist as part of strong, unfrightened and affirmative attitudes to living.[9]

Likewise, we must develop strong, unfrightened, affirmative attitudes toward the risk of nuclear war. Only then can we disenthrall ourselves from myths and perhaps lessen the danger. We must see the threat of nuclear war as it is: of large but still human dimensions; a very difficult but ultimately tractable problem. But like all really important problems of human existence, the solution will come in bits and pieces to be slowly and patiently assembled: a more secure deterrent force replacing a vulnerable one here; a mutually adopted measure against accidental war there. In this painstaking process, we must dare to bear the risk of nuclear war if we are ever to make that risk go away.

Finally, we must think enough of ourselves and our civilization that we refuse to settle for either slavery or death. We must understand that it is the United States that will have to bear the primary responsibility for movement toward a safer world. In principle, the Soviets are equally well positioned to do so. But they will not. They are at once too amoral, too bellicose, and too frightened. It falls to the world's great, free democracy to close the path to Armageddon. Much of what we do might be misunderstood by the ignorant and by advocates of expedience. When we engage the Soviet Union in dialogue to limit the danger of accidental war, for example, there are those who will say that they cannot be dealt with, ever or on any issue. On the other hand, when we rebuild a secure deterrent as we must, some will call us warmongers and say we are arming to the teeth. We must persevere.

The United States must shoulder this burden not only for its own safety, but for the peace and safety of the world. That our burden is so heavy should neither surpirse nor confound us, for the great man spoke more truly than ever even he could know when he called us the last best hope.

ENDNOTES

Chapter II

1. The best history of just war theory is James Turner Johnson, *Just War and the Restraint of War* (Princeton, NJ: Princeton University Press, 1981). Another is Donald A. Wells, *War Crimes and Laws of War* (Lanham, MD: University Press of America, 1984). Shorter treatments include James E. Dougherty, *The Bishops and Nuclear Weapons* (Handen, CT: Archon Books, 1984), Chapter 2; and Telford Taylor, *Nuremberg to Viet Nam* (New York: New York Times Book Co., 1970), Chapter 3.

2. St. Augustine *The City of God,* trans. Marcus Dods, *The Confessions, The City of God, On Christian Doctrine* (Chicago, IL: Encyclopedia Britannica, Inc., 1952), esp. Book IV, Chapter 15, and Book XIX, Chapter 12.

3. *ibid.,* p. 196.

4. St. Thomas Aquinas, "Summa Theologica, Part II, Question 40," Kenneth E. Alrutz, *et al.,* eds., *War and Peace* (Lanham, MD: University Press of America, 1982), pp. 3-12.

5. *ibid.,* pp. 10-12.

6. Thomas More, *Utopia* (New York: E.P. Dutton, 1951), pp. 107-117.

7. Johnson, *Just War,* pp. 125-129.

8. See Wesley L. Gould, *An Introduction to International Law* (New York: Harper & Row, 1957), pp. 31-100; Morton Kaplan and Nicholas Katzenbach, *The Political Foundations of International Law* (New York: John Wiley & Sons, 1961), pp. 56-80; Gerhard von Glahn, *Law Among Nations,* 4th ed. (New York: Macmillan, 1981), pp. 41-55.

9. Hugo Grotius, *The Law of War and Peace,* trans. Louise Loomis (Roslyn, NY: Walter J. Black, Inc., 1949).

10. A brief survey of natural law theory is provided in Richard Wollheim, "Natural Law," *The Encyclopedia of Philosophy,* vol. 5, pp. 450-454. Far more thorough discussions are provided by A.P. D'Entreves, *Natural Law: An Historical Survey* (New York: Harper & Row, 1965); and John Finnis, *Natural Law and Natural Rights* (Oxford: Clarendon Press, 1980).

11. See, for example, John Colman, *John Locke's Moral Philosophy* (Edinburgh: Edinburgh University Press, 1983), Chapters II and VII; Morton White, *The Philosophy of the American Revolution* (Oxford: Oxford University Press, 1978).

12. On the application of natural law to nations and their behavior, see Marshall Cohen, "Moral Skepticism and International Relations," *Philosophy and Public Affairs,* vol. 13, no. 4 (Fall 1984), pp. 299-346; E.B.F. Midgley, *The Natural Law Tradition and International Relations* (New York: Barnes and Noble, 1973).

13. Grotius, *The Law of War and Peace.*

14. Emeric de Vattel, "Of the Law of Nations," Section 7, Alrutz, *et al.,* eds., *War and Peace,* p. 54.

15. Wells, *War Crimes,* pp. 41-48.

16. See Paul Fussell, *The Great War and Modern Memory* (New York: Oxford University Press, 1975); and Eric J. Lead, *No Man's Land: Combat and Identity in World War I* (Cambridge: Cambridge University Press, 1979).

17. Wells, *War Crimes,* pp. 48-52.

18. Reinhold Niebuhr, *Christianity and Power Politics* (New York: Charles Scribner and Sons, 1940), pp. 8-18 and *passim.*

19. Paul Ramsey, *The Just War* (New York: Charles Scribner and Sons, 1968); and *War and the Christian Conscience* (Durham, NC: Duke University Press, 1961).

20. John Courtney Murray, *Morality and War* (New York: Church Peace Union, 1959); and "Theology and Modern War," *Theological Studies,* vol. 20 (1959), pp. 41-60.

21. Michael Walzer, *Just and Unjust Wars* (New York: Basic Books, 1977).

22. William V. O'Brien, *The Conduct of Just and Limited War* (New York: Praeger, 1981).

23. James Turner Johnson, *Can Modern War be Just?* (New Haven: Yale University Press, 1984); and *Just War Tradition and the Restraint of War* (Princeton, NJ: Princeton University Press, 1981).

24. "The Challenge of Peace: God's Promise and Our Response," 3rd Draft, *Origins,* vol. 12 (April 14, 1983), pp. 687-728.

25. O'Brien, *The Conduct of Just and Limited War,* p. 16.

26. See, *inter alia:* O'Brien, *The Conduct of Just and Limited War,* Chapter 2; von Glahn, *Law Among Nations,* Chapter 24; Walzer, *Just and Unjust Wars,* Chapters 2, 4, 7, and *passim;* Wells, *War Crimes,* pp. 16-20.

27. The whole sad tale of the moral failure of the Third Republic and its lost potential to stop Hitler is told in many places. The best are accounts by William Shirer who, in addition to being a superb popular historian, was a reporter on the scene covering both the German and French sides of developments. For the French side, see his *The Collapse of the Third Republic* (New York: Simon & Schuster, 1969), especially Chapter 11 and Books Three and Four. For the definitive account of the German side, see his *The Rise and Fall of the Third Reich* (New York: Simon & Schuster, 1960), Chapters 12-31. For a more reportorial picture of the developments from both sides see his *The Nightmare Years* (Boston: Little Brown, 1984), Book Three and Chapters 14, 15, and 16.

For another excellent account of a crucial part of the story, see Telford Taylor, *Munich: The Price of Peace* (New York: Doubleday, 1979); France's role is covered in Chapters 7, 19, 20, and 21.

28. Quoted in Richard Wasserstrom, "On the Morality of War," Richard Wasserstrom, ed., *War and Morality* (Belmont, CA: Wadsworth, 1970), p. 88.

29. Telford Taylor "Just and Unjust Wars," Malham M. Wakin, ed., *War, Morality and the Military Profession* (Boulder, CO: Westview Press, 1979), pp. 245-258.

30. O'Brien, *The Conduct of Just and Limited War,* pp. 131-133.

31. *ibid.,* pp. 24-27.

32. *ibid.,* p. 65.

33. *ibid.,* pp. 66-67, 226-228.

34. Richard Wasserstrom, "Conduct and Responsibility in War," *Philosophy and Social Issues: Five Studies* (Notre Dame, IN: University of Notre Dame Press, 1980), pp. 152-187.

35. Murray, *Morality and War;* O'Brien, *The Conduct of Just and Limited War,* pp. 127-153.

36. Antony Flew, ed., *A Dictionary of Philosophy* (New York: St. Martin's Press, 1979), p. 91.

37. Wasserstrom, "On the Morality of War," p. 78.

38. Quoted in *ibid.,* pp. 78-79.

39. Quoted in Russell F. Weigley, *The American Way of War* (Bloomington, IN: Indiana University Press, 1977), p. 152.

40. *ibid.,* pp. 145-152; Wasserstrom, "On the Morality of War." See also Walzer, *Just and Unjust Wars,* pp. 3-20, for a different but equally compelling refutation of moral nihilism in regard to war.

41. This is very close to Michael Walzer's view; see *Just and Unjust Wars,* pp. 269-283.

42. See Philip Devine, *The Ethics of Homocide* (Ithaca, NY: Cornell University Press, 1978), pp. 134-138; Jonathan Glover, *Causing Death and Saving Lives* (London: Pelican, 1977), pp. 255-258.

43. Reinhold Niebuhr, *Christianity and Power Politics.* Tom Regan, "A Defense of Pacifism," *Canadian Journal of Philosophy,* vol. 11 (1972), pp. 73-86; the author defends pacifism only against logical incoherence. The title to the contrary, he finds it lacking a "fully developed moral sensitivity to the vagaries and complexities of human existence" (p. 86).

44. Jan Narveson, "Pacifism: A Philosophical Analysis," *Ethics,* vol. 75 (1965), pp. 259-271.

45. James W. Child, "On the Immorality of Pacifism," paper read at the Ohio Philosophical Association Annual Meeting, The Ohio State University, Columbus, Ohio, April 20, 1985.

46. William L. Prosser, *Law of Torts,* 3rd ed., (St. Paul, MN: West Publishing Co., 1964), pp. 110-115; Rollin M. Perkins, *Perkins on Criminal Law,* 2nd ed. (Mineola, NY: The Foundation Press, 1969), pp. 993-1022.

47. Charles Fried, *Right and Wrong* (Cambridge, MA: Harvard University Press, 1978), pp. 44-45.

48. Prosser, *Law of Torts,* p. 111; Perkins, *Perkins on Criminal Law,* p. 993.

49. There are two good survey articles on social contract theory for the general reader. Each explains in clear terms the intricate historical and philosophical relationships among the concepts of natural law, natural rights, and the social contract. They are Peter Laslett, "Social Contract," Paul Edwards, ed., *The Encyclopedia of Philosophy,* vol. 7 (New York: Macmillan, 1967), pp. 465-467; and Michael Levin, "Social Contract," Philip Weiner, ed., *Dictionary of the History of Ideas,* vol. IV (New York: Scribner's, 1973), pp. 251-263.

50. The theory here is John Locke's almost without modification. See his "Second Treatise," *Two Treatises of Government* (New York: Cambridge University Press, 1960),

esp. Chapters 2 and 8. A good secondary source for the theory is Richard H. Cox, *Locke on War and Peace* (Washington, DC: University Press of America), esp. Chapters 3 and 4.

51. Vattel, "Of the Law of Nations," Alrutz, et al., eds., *War and Peace,* pp. 67-68.

52. von Glahn, *Law Among Nations,* p. 126.

53. *ibid.,* p. 90.

54. See, however, Baruch A. Brody's excellent paper, "The International Defense of Liberty," *Social Philosophy and Policy,* vol. 3, no. 1 (Autumn 1985), pp. 27-42. Brody goes beyond alliances and analyzes one nation's rights to defend the liberty of another in terms of rights and duties to aid third parties who are not alliance partners. He assumes that there exists a right where there are preexisting promises or contracts, i.e., alliance treaties.

Chapter III

1. Robert McNamara and Hans Bethe, "Reducing the Risk of Nuclear War," *Atlantic* (July 1985), p. 43.

2. Nevil Shute, *On the Beach* (New York: Morrow, 1957).

3. OTA, *The Effects of Nuclear War* (Washington, DC: U.S. Government Printing Office, 1979).

4. Jonathon Schell, *The Fate of the Earth* (New York: Alfred Knopf, 1982).

5. Eric Chivian, *et al.,* eds., *Last Aid* (New York: William H. Freeman and Co., 1982).

6. Ruth Adams and Susan Cullen, eds., *The Final Epidemic* (Chicago: Educational Foundation for Nuclear Science, 1981).

7. Sir John Hackett, *The Third World War* (New York: Macmillan, 1978).

8. Whitley Strieber and James Kunetka, *Warday* (New York: Holt, Rinehart and Winston, 1984).

9. Anyone familiar with utility theory knows that there are profound foundational issues about actually measuring utility (cardinal utility) versus merely ordering preferences (ordinal utility). There are even worse problems with interpersonal comparisons of utility. Here, I clearly oversimplify. However, practitioners, e.g., economists and business planners, find utility theory to be a useful aid in making decisions. For a good overview of the foundational problems, see two articles in the *Dictionary of the History of Ideas,* vol. IV: Kenneth Arrow, "Formal Theories of Social Welfare," and Nicholas Georgescu-Roegen, "Utility and Value in Economic Thought". For an example of the ease of application of utility theory in spite of the conceptual problems, see Ralph O. Swalm, "Utility Theory: Insights into Risk Taking," *Harvard Business Review* (Nov.-Dec. 1966); reprinted in Douglas Dickson, *Using Logical Techniques for Making Better Decisions* (New York: Wiley, 1983), pp. 73-84.

10. Michael Dummett, "Nuclear Warfare," Nigel Blake and Kay Pole, eds., *Objections to Nuclear Defense* (London: Routledge and Kegan Paul, 1984), p. 40.

11. Helen Caldicott, *Missile Envy* (New York: William Morrow, 1984), p. 203.

12. Napoleon A. Chagnon, *Yanomamo, The Fierce People,* 2nd ed. (New York: Holt, Reinhart and Winston, 1977), esp. Chapter 5.

13. C.V. Wedgewood, *The Spoils of Time* (New York: Doubleday, 1985), p. 100. The intimate causal relationship between the twin scourges of war and disease indicates that we perhaps ought to think of them as one, where the human cost of consequent epidemics is treated as part of the human cost of war. Indeed, this is a key theme in William H. McNeill, *Plagues and People* (New York: Doubleday, 1976), pp. 1-5 and *passim.*

14. James Chambers, *The Devil's Horsemen* (New York: Atheneum, 1979), pp. 14-17.

15. Desmond Seward, *The Hundred Years' War: The English in France 1337-1453* (New York: Atheneum, 1978), pp. 58-59.

16. William McNeill, *The Pursuit of Power* (Chicago: The University of Chicago Press, 1982), p. 315.

17. Grotius, *The Law of War and Peace,* pp. 304-305.

18. Michael Howard, *War in European History* (Oxford: Oxford University Press, 1976), pp. 70-74. Howard's book is a good one for a historical overview of modern war, although it concentrates upon administrative and political development. McNeill's *The Pursuit of Power* is also excellent, although its emphasis is on weapons technology and, especially, the causal interplay between economic institutions and military capacity. For a balanced overview, see Richard Preston and Sydney Wise, *Men in Arms,* 4th ed. (New York: Holt, Reinhart and Winston, 1978); or Hew Strachan, *European Armies and the Conduct of War* (London: George Allen and Unwsin, 1983). Gwynne Dyer's *War* (New York: Crown, 1985), is written for more popular appeal and is highly idiosyncratic, but a very good read.

19. There are three adequate popular accounts of the Black Death. They are McNeill, *Plagues and People,* Chapter IV, especially pp. 156-169; Barbara Tuchman, *A Distant Mirror* (New York: Knopf, 1978), Chapter 5; and, the best, Philip Ziegler, *The Black Death* (Hammondsworth: Penguin Books, 1969).

20. Ziegler, *The Black Death,* p. 239.

21. McNeill, *Plagues and People,* p. 166.

22. *ibid.,* p. 178; Ziegler, *The Black Death,* p. 238 and Chapter 14, *passim.*

23. Good surveys are Hanson Baldwin, *World War I* (New York: Harper and Row, 1962); Keith Robbins, *The First World War* (Oxford: Oxford University Press, 1984); James L. Stokesbury, *A Short History of World War I* (New York: Morrow, 1981).

24. Bernard and Fawn Brodie, *From Crossbow to H-Bomb,* 2nd ed. (Bloomington, IN: Indiana University Press, 1973), Chapters 6 and 7; Dyer, *War,* Chapter IV; Preston and Wise, *Men in Arms,* Chapter 15.

25. Stokesbury, *A Short History of World War I,* p. 156.

26. Chivian, *et al.,* eds., *Last Aid,* Chapter 16.

27. General overviews include Paul Carell, *The Scorched Earth: The Russian German War 1943-1944,* trans. Ewald Osers (Boston: Little Brown, 1970); Albert Seaton, *The Russian German War 1941-45* (New York: Praeger, 1971); Alexander Werth, *Russia at War, 1941-1945* (New York: Carroll and Graf, 1964). Excellent discussions of specific events are William Craig, *Enemy at the Gates: The Battle for Stalingrad* (New York: Dutton, 1973); Harrison Salisbury, *The 900 Days: The Siege of Leningrad* (New York: Harper and Row, 1969); Col. Albert Seaton, *The Battle for Moscow* (New York: Stein and Day, 1971).

28. Many of these horrors are detailed in Nikolai Tolstoy, *Stalin's Secret War* (London: Pan Books, 1981), esp. Part II.

29. Salisbury, *The 900 Days,* pp. 506-520.

30. *ibid.,* pp. 452-453, 474-476.

31. Dick Wilson, *When Tigers Fight: The Story of the Sino-Japanese War, 1937-1941* (New York: Viking, 1982), p. 82.

32. See Andre Ryerson, "The Cult of Hiroshima," *Commentary,* vol. 80, no. 4 (October 1985), pp. 36-40 for a compelling argument for the use of the atomic bomb on Japan.

33. OTA, *The Effects of Nuclear War,* p. 10, table 2, and pp. 81-94.

34. Reinhold Niebuhr, *The Nature and Destiny of Man, Vol. II Human Destiny* (New York: Scribner, 1944), pp. 51-52.

35. Kosta Tsipis, *Arsenal* (New York: Simon and Schuster, 1983), p. 44.

36. David Ziegler, *War, Peace and International Relations,* 2nd ed. (Boston: Little Brown, 1981), p. 224.

37. *ibid.*

38. Harold Willens, *The Trimtab Factor* (New York: Morrow, 1984).

39. Christopher Chant and Ian Hogg, compilers, *Nuclear War in the 1980's* (New York: Harper and Row, 1983), p. 26.

40. P.M.S. Blackett, "Is the Atomic Bomb an Absolute Weapon," *Scientific American* (March 1949), p. 15.

41. Jonathan Schell, *The Fate of the Earth* (New York: Alfred Knopf, 1982). Hereafter, references to page numbers are in the text.

42. Other examples are Helen Caldicott, *Missile Envy,* esp. pp. 267-286; and Harold Freeman, *If You Care about Life* (New York: Dodd-Mead, 1985), Chapter 2.

43. Among others Eric Chivian, *et al.,* eds., *Last Aid,* pp. 41-107.

44. John Toland, *The Rising Sun* (New York: Bantam, 1970), pp. 756-769. See also Gordon Musgrave, *Operation Gomorrah; The Hamburg Firestorm Raids* (London: Jane's, 1981).

45. The definitive text in this area is Samuel Glasstone and Philip J. Dolan, eds., *The Effects of Nuclear Weapons,* 3rd edition (Washington, DC: United States Departments of Defense and Energy, 1977). Indeed, this work represents a touchstone for our consideration of Schell, for he cites it as "the indispensable classic textbook," (pp. 4-5) and, though he seems to honor its authority in the breach of it, he is correct in his evaluation.
The 3rd Edition of Glasstone and Dolan comes with a manual analogue computer (a kind of slide rule) called the "Nuclear Bomb Effects Computer," developed by E. Royce Fletcher of the Lovelace Biomedical and Environmental Research Institute Inc., Albuquerque, New Mexico, based upon data in the Glasstone and Dolan book. Author's calculations cited in this note and hereafter are done with the aid of this computer.

46. *ibid.,* p. 563. Indeed, *The Effects of Nuclear War* limits third degree burns to a 5 mile radius (p. 21), which would mean that Schell overstates the area by *3.2 times.*

47. Takeshi Ohkita, "Acute Medical Effects at Hiroshima and Nagasaki," Eric Chivian, *et al.,* eds., *Last Aid: The Medical Dimensions of Nuclear War,* pp. 71-72.

48. Glasstone and Dolan, *The Effects of Nuclear Weapons,* p. 31 and table 5, p. 32. See also Andrew Haines, "The Possible Consequences of a Nuclear Attack on London," Eric Chivian *Last Aid,* p. 167.

49. Glasstone and Dolan, *The Effects of Nuclear Weapons,* p. 299.

50. *ibid.,* p. 504.

51. *ibid.,* pp. 299-300.

52. *ibid.,* p. 304.

53. Kosta Tsipis, *Arsenal,* "The Physical Effects of a Nuclear Explosion, pp. 44-74;" Eric Chivian, *Last Aid,* p. 34. For a far more thorough analysis of the Hamburg firestorm, see Gordon Musgrave, "The Firestorm Phenomenon," Eric Chivian, *Last Aid,* pp. 102-116.

54. Chivian, *Last Aid, op. cit.,* p. 130.

55. Glasstone and Dolan, *The Effects of Nuclear Weapons,* pp. 22, 299.

56. Author's calculations with Nuclear Bomb Effects Computer.

57. Kosta Tsipis, *Arsenal,* p. 64, figure 8; this is based also on author's calculations and data provided by Glasstone and Dolan, pp. 422-432, esp. figure 9.866, p. 426.

58. *ibid.*

59. *The Military Balance, 1982-1983* (London: The International Institute for Strategic Studies, 1981).

60. Bill Gunston, ed., *The Encyclopedia of World Air Power* (New York: Crescent Books, 1980), p. 338.

61. Caspar Weinberger, *Annual Report to Congress, Fiscal Year 1986* (Washington, DC: U.S. Government Printing Office, 1985), p. 210.

62. Chant and Hogg, *Nuclear War in the 1980's,* p. 89.

63. *The Military Balance, 1982-1983,* p. 13.

64. See John M. Collins, *U.S.-Soviet Military Balance 1980-1985* (New York: Pergamon-Brassey's, 1985), p. 183; *The Military Balance: 1984-1985* (London: International Institute for Strategic Studies, 1985), p. 17.

65. Author's calculations with Nuclear Bomb Effects Computer.

66. Glasstone and Dolan, *The Effects of Nuclear War,* p. 18.

67. Arthur M. Katz, *Life after Nuclear War* (Cambridge, MA: Ballinger, 1982), p. 21; and Glasstone and Dolan, *The Effects of Nuclear Weapons,* p. 69.

68. Glasstone and Dolan, *The Effects of Nuclear Weapons,* p. 552.

69. OTA, *The Effects of Nuclear Weapons,* figure 2, p. 24 and figure 3, p. 25.

70. Glasstone and Dolan, *The Effects of Nuclear Weapons,* figure 9.266, p. 426.

71. Tsipis, *Arsenal,* figures 7 and 8, p. 64.

72. Glasstone and Dolan, *The Effects of Nuclear Weapons,* p. 428.

73. This and the following information on shielding and shelters can be found in Joseph Rotblat, *Nuclear Radiation in Warfare* (Solna, Sweden: Stockholm International Peace Research Institute, 1981), pp. 118-120; Glasstone and Dolan, *The Effects of Nuclear Weapons,* table 9.12, p. 441, and "United States and Soviet City Defense" (Washington, DC: Congressional Research Service, Library of Congress, 1976), p. 35.

74. See Joseph D. Douglass, Jr. and Amoretta M. Hoeber, *Soviet Strategy for Nuclear War* (Stanford, CA: Hoover Institution Press, 1979), pp. 58-66.

75. Chant and Hogg, *Nuclear War in the 1980's,* p. 27.

76. Frank Barnaby and Randall Foresberg, "Strategic Nuclear Weapons," *The Arms Race and Arms Control* (Solna, Sweden: Stockholm International Peace Research Institute, 1982), table 4.1, p. 85.

77. John M. Collins, *U.S.-Soviet Military Balance, Concepts and Capabilities 1960-1980* (New York: McGraw Hill, 1980), p. 129.

78. *ibid.,* p. 29.

79. Andrew Cockburn, *The Threat: Inside the Soviet Military Machine* (New York: Random House, 1983), Chapter 12, esp. pp. 198-199. See also James Fallows, *National Defense* (New York: Random House, 1981), pp. 148-157.

80. See, for example, Bernard Feld and Kosta Tsipis, "Land Based Intercontinental Ballistic Missiles," *Scientific American* (November 1979), pp. 51-61; and Thomas Garwin and John Steinbruner, "Strategic Vulnerability," *International Security* (Summer 1976), pp. 138-200, esp. pp. 141-142.

81. OTA "Summary of Results," *The Effects of Nuclear War,* pp. 140-145.

82. *ibid.,* table D-1, p. 140.

83. Herbert Abrams and William von Kaenel, "Medical Problems of Survivors of Nuclear War," *New England Journal of Medicine* (November 12, 1981), pp. 1226-1232.

84. Tsipis, *Arsenal,* p. 80.

85. "Public Interest Report," *Journal of the Federation of American Scientists,* vol. 34 (February 1981), p. 1.

86. Chivian, *Last Aid,* p. 115.

87. The somewhat less than typical scholarly events surrounding the announcement of the nuclear winter hypothesis are chronicled in Brad Sparks, "Lysenko's Ghost: The Scandal of Nuclear Winter," *National Review* (November 15, 1985), pp. 28-38.

88. The primary article was R.P. Turco, O.B. Toon, T.P. Ackerman, J.B. Pollack, Carl Sagan, "Nuclear Winter: Global Consequences of Multiple Nuclear Explosions," *Science,* vol. 222 (December 23, 1983), pp. 1283-1292. (This article is universally referred to in the literature as the TTAPS study, making an acronym of the first letter of the authors' last names. I adopt that convention here.) A nearly identical article by the same authors, "The Climatic Effects of Nuclear War," appeared in *Scientific American,* vol. 251 (August 1984), pp. 33-43. See also Paul R. Ehrlich, *et al.,* "Long-Term Biological Consequences of Nuclear War," *Science,* vol. 222 (December 23, 1983), pp. 1293-1300; Paul R. Ehrlich, Carl Sagan, Donald Kennedy, and William Orr Roberts, *The Cold and the Dark: The World after Nuclear War* (New York: Norton, 1984).

89. TTAPS, p. 1284 and table 1.

90. TTAPS, figure 4, p. 1287.

91. Turco, *et al.,* "The Climatic Effects of Nuclear War," p. 40; Erlich, *et al., The Cold and the Dark,* p. 20.

92. Erlich, *The Cold and the Dark,* p. 20.

93. Turco, *et al.,* "The Climatic Effects of Nuclear War," p. 40.

94. See TTAPS, p. 1284, and Erlich, *The Cold and the Dark,* case 17, p. 19.

95. National Research Council, "The Effects on the Atmosphere of a Major Nuclear Exchange," (Washington, DC: National Academy Press, 1985), pp. 13-16.

96. Erlich, *The Cold and the Dark,* p. 16.

97. *ibid.,* figure 2, p. 17.

98. Turco, "The Climatic Effects of Nuclear War," p. 40.

99. Erlich, *The Cold and the Dark,* p. 59.

100. As quoted in Brad Sparks, "Lysenko's Ghost," p. 32.

101. Howard Maccabee, "Nuclear Winter: How Much Do We Really Know?" *Reason* (May 1985), pp. 26-35.

102. National Research Council, "The Effects on the Atmosphere," pp. 10-12.

103. *ibid.,* and Caspar Weinberger, "The Potential Effects of Nuclear War on the Climate: A Report to the United States Congress," mimeographed, released March 1985.

104. National Research Council, "The Effects on the Atmosphere," pp. 6-7.

105. Turco, "The Climatic Effects of Nuclear War," pp. 39-40.

106. Erlich, *The Cold and the Dark,* p. 20.

107. Howard Maccabee, "Nuclear Winter," p. 31.

108. *ibid.*

109. Erlich, *The Cold and the Dark,* p. 16.

110. Howard Maccabee, "Nuclear Winter," p. 31.

111. Caspar Weinberger, "The Potential Effects," p. 4.

112. Turco, "The Climatic Effects of Nuclear War," p. 43.

113. OTA, *The Effects of Nuclear War,* p. 115.

Chapter IV

1. My treatment oversimplifies this distinction considerably. It ignores, for example, moral duties one might have to oneself. See Alan Donagan, *The Theory of Morality* (Chicago: University of Chicago Press, 1977), Chapter 3.2; Hardy Jones, "Treating Oneself Wrongly," *Journal of Value Inquiry,* vol. 7 (1983); Rolf Sartorius, "Utilitarianism, Rights, and Duties to Self," *American Philosophical Quarterly,* vol. 22 (July 1985).

Furthermore, one can be prudent as regards other peoples' interests because considering those interests in the near term affects your own interests in the long term. There are other complications. However, for our purposes this rough and ready distinction will serve well.

2. This assumption not only oversimplifies, it conflates several problems. First, there is the social scientific question of what people or what sorts of social institutions act when a government is said to act. See Graham T. Allison, *Essence of Decision* (Boston: Little Brown, 1971). It also glosses over the related philosophic problem of just what sorts of entities can be said to have reasons or motives for action. Does it make sense to ascribe reasons, motives, or actions to social institutions and organizations at all? For an examination of this issue see, for example, Peter French, "The Corporation as a Moral Person," *American Philosophical Quarterly,* vol. 16 (1979); and John Ladd, "Morality and the Ideal of Rationality in Formal Organizations," *The Monist,* vol. 54 (1970).

However, important as these issues are, ignoring them in this context does not vitiate the conclusions reached here. I shall adopt the harmlessly simplistic view of nations as actors.

3. Carl von Clausewitz, *On War,* ed. and trans. Michael Howard and Peter Paret (Princeton, NJ: Princeton University Press, 1976), pp. 86-87.

4. *ibid.,* p. 87.

5. See, for example, *Clark and Marshall on Crimes,* 7th edition (Mundelin, IL: Callaghan and Co., 1967), Chapters 6 and 7; *Perkins on Criminal Law,* 2nd edition (Mineola, NY: The Foundation Press, 1969), Chapter 9.

6. Thomas Schelling, *The Strategy of Conflict* (New York: Oxford University Press, 1960), p. 86.

7. To be sure, there are other nuclear powers in the world, and there are other nations that possess significant conventional forces. However, the American and Soviet nuclear forces so totally outstrip other nuclear arsenals in size, destructive power, and flexibility of use as to make the world essentially bipolar. There are other significant conventional powers, although many of them are allied with us in NATO or with the Soviet Union in the Warsaw Pact and thus essentially bipolar. A look at a recent issue of the international Institute for Strategic Studies' *The Military Balance* will confirm this. China, Vietnam, both Koreas's, etc., have substantial numbers of men under arms. However, their nearly complete lack of air and sea lift capacity reduces threats of projected force to virtually nothing. Of course, they can be most troublesome in their immediate areas.

The bipolar model serves well for most purposes, ours here included, but it does not give sufficient emphasis to the terrible dangers of nuclear proliferation and consequent "catalytic war." For more on this problem, see Henry S. Rowen, "Catalytic Nuclear War,"

Graham T. Allison, *et al.,* eds., *Hawks, Doves and Owls* (New York: Norton, 1985), pp. 148-163.

8. One approach to it is a good bibliography. The best I know is Michael Intriligator, "Research on Conflict Theory," *The Journal of Conflict Resolution* (June 1982), pp. 307-327.

9. The classic and still the best volume in the area is Thomas Schelling, *The Strategy of Conflict.* See also Thomas Schelling, *Arms and Influence* (New Haven: Yale University Press, 1966) and the much more recent book by Steven J. Brams, *Superpower Games* (New Haven, CT: Yale University Press, 1985).

10. E.P. Thompson, *Beyond the Cold War* (New York: Pantheon Books, 1982), pp. 1-23.

11. Fred Kaplan, *The Wizards of Armageddon* (New York: Simon and Schuster, 1983).

12. *ibid.,* p. 67.

13. Derek Parfit, "Prudence, Morality and the Prisoner's Dilemma," *Proceedings of the British Academy,* vol. LXV (1979).

14. Thomas Schelling, *Choice and Consequence* (Cambridge, MA: Harvard University Press, 1984), note, p. 109.

15. Indeed, the theory need not even assume intelligent agents in any real sense. It will suffice that the game "players" behave as if they are intelligent agents. For the application of game theory to the "strategies" genes follow in evolution, see Richard Dawkins *The Selfish Gene* (New York: Oxford University Press, 1976), esp. Chapters 5 and 6.

16. The theory is best covered in Glenn H. Snyder and Paul Diesing, *Conflict Among Nations* (Princeton, NJ: Princeton University Press, 1977). Excellent discussions of historical examples occur in Alexander L. George and Richard Smoke, *Deterrence in American Foreign Policy* (New York: Columbia University Press, 1974); John J. Mearsheimer, *Conventional Deterrence* (Ithaca, NY: Cornell University Press, 1983); and Richard Smoke, *War* (Cambridge, MA: Harvard University Press, 1977).

17. Jonathan Schell, *The Fate of the Earth* (New York: Alfred Knopf, 1982), p. 226.

18. The most authoritative treatment is R. Duncan Luce and Howard Raiffa, *Games and Decisions* (New York: John Wiley and Sons, 1957), pp. 94-97. An excellent, elementary treatment is Morton D. Davis, *Game Theory: A Nontechnical Introduction,* revised edition (New York: Basic Books, 1983), pp. 108-130.

19. The best recent treatment is Brams, *Superpower Games,* esp. Chapters 1 and 3. See also Nicholas Measor, "Games Theory and the Nuclear Arms Race," Nigel Blake and Kay Pole, eds., *Dangers of Deterrence* (London: Routledge and Kegan Paul, 1983), pp. 132-156; and Bruce Russett, *The Prisoner's of Insecurity* (New York: W.H. Freeman, 1983), pp. 99-106 and 115-132.

20. In fact, I would argue that the United States has for the most part in the last decade resisted the tendency to race, to its own strategic detriment. For example, the American stockpile of nuclear devices is at a twenty-year low; it was one third higher in 1967. Total megatonnage is at a twenty-five-year low and is only 25% of the 1960 high. See Caspar Weinberger, *Annual Report to the Congress: Fiscal Year 1985* (Washington, DC: U.S. Government Printing Office, 1984), p. 33. For a thorough critique of the very notion of an "arms race," see Albert Wohlstetter, "Legends of the Arms Race," *USSI Report 75-1* (Washington, DC: United States Strategic Institute, 1975). Keep in mind, however, that all observers would agree that there exists a strong *tendency to race* and that such tendency is explained by the Prisoner's Dilemma.

21. Gwynne Dyer, *War* (New York: Crown, 1985), Chapter 11; and Jonathon Schell, *The Fate of the Earth,* part III, esp. pp. 219-231.

22. This particularly frightening version of a "game" played between the Soviet Union and ourselves was first clearly stated in Schelling, *The Strategy of Conflict,* esp. Chapter 9, "Reciprocal Fear of Surprise Attack," pp. 207-228.

23. The terrifying logic of this particular game-theoretic situation was formulated by Thomas Schelling in *The Strategy of Conflict* long before the technology of MIRVing or the development of ICBM accuracies sufficient to knock out silos. In Chapter 9 entitled, "The Reciprocal Fear of Surprise Attack," pp. 207-229, he delineates what can only be described as the most likely road to nuclear war in our time. All concerned, educated citizens should read it.

24. This vulnerability describes the much discussed "window of vulnerability." Experts disagree on its practical existence; i.e., would the Soviets ever take the terrible risk of an unsuccessful attack? However, no one argues against its theoretical existence; the logic is irrefragable. One of the earliest treatments was in *Strategic Survey 1974* (London: International Institute for Strategic Studies, 1975), pp. 46-50. Other useful technical treatments, though ones not necessarily in agreement with my views, include John D. Steinbruner and Thomas M. Garwin, "Strategic Vulnerability: The Balance between Prudence and Paranoia," *International Security* (Summer 1976); Colin Gray, "The Future of Land Based Missiles," *Adelphi Paper* (London: International Institute for Strategic Studies, 1977); and Bernard Feld and Kosta Tsipis, "Land-based Intercontinental Ballistic Missiles," *Scientific American* (November 1979), pp. 51-61.

25. Both the MX and the Trident II (also called D-5) have sufficient accuracy for hard kill capability. Because the present intent is to base the MX in old Minuteman silos, it is far more destabilizing than Trident II, which is to be based on the virtually invulnerable *Ohio* class submarine.

26. This argument does not constrain one to the dubious notion often called "assured destruction," under which civilian population and urban areas are threatened with destruction. If both sides adopt this strategy, the famous Mutual Assured Destruction (MAD) doctrine results, which is endorsed by Robert MacNamara, McGeorge Bundy, and Theodore Draper, among others. I explicitly reject this view. In order to make deterrence work, you have only to threaten, from an invulnerable position, the destruction of whatever your adversary holds dear. I shall argue below that this is his military forces, his state security apparatus, and his command and control structure, not, in the case of the Soviet Union, cities and civilian population.

27. Bernard Brodie, *Strategy in the Missile Age* (Princeton, NJ: Princeton University Press, 1965), p. 281.

28. *ibid.,* p. 283.

29. See especially the excellent book by Roberta Wohlstetter, *Pearl Harbor: Warning and Decision* (Stanford, CA: Stanford University Press, 1962), particularly pp. 230-231. Also see Richard K. Betts, *Surprise Attack* (Washington, DC: The Brookings Institution, 1982), p. 47.

30. Bertrand Russell, *Common Sense and Nuclear Warfare* (New York: Simon & Schuster, 1959), p. 28.

31. P.H. Vigor, *The Soviet View of War, Peace and Neutrality* (London: Routledge and Kegan Paul, 1975), pp. 25-57. Vigor's book is by far the best in this area, but see also W.B. Gallie, *Philosophers of Peace and War* (Cambridge: Cambridge University Press, 1978), Chapter 5 (Marx and Engles); E. Kardelj, *Socialism and War* (New York: McGraw Hill, 1960); M. Michalik, "The Marxist Theory of War," *Dialetics and Humanism,* vol. 9 (August 1982).

32. Vigor, *The Soviet View of War*, p. 72.

33. *ibid.*, p. 73.

34. V.D. Sokolovskiy, *Soviet Military Strategy*, 3rd edition, ed. Harriet Fast Scott (New York: Crane and Russak, 1975), pp. 174-175.

35. *ibid.*, p. 176.

36. Excerpted from "The Soviet Strategic View," *Strategic Review* (Fall 1980), compiled and edited by Leon Goure and Michael Deane, pp. 81-82. Goure and Deane compile "The Soviet Strategic View" for each issue of *Strategic Review*. It is made up primarily of translations of recent Soviet statements on all facets of military strategy and is an invaluable source "from the horses mouth," so to speak.

37. The single exception might be conventional naval clashes. This type of war between the United States and the Soviet Union does not have a particularly good foundation in Marxist-Leninist theory. Instead, it seems to have arisen with the enormous growth in importance of the Soviet Navy over the last two decades and the concommitant prestige of the great Admiral S.G. Groshkov, father of the modern Soviet Navy. Groshkov believed such engagements were genuine possibilites. See his book, *The Sea Power of the State* (New York: Pergamon, 1979), Chapter 4.

38. Vigor, *The Soviet View of War*, p. 93.

39. N.V. Karaborov, *The Philosophical Heritage of V.I. Lenin and the Problem of Contemporary War* (Moscow: Vonzidat, 1972), pp. 17-18.

40. As quoted in Richard Soll, "The Soviet Union and Protracted Nuclear War," *Strategic Review,* vol. 8 (Fall 1980), p. 17.

41. Richard Pipes, "Why the Soviet Union Thinks it Could Fight and Win a Nuclear War," *Commentary* (July 1977); "Soviet Global Strategy," *Commentary* (April 1980); and *Survival is not Enough* (New York: Simon & Schuster, 1984), pp. 83-102.

42. Pipes, *Survival is not Enough,* p. 91.

43. Pipes, "Why the Soviet Union Thinks it Could Fight and Win a Nuclear War," p. 30.

44. Benjamin Lambeth and Kevin Lewis, "Economic Targeting in Nuclear War," *Orbis,* vol. 27 (Spring 1983), p. 144; John Erickson, "The Soviet View of Deterrence: A General Survey," *Survival,* vol. 24 (Nov./Dec. 1982), p. 246.

45. Pipes, "Why the Soviet Union Thinks it Could Fight," pp. 28-29; John Erickson, "The Soviet Military System, Doctrine, Technology and Style," John Erickson and E.J. Fenchtwanger, eds., *Soviet Military Power and Performance* (Hamden, CT: Archon Books, 1979), pp. 25-26.

46. Edward L. Warner III, *The Military in Contemporary Soviet Politics* (New York: Praeger, 1977), pp. 137-146.

47. Bernard Brodie, *Strategy in the Missile Age,* pp. 160-165.

48. Raymond L. Garthoff, "Mutual Deterrence and Strategic Arms Limitation in Soviet Policy," *International Security* (Summer 1978), pp. 112-147; Benjamin Lambeth, "How to Think About Soviet Military Doctrine," *Rand Paper Series* (Santa Monica: Rand Corp., 1978); Fritz W. Ermath, "Contrasts in American and Soviet Strategic Thought," *International Security* vol. 3 (Fall 1978), pp. 138-155; Helmut Sonnenfeldt and William Hyland, "Soviet Perspectives on Security," *Adelphi Paper 150* (London: International Institute for Strategic Studies, 1979).

49. Lambeth, "How to Think," p. 2.

Chapter V

1. Third Draft of the Pastoral Letter of the U.S. Bishops on War and Peace, "The Challenge of Peace: God's Promise and Our Response," *Origins,* vol. 12 (April 14, 1983).

2. Germain G. Grisez, "Toward a Consistent Natural Law Ethics of Killing," *American Journal of Jurisprudence,* vol. 15 (1970), p. 93.

3. George Kennan, *The Nuclear Delusion* (New York: Pantheon, 1982), pp. 194-195.

4. Anthony Kenny, " 'Better Dead than Red'," Nigel Blake and Kay Pole, eds., *Objections to Deterrence* (London: Routledge and Kegan Paul, 1984), pp. 18-19.

5. *ibid.,* p. 27.

6. Albert Wohlstetter, "Between an Unfree World and None," *Foreign Affairs,* vol. 63 (Summer 1985), pp. 993-994.

7. John M. Collins, *U.S.-Soviet Military Balance 1980-1985* (New York: Pergammon-Brassey's, 1985, pp. 53-86; *The Military Balance 1984-1985* (London: The International Institute for Strategic Studies, 1985), pp. 4-6, 17-18.

8. Collins, pp. 99-127, and *The Military Balance,* pp. 6-12, 18-22.

9. See Barry Nicholas, *An Introduction to Roman Law* (Oxford: Oxford University Press, 1962), pp. 69-76; M.I. Finley, *Ancient Slavery and Modern Ideology* (New York: Viking, 1980), Chapter 3.

10. 45 *American Jurisprudence, 2nd Edition,* p. 928.

11. 80 *Corpus Juris Secundum,* p. 1317.

12. *ibid.,* p. 1324. It should be noted that while slaves in America were regarded as chattel for the purposes of the civil law, they were persons under the criminal law. Excellent discussions of the history of the legal concept of slavery occur in David Brion Davis, *The Problem of Slavery in the Age of Revolution* (Ithaca, NY: Cornell University Press, 1975), Chapter 10, esp. pp. 471-489; and Don E. Fehranbacher, *The Dred Scott Case: Its Significance in American Law and Politics* (New York: Oxford University Press, 1975), Chapter 2.

13. Thomas Hobbes, *The Leviathan* (New York: Dutton, 1950), Chapter XX, pp. 170-172.

14. Baron de Montesquieu, *The Spirit of the Laws,* trans. Thomas Nugent (New York: Scribner's, 1949), Book XV, pp. 235-237.

15. John Locke, "Second Treatise," *Two Treatises of Government* (New York: Cambridge University Press, 1960), Sections 17, 22, 23, 135, 137; and Jean Jacques Rousseau, "The Social Contract," *The Social Contract and Discourses,* trans. G.D.H. Cole (New York: Dutton, 1950), Book I, Chaper IV, pp. 7-12; see also "A Discourse on the Origin of Inequality," *ibid.*

16. An excellent general discussion of definitional issues involving slavery is David Brion Davis, *Slavery and Human Progress* (New York: Oxford University Press, 1984), Chapter 2. The same author's *The Problem of Slavery in Western Culture* (Ithaca, NY: Cornell University Press, 1966), Chapters 13 and 14, offers an excellent discussion of the notion of slavery in modern Western political philosophy.

17. I would argue that Locke, Montesquieu, and Rousseau would see such attempted surrender as morally wrong. For an excellent historical review of this exact point, plus additional arguments by the author, see Arthur Kuflik, "The Inalienability of Autonomy," *Philosophy and Public Affairs,* vol. 13 (Fall 1984).

18. Douglas Lackey, "Missiles & Morals; A Utilitarian Look at Nuclear Deterrence," *Philosophy and Public Affairs,* vol. II (Summer 1982), pp. 189-231.

19. *ibid.*, p. 210.

20. *ibid.*, p. 212.

21. *ibid.*, p. 221, note 29.

22. *ibid.*, p. 212.

23. *ibid.*, p. 221.

24. This and other decision-theoretic mistakes in the paper are pointed out by Russell Hardin and Gregory Kavka responding to Lackey in *Philosophy and Public Affairs,* vol. 21 (Summer 1983), pp. 236-260.

25. Lackey, "Missiles & Morals," p. 214.

26. *ibid.*, p. 211.

27. *ibid.*, p. 211. Lackey also has his facts wrong. Both RAF Bomber Command and the U.S. Air Force long-range bombers in the Pacific used thermite fire bombs, not napalm, which was used for tactical and close ground support applications only; see Lee Kennett, *A History of Strategic Bombing* (New York: Scribners, 1982), pp. 169-177 *passim.*

28. This brute and, one would think, obvious fact of the revolutionary character of nuclear weapons has been amply discussed over the years. The first and still one of the best discussions is Bernard Brodie, ed., *The Absolute Weapon* (New York: Harcourt Brace, 1946), particularly Brodie's own essay. A recent and also excellent treatment is Michael Mandebaum, *The Nuclear Revolution* (New York: Cambridge University Press, 1981), esp. Chapters 1 and 8.

29. David Hoekema, "The Moral Status of Deterrent Threats," *Social Philosophy and Policy,* vol. 3 (Autumn 1985).

30. *ibid.*, p. 116.

31. Here I gloss over the important quantitative distinction between megatons and equivalent megatons. However, this gloss has the effect of *understating* rather than *overstating* the difference between nuclear and conventional weapons.

32. The MX, for example, is thought to have a circular error probable of from 200 to 300 feet. A "circular error probable" means the radius of a circle into which at least 50 percent of the warheads would impact, at full range.

33. Jeff McMahan, "Nuclear Blackmail," Nigel Blake and Kay Pole, eds., *Dangers of Deterrence* (London: Routledge and Kegan Paul, 1983), pp. 84-111.

34. *ibid.*, pp. 109-110.

35. Lackey, "Missiles & Morals," p. 221.

36. *ibid.*, p. 211.

37. Lawrence Freedman, *The Evolution of Nuclear Strategy* (London: Macmillan, 1981) pp. 45-62; and especially Gregg Herken, *The Winning Weapon* (New York: Knopf, 1980).

38. Typical examples of this easy moral equation are Edmund G. Brown, Jr., "Nuclear Addiction: A Response," *Thought,* vol. 59 (March 1984), p. 11; and Bruce Kent, "A Christian Unilateralism From a Christian Background," Goeffrey Goodwin, ed., *Ethics and Nuclear Deterrence* (London: Croom and Helms, 1982), p. 59.

39. See, for example, Jerry L. Folk, "The Case for Pacifism," Charles P. Lutz and Jerry L. Folk, eds., *Peaceways* (Minneapolis: Augsburg, 1983); and Bruce Kent, "A Christian Unilateralism."

40. Kennan, *The Nuclear Delusion,* p. 71.

41. *ibid.*

42. For technical characteristics of the weapon, see Fred M. Kaplan, "Enhanced-Radiation Weapons," *Progress in Arms Control?* (San Francisco: W.H. Freeman, 1978); and Herbert Scoville, Jr., "The Neutron Bomb," Stockholm International Peace Research Institute, *The Arms Race and Arms Control* (London: Taylor and Francis, 1982).

43. Charles Krauthammer, "On Nuclear Morality," R. James Woolsey, ed., *Nuclear Arms: Ethics, Strategy, Politics* (San Francisco: Institute for Contemporary Studies, 1984).

44. The issue of limiting nuclear war blends into a cluster of other strategic issues including flexible targeting options, counterforce capacity, command and control vulnerability, and control of escalation. A small sample of the literature is all we can possibly provide. The best work directly on point is Desmond Ball, "Can Nuclear War be Controlled?," *Adelphi Paper: 169* (London: International Institute for Strategic Studies, 1981). Lawrence Freedman, *The Evolution of Nuclear Strategy,* is the very best history of the evolution of counterforce and flexible response. An excellent short discussion of the evolution of counterforce and limited war theory is Donald M. Snow, *Nuclear Strategy in a Dynamic World* (University, AL: University of Alabama Press, 1981), Chapter 3. For the vulnerability of command and control systems, see Ball and Paul Bracken, *The Command and Control of Nuclear Forces* (New Haven, CT: Yale University Press, 1981); and the more popularly written volume by Daniel Ford, *The Button* (New York: Simon & Schuster, 1985).

45. Freedman, *The Evolution of Nuclear Strategy,* esp. Chapters 15, 25.

46. Ball, "Can Nuclear War Be Controlled?," and Bracken, *The Command and Control of Nuclear Forces.*

47. Freedman, *The Evolution of Nuclear Strategy,* Chapter 14.

48. One cannot reach this conclusion without at least citing powerful, yet finally unconvincing, arguments by Albert Wohlstetter (with whom the author so often agrees) that escalation is not automatic and might not occur. All of his work (much of which is cited elsewhere here) is imbued with this conviction, but his most effective arguments can be found in "Between an Unfree World and None," pp. 980-989.

49. Gwynne Dyer, *War* (New York: Crown, 1985), p. 94.

50. *ibid.,* p. 262 and p. 263 respectively.

51. Colin S. Gray and Keith Payne, "Victory is Possible," *Foreign Policy,* vol. 39 (Summer 1980), p. 20.

52. Jeff McMahan, "Nuclear Blackmail," p. 111, note 8.

53. Anthony Kenny, "Better Dead Than Red," pp. 20-21.

54. George Kennan, *The Nuclear Delusion,* p. 176.

55. Freedman, *The Evolution of Nuclear Strategy,* Chapters 22-25.

56. It is clear that many of those ten million lives saved would be lost in subsequent strikes. The Soviets have substantial overkill capability. Still, many of the factors considered in Chapter III, e.g., mechanical failure, will cut down the margin of overkill, perhaps substantially. In any case, a substantial reduction of the number of warheads impacting the United States will save a large number of lives, the exact number being dependent on a whole range of variables.

57. Joseph D. Douglass, Jr. and Amoretta M. Hoeber, *Soviet Strategy for Nuclear War* (Stanford, CA: Hoover Institution Press, 1979), pp. 58-66.

58. *Perkins on Criminal Law,* 2nd edition (Mineola, NY: Foundation Press, 1969) pp. 1006-1007.

59. *ibid.*

60. John Locke, "Second Treatise," Chapter III, section 17.

61. Robert Fullinwider, "War and Innocence," *Philosophy and Public Affairs,* vol. 5 (1975); Jeffrie G. Murphy, "The Killing of the Innocent," *The Monist,* vol. 57 (1973); and Thomas Nagel, "War and Massacre," *Philosophy and Public Affairs,* vol. 1 (1972).

62. There exists the simple and, I would say, simple-minded argument based upon cost and benefit that the purposive killing of civilians "breaks the will of the people," hastens an end to the war, and thus, according to the Rule of Proportionality, is justified. This argument was central to the evolution of the doctrine of strategic bombardment. Both Mitchell and Douhet made it. Nonetheless, almost no one holds it today.

I assert a near consensus against the purposive killing of civilians because of a number of excellent papers published some time ago which have, to my knowledge, never been responded to by members of the philosophic community. These include Anscombe, "War and Murder," reprinted in Malham Wakin, *War, Morality, and the Military Profession* (Boulder, CO: Westview, 1979), pp. 285-298, and the articles cited in note 61 above.

63. Murphy, "The Killing of the Innocent," pp. 347-351.

64. Thomas M. Coffey, *Decision Over Schweinfurt: The U.S. 8th Air Force Battle for Daylight Bombing* (New York: McKay, 1977); Lee Kennett, *A History of Strategic Bombing* (New York: Scribner's, 1982), Chapters 7-10. For a stirring testimony to the heroism and sacrifice such a strategy called for, see Elmer Bendiner's critically acclaimed memoir, *The Fall of Fortresses* (New York: Putnam, 1980). Bendiner himself was a B-17 navigator and recipient of the Distinguished Flying Cross.

65. Paul Ramsey, *The Just War* (New York: Scribner's, 1968), Chapter II, pp. 248-258 and Chapters 14-15.

66. Anscombe, "War and Murder," pp. 294-296; and Michael Walzer, *Just and Unjust Wars* (New York: Basic Books, 1977), pp. 278-283.

67. Thomas Schelling, *The Strategy of Conflict* (New York: Oxford University Press, 1963), Chapters 2, 3, 5, 7, and 8, and *passim.*

68. *Restatement of Agency,* 2nd (1958), Section 1; and Warren A. Seavey, *Agency* (St. Paul: West, 1964), pp. 2-4.

69. *Restatement* Section 7(c) and Section 35; Seavey, *Agency,* pp. 12-13.

70. For a radically different kind of argument which nonetheless would support *B*'s actions and impose responsibility upon *A,* see Eric Mack, "Three Ways to Kill Innocent Bystanders: Some Conundrums Concerning the Morality of War," *Social Philosophy and Policy,* vol. 3 (Autumn 1985). Mack bases his highly relevant and compelling argument on broadened notions of the causation of harm worked out by Judith Jarvis Thomson in "Killing and Letting Die and the Trolley Problem," *The Monist,* vol. 59 (Spring 1976), and his own "Bad Samaritanism and the Causation of Harm," *Philosophy and Public Affairs,* vol. 9 (Summer 1980). I consider the Thomson-Mack line of argument ultimately compelling and do not mean to reject it here. It is merely that I find the notions of agency and responsibility based upon agency more easily understood and appealing (perhaps only to this lawyer's mind). In any case, Mack is on to something very deep in the issue of noncombatant immunity and pursuit of it would yield great rewards.

71. Robert Nozick discusses the problem of innocent shields in *Anarchy State and Utopia* (New York: Basic Books, 1974), pp. 34-35. He finds no ultimately satisfying answer to it.

72. George Kennan, in *The Nuclear Delusion* (New York: Pantheon, 1982), pp. 84-85, hardly the type to seek justification for attacking Soviet civilians, has noted "indifference" and "a curious sort of boredom and spiritlessness" as the primary feelings elicited on the part of the people by the Soviet government's claims of legitimacy and its ideological justifications of its actions.

73. Gerhard von Glahn, *Law Among Nations,* 4th ed. (New York: Macmillan, 1981), pp. 90-116, esp. pp. 98-99.

74. *Restatement,* Section 8 and Section 27; Seavey, *Agency,* p. 43.

75. *ibid.*

76. Kennan, *The Nuclear Delusion,* pp. 83-84; and Seweryn Bialer, "Danger in Moscow," *The New York Review of Books,* February 16, 1984, p. 9.

77. See Theodore M. Benditt, *Rights* (Totowa, NJ: Rowman and Allanheld, 1982), p. 15.

78. "Culpable ignorance" has been defined as "such ignorance as results from the failure to exercise ordinary care to acquire knowledge." 25, *Corpus Juris Secundum,* 29.

79. What seems to be suggested (although certainly not demonstrated) by this is that people may not morally owe it to themselves to be governed by an open democracy, but that they owe it to third parties. Or, at least, they owe it to third parties to maintain the ability to control their government. Perhaps that requires a constitution, or perhaps merely keeping a rifle in the closet, for one can, following John Locke, rise against a despotic government "....as soon as God shall give those under their subjection courage and opportunity to do it" (*Second Treatise* section 196, pp. 443-444).

80. The best popular account of this phenomenon is "Nuclear Weapons: Another Age?", *The Economist,* pp. survey 3 - survey 18, 1-7, September 1984.

81. Robert Jastrow, "Reagan vs. The Scientists," *Commentary,* January 1984, pp. 31-32 and *The Economist,* survey p. 11.

82. Far and away the most authoritative and exhaustive compilation of the literature on SDI can be found in "Briefing Packet: The Strategic Defense Initiative, Technical and Strategic Aspects," in two volumes prepared by the Institute for Foreign Policy Analysis, Inc., Cambridge, MA.

83. Only recently has the literature begun to reflect consideration of the political and strategic implications of the nuclear winter. Among the more interesting are: Anne Ehrlich, "Nuclear Winter," *The Bulletin of the Atomic Scientist* (April 1984); Colin S. Gray, "The Nuclear Winter Thesis and U.S. Strategic Policy," *The Washington Quarterly* (Summer 1985); Thomas Powers, "Is Nuclear War Impossible?," *The Atlantic* (November 1984); Carl Sagan, "Nuclear War and Climatic Catastrophe," *Foreign Affairs* (Winter 1983/84); Albert Wohlstetter, "Between an Unfree World and None," *Foreign Affairs,* vol. 63 (Summer 1985), pp. 962-994. The least polemical and most balanced is Dan Horwitz and Robert J. Lieber, "Nuclear Winter and the Future of Deterrence," *The Washington Quarterly,* Summer 1985.

84. R.P. Turco, *et al.,* "Nuclear Winter: Global Consequences of Multiple Nuclear Explosions," *Science,* vol. 222 (December 23, 1983).

85. *ibid.*

86. Sagan, "Nuclear War and Climatic Catastrophe," pp. 279-280.

87. *Perkins on Criminal Law,* p. 994.

88. Wayne R. LaFave and Austin W. Scott, Jr., *Criminal Law* (St. Paul: West, 1972), p. 394.

89. *ibid.*

90. Nagel, "War and Massacre," p. 387.

91. See Desmond Ball, *Targeting for Strategic Deterrence,* Adelphi Paper, No. 185 (London: International Institute for Strategic Studies, 1983), pp. 29-31; Colin S. Gray, *Nuclear Strategy and Strategic Planning* (Philadelphia: Foreign Policy Research Institute, 1984), pp. 76-77; Gray, "Nuclear Strategy: A Case for a Theory of Victory," *International*

Security, Summer 1979), pp. 65-67; Benjamin Lambeth and Kevin N. Lewis, "Economic Targeting in Nuclear War: U.S. and Soviet Approaches," *Orbis* (Spring 1983), pp. 127-149.

92. See George I. Mavrodes, "Conventions and the Morality of War," *Philosophy and Public Affairs,* vol.5 (Winter 1975); Mavrodes argues that the combatant/noncombatant distinction is essentially conventional. I have argued that it is not. However, the inherent fuzziness of the border may make its exact location conventional.

93. Gray, "Nuclear Strategy: A Case for a Theory of Victory," pp. 67-69; *Nuclear Strategy and Strategic Planning,* pp. 71-76; with Keith Payne, "Victory is Possible," *Foreign Policy,* vol. 39 (Summer 1980) p. 24.

94. The obsession of the Soviet society and system with authority, order, centralized control, and security (both internal and external) seems to be a universal theme running through their history, culture, ideology, and political and social life. The author is by no means a Soviet scholar or expert. He does not read Russian. But the point comes home over and over in what has been a fairly extensive lay investigation of the field. As a layman leading laymen, I would recommend the following analyses of the Soviet Union: Heddrick Smith, *The Russians* (New York: Ballantine, 1976), especially Chapter X and the wonderful diagrammatic metaphor on p. 336, using a ball and two containers to illustrate the differing characters of the U.S. and the Soviet Union. It is not Smith's own thought, but that of a Soviet scientist with whom he became friends. I find myself returning over and over to it as I investigate Soviet society further. Robert Kaiser, *Russia: The People and the Power* (New York: Atheneum, 1976), is also very good, especially Chapters 3 and 4.

The power of the notions of authority, central control, and security pervades a number of other good accounts of Soviet society by American journalists who have lived in the Soviet Union. Kevin Klose, *Russia and the Russians: Inside the Closed Society* (New York: Norton, 1984); Elizabeth Pond, *From the Yaroslavsky Station: Russia Perceived,* Revised edition (New York: Universal Books, 1984); David K. Shipler, *Russia: Broken Idols, Solemn Dreams* (New York: Times Books, 1983).

Similar themes comes through strongly in the accounts of Russian emigres, particularly in the areas of their society with which they are most familiar. See Dina Kaminskaya, *Final Judgement: My Life as a Soviet Defense Attorney* (New York: Simon & Schuster, 1982), for the criminal justice system; Arkady N. Shevchenko, *Breaking with Moscow* (New York: Knopf, 1985), for the political and foreign policy establishment; Konstantin Simis, *USSR: The Corrupt Soviety* (New York: Simon & Schuster, 1982), for the economy and industry; Viktor Suvorov, *Inside the Soviet Army* (New York: MacMillan, 1982), for the defense establishment.

Any good text on the Soviet political system covers the government and, especially, the party and state security apparatus which is both the most visible manifestation of this obsession with authority and central control, and what makes it possible in practice. See, for example, Donald D. Barry and Carol Barner-Barry, *Contemporary Soviet Politics* (Englewood Cliffs, NJ: Prentice Hall, 1978); Jerry F. Hough and Merle Fainsod, *How the Soviet Union is Governed,* Revised edition (Cambridge, MA: Harvard University Press, 1979); John N. Hazard, *The Soviet System of Government,* 4th edition (Chicago: The University of Chicago Press, 1968).

Two works on the Soviet Union's problems of transferring leadership point out how the obsession with control and authority makes such transfer far more difficult than it is in the West. They are Seweryn Bialer, *Stalin's Successors* (New York: Cambridge University Press, 1980); and Jerry F. Hough, *Soviet Leadership in Transition* (Washington, DC: The Brookings Institution, 1980).

My own personal contacts with Soviet citizens have been limited to a number of commercial representatives and agricultural experts (and a few severe looking gentlemen who seemed expert in neither area). However, in general discussions, away from immediate business and technical subjects, they certainly manifested concerns with order and central authority as basic to their conception of their society and of organized social life altogether. Their view of the United States is of a society rapidly falling into chaos. That we have always been as we are they simply disbelieve.

Although there is a virtual consensus, almost regardless of political viewpoint, as to the importance of these themes in Soviet society, accounts differ as to the reasons for it. There are primarily two competing explanations. The first emphasizes the historical and cultural experience of the ethnic Russians. One Soviet expert who consults extensively with several American intelligence services told me that in his mind, the entire story of the comparison of the Soviet Union and the United States could be derived from the contrast brought out by two nineteenth-century Frenchmen's accounts of the two societies—Alexis de Tocqueville's accounts of his travels in the United States, and the Marquis ce Custine's accounts of his travels in czarist Russia. While this might be a bit overstated, it is certainly true that Custine observed a society which put a high priority on authority and security, along with a related obsessive concern with secrecy and the presentation of a false picture of itself. See *Custine' Eternal Russia,* ed. and trans. Phyllis Kohler (Coral Gables, FL: University of Miami Press, 1976). Richard Pipes very much takes this approach in *Russia Under the Old Regime* (New York: Scribner's, 1974). It is hard not to see this theme in Russian history even when the author himself is not quite so consciously arguing for it. See, for example, Nicholas V. Riasanovsky, *A History of Russia,* 3rd edition (New York: Oxford University Press, 1977).

Two scholars who argue that it is Marxism-Leninism, rather than Russian culture, which accounts for this aspect of Soviet society are James L. Payne, "Marxism and Militarism," forthcoming in *Polity;* and Aaron Wildavsky, "No War Without Dictatorship, No Peace Without Democracy," *Social Philosophy, and Policy,* vol. 3 (Autumn, 1985); and his "The Soviet System" Aaron Wildavsky, ed. *Beyond Containment* (San Francisco: Institute for Contemporary Studies, 1983).

Perhaps the correct explanation is that both their ideology and their culture cause the Soviets to be obsessive about central authority, control, and security. This seems to be Richard Pipes's most recent view; see *Survival is not Enough* (New York: Simon & Schuster, 1984). In any case, one cannot deny that this is a deep and persistent part of their society and, as such, a feature of paramount value to them. A deterrent force that can credibly threaten to destroy their political command and, control and security apparatus seems to be the most effective possible means to prevent Soviet nuclear adventurism.

95. Gray, *Nuclear Strategy and Strategic Planning,* p. 62.

96. On these points, in addition to Gray's work cited above, see his *The Soviet-American Arms Race* (London: D.D. Heath Ltd., 1976) esp. Chapter 5.

97. See Pipes, *Survival is not Enough,* Chapters 1 and 2; Wildavsky, "No War Without Dictatorship."

98. H.L.A. Hart, *Punishment and Responsibility* (Oxford: Oxford University Press, 1968), pp. 8-10, 71-83; Herbert Packer, *The Limits of the Criminal Sanction* (Stanford, CA: Stanford University Press, 1968), pp. 38-39.

99. John Steinbrunner, "Nuclear Decapitation," *Foreign Policy,* vol. 45 (Winter 1981-82), pp. 16-28.

100. Sam Nunn and John W. Warner, "Reducing the Risks of Nuclear War," *The Washington Quarterly,* Spring 1984. See also an excellent new book by William L. Ury, *Beyond the Hotline* (New York: Houghton Mifflin Co., 1985).

101. This is, of course, one aspect of the long and loud debate between those who believe in countervalue threats and nuclear weapons for deterrence only, on the one hand, and those who believe in counterforce threats and rationally fighting a nuclear war if one unavoidably comes, on the other. Suffice it to say that, with the possible exception of Colin Gray, no counterforce theorist recommends first-strike counterforce warfare, although many partisans of countervalue deterrence keep attacking a strawman who does. For one countervalue deterrence theorist who is especially concerned about the temptation to initiate a nuclear war, see Theodore Draper's aptly titled "Nuclear Temptations," *The New York Review of Books,* January 19, 1984, and his later rejoinder to Wohlstetter, "Nuclear Temptations: An Exchange," *The New York Review of Books,* May 31, 1984. For a closely related argument, see Robert S. McNamara, "The Military Role of Nuclear Weapons," *Foreign Affairs* (Fall 1983).

102. See Wohlstetter, "Between an Unfree World and None"; "Bishops, Statesmen and Other Strategists?," *Commentary,* June 1983; his response to his critics in "Morality and Deterrence: An Exchange," *Commentary,* December 1983; and his response to Draper in "Nuclear Temptations: An Exchange," *The New York Review of Books,* May 31, 1984.

103. *Report of the President's Commission on Strategic Forces,* April 1983.

104. McGeorge Bundy, "Existential Deterrence and Its Consequences," Douglas MacLean, ed., *The Security Gamble* (Totowa, NJ: Rowman and Allenheld, 1984).

105. "Third Draft of the Pastoral Letter" (Washington, DC: U.S. Catholic Conference, 1983).

106. Walzer, *Just and Unjust Wars,* p. 283.

107. Albert Wohlstetter, "Bishops, Statesmen and Other Strategists on the Bombing of Civilians," p. 16.

108. Gregory S. Kavka, "Some Paradoxes of Deterrence," *Journal of Philosophy,* vol. 75, as reprinted in Molham M. Wakin, ed., *War, Morality and the Military Profession* (Boulder, CO: Westview, 1979), pp. 505-525. See also his "Deterrence, Utility and Rational Choice," *Theory and Decision* (March 1980).

109. But see David Gauthier, "Deterrence, Maximization, and Rationality," *Ethics,* vol. 94 (April 1984), pp. 474-495 for a brilliant attempt, largely successful I believe, to reconcile countervalue (and therefore immoral) deterrent threats with morality and rationality. It does not thereby morally redeem countervalue warfare, however. Nor is it clear that Gauthier believes that it does.

Conclusion

1. Jonathan Schell, *The Fate of the Earth* (New York: Alfred A. Knopf, 1982), p. 195.

2. Helen Caldicott, *Missile Envy* (New York: William Morrow, 1984), pp. 293-301.

3. Some recent excellent efforts in that direction have been made and deserve note, even if the writers do not always agree with the author. See the Harvard Study Group, *Living with Nuclear Weapons* (Cambridge, MA: Harvard University Press, 1983), Part III; and Carnesdale, Nye, and Allison's, "An Agenda for Action" in their excellent anthology *Hawks, Doves and Owls* (New York: Norton, 1985).

4. For a frightening comparison between the risk of inadvertent war today and the start of World War I, see Miles Kahler, "Rumors of War: The 1914 Analogy," *Foreign Affairs* vol. 58 (Winter 1979/80), pp. 374-396. For a study of just how confusion and miscommunication increased under increasing tension in this confrontation, see Ola R. Holsti, "The 1914 Case," *American Political Science Review,* vol. 49 (June 1965), pp. 365-378.

5. Ernest Becker, *The Denial of Death* (New York: The Free Press, 1973), p. 69.

6. Paul Tillich, *The Courage to Be* (New Haven, CT: Yale University Press, 1952), p. 155.

7. *ibid.,* p. 27.

8. *ibid.*

9. L.C. Knights, "Hamlet and Death," John Jump, ed., *Shakespere: Hamlet* (London: MacMillan, 1969), p. 152.